The First Sail: J. Hillis Miller

# The First Sail: J. Hillis Miller
## A Film Book

*Dragan Kujundžić*

OPEN HUMANITIES PRESS

*London 2015*

First edition published by OPEN HUMANITIES PRESS 2015

Copyright © 2015 Dragan Kujundžić. Chapters by respective authors.

Book freely available online at http://openhumanitiespress.org/books/the-first-sail.html

Film freely available at: https://archive.org/details/TheFirstSail

This is an open access book, licensed under Creative Commons By Attribution Share Alike license. Under this license, authors allow anyone to download, reuse, reprint, modify, distribute, and/or copy their work so long as the authors and source are cited and resulting derivative works are licensed under the same or similar license. No permission is required from the authors or the publisher. Statutory fair use and other rights are in no way affected by the above.

Read more about the license at creativecommons.org/licenses/by-sa/4.0

Cover Art, figures, and other media included with this book may be under different copyright restrictions. Please see the *Permissions* section at the back of this book for more information.

PRINT ISBN 978-1-78542-003-0
PDF ISBN 978-1-78542-019-1

Open Humanities Press is an international, scholar-led open access publishing collective whose mission is to make leading works of contemporary critical thought freely available worldwide. More at http://openhumanitiespress.org

OPEN HUMANITIES PRESS

# Contents

| | |
|---|---|
| Avant-propos<br>*Dragan Kujundžić* | 9 |
| Introduction<br>*Henry Sussman* | 14 |

## Part 1

| | |
|---|---|
| Film Transcript | 27 |
| Interview<br>*Taryn Devereux* | 71 |

## Part 2

| | | |
|---|---|---|
| 1. | "Talking about the same questions but at another rhythm": Deconstruction and Film<br>*Sarah Dillon* | 86 |
| 2. | Just a Miracle<br>*Charlie Gere* | 102 |
| 3. | Up<br>*Nicholas Royle* | 111 |
| 4. | Miller's Idle Tears<br>*Éamonn Dunne and Michael O'Rourke* | 121 |
| 5. | Envoiles (Post It)<br>*Dragan Kujundžić* | 139 |
| 6. | Memory to come (tba) or, towards a poetics of the spectral<br>*Julian Wolfreys* | 152 |

**Part 3**

7. "Like a Beginning of an Interminable Waterway":
   J. Hillis Miller and the Theory to Come                    173
   *Dragan Kujundžić*

8. Thanks a Lot and What I Would Say Now                      210
   *J. Hillis Miller*

*Riddled with light. Ah!*
   "Cold Heaven," W. B. Yeats

*Avant-propos*

Dragan Kujundžić

## *A Limitless Yes: The First Sail* With J. Hillis Miller at the Time of Critical Climate Change (Thank you, Hillis, or What I Would Ask Hillis now)

*A note on the volume: this film-book is part of an installation, and is related to the video* The First Sail: J. Hillis Miller,[1] *available on the Internet Archive. While the book can stand alone, the reader is encouraged to view the film.*

The film-book, *The First Sail: J. Hillis Miller*, is based on the documentary film by the same name which I made in 2010, filming with J. Hillis Miller in Florida (Gainesville, University of Florida), and Deer Isle (summer residence), and Sedgwick, Maine (winter residence) where Hillis lives in his family houses with his wife, Dorothy. The film also includes footage from academic events in which J. Hillis Miller was a plenary speaker ("Who? or What?—Jacques Derrida", University of Florida, 2006),[2] as well as the exclusive footage of the plenary lecture Jacques Derrida read at the conference on "J" in honor of J. Hillis Miller, in 2003.[3] I was the

---

1   The film, *The First Sail: J. Hillis Miller*. Documentary Film, 85 Minutes. Deer Isle Productions, 2011. The film opened at the Harn Museum, University of Florida, on October 25, 2011. It is archived at https://archive.org/details/TheFirstSail. The DVD is available at Amazon.com.

2   "'Who?' or 'What?': Jacques Derrida." Dragan Kujundžić Guest Editor. Essays by Jacques Derrida, Hélène Cixous, J. Hillis Miller, et al. *Discourse* (Summer 2009).

3   *Provocations to Reading. Essays For a Democracy To Come*. Introduction, Co-edited with Barbara Cohen (conference co-organizer and co-director of "J"), New York: Fordham University Press (Fall 2005). "J"', Special Issue, Dragan Kujundžić Guest Editor, and Introduction, *Critical Inquiry,* University of

organizer and conference (co)director of both of these events, which are thus in their own way early attempts at "directing," resulting in preliminary footage of what was to become a documentary film. The film thus operates as an installation, a work as a net-work of conference directing and presentations, edited volumes based on these conferences, filming J. Hillis Miller with an explicit intention of making a documentary film, and then editing the film, and screening it at various events which have become part of this volume and as-of-yet-emerging projects. Two conferences where the film was screened are of particular relevance. "J. Hillis Miller and the Theory to Come," an international conference dedicated to the work of J. Hillis Miller, at Lancaster University, England, in May 2012, where I had an honor to be the plenary speaker, together with J. Hillis Miller; and "The First Sail: J. Hillis Miller," the film screening and post-screening lecture, roundtable and conference dedicated to the film, University College, Dublin, Ireland, in May, 2012, also with the participation of J. Hillis Miller. The proceedings of these two conferences form most but not all of the essays in this book. The book is therefore a product or still evolving effect of a wide network of places, from California, Florida, Deer Isle, Maine, Paris, Lancaster, Dublin, New Haven (Yale University) but also Brown University (Providence, Rhode Island) where I appeared on stage with J. Hillis Miller (Miller via Skype) for the screening of the film. Hillis Miller's presentation at the Brown screening became the concluding chapter (updated in the Fall of 2014 with latest bibliography) of this volume.

The film and the book are thus a quasi-interminable project that spans more than a decade (in fact much more than that) and includes numerous institutions, email exchanges, academic encounters, lectures, essays, conference organization, directing and participation, volume editing, interviews, film screenings and discussions, etc., spanning from Moscow and Berlin (my collaborative project with Natalia Pschenichnikova who wrote the sound and music for the film) to China and Australia where the collective interview with J. Hillis Miller from the Dublin conference, which took place after the screening of the film, has been published.[4] The film has had other screenings, most notably at the University

---

Chicago Press, Spring, 2005.

4 "You see you ask an innocent question and you've got a long answer," J.Hillis

of California, Berkeley, University of Florida, SUNY Albany, Museum of Modern Art in Novi Sad, Serbia, in Esslingen am Neckar, Germany, Tulane University, New Orleans, and Stanford University. The current book carries the inscription of all these and many more events, as well as contributions from numerous colleagues who participated in the venture. (The extensive list of institutions and colleagues who contributed to *The First Sail* is listed in the credits of the film in the film transcript). The film and the book are also a site of a communal gathering around the work of J. Hillis Miller. This aspect of the book has been addressed in Henry Sussman's introduction, and the essays by the contributors to the volume testify to this. All these complex intersections testify in an exemplary way to the new world of jet travel and ubiquitous digital media, which is the way we live now.

In all these ventures J. Hillis Miller, who had the kindness to accept the invitation to be part of this experiment, has generously supported this sailing. Without his generosity to which many, like the contributors to this volume, joined enthusiastically, this project would not have been possible. His kindness allowed me to continue our collaboration, which started more than three decades ago when I first edited his work in Serbian and when I had not met Hillis Miller yet,[5] and continued in personal contacts on numerous occasions at the University of California at Irvine, where we worked in the same department together on numerous conferences, lectures and events, as well as at the University of Florida where J. Hillis Miller is a Doctor Honoris Causa and which he has visited frequently. This project provided me with a singular opportunity to continue working with J. Hillis Miller, while preparing to film and during the filming of the documentary, reading his current work which he has generously made available for me in digital form (listed at the end of Miller's afterword to this volume), and including joint appearances in various venues in the US and overseas where Hillis presented his

---

Miller in discussion with Éamonn Dunne, Michael O'Rourke, Martin McQuillan, Dragan Kujundžić, Graham Allen and Nicholas Royle, *Australian Humanities Review*, Issue 56, May 2014, http://www.australianhumanitiesreview.org/archive/Issue-May-2014/miller.html

5 "Deconstruction, a Merry Science," (Essays by J. Hillis Miller, Jacques Derrida, Jonathan Culler, Cynthia Chase et al.), *Letopis Matice srpske*, special issue, Dragan Kujundžić Guest Editor, Summer 1985 (in Serbian).

latest work. This work thus in itself forms a vast network of references, and Hillis Miller's theoretical interventions, which are fascinating, and politically urgent. They are energized by Hillis Miller's current interest in the critical climate change (a topic raised in the film on several occasions), his work on the Holocaust in his recent book *The Conflagration of Community*,[6] his essays on Stevens and Kafka, his numerous landmark and anthologized essays on Conrad, and last but not least his latest book, on George Eliot. His newest book, *Communities in Fiction*, with chapters on novels by Anthony Trollope, Thomas Hardy, Joseph Conrad, Virginia Woolf, Thomas Pynchon, and Miguel de Cervantes, will appear in early 2015 from Fordham University Press, and other books are in the works.

But if anything, this volume and film are, to quote and paraphrase the conclusion of Hillis Miller's book on George Eliot[7] in reference to Dorothea Brooke, a "limitless yes" to his work, an attempt to share with the reader and the viewer some aspects of this immense oeuvre which are not visible to those who do not know J. Hillis Miller. I hope this volume and film reveal something that Jacques Derrida called "the taste of J. Hillis Miller." The material filmed could make several documentaries, so strictly speaking little new would remain to ask Hillis now, which he has not already responded to during the two weeks of the filming at Deer Isle. Miller has addressed what he would say today at the end of this book. At the same time, the political, academic and environmental context surrounding this film since its release proves with more and more urgency the need to read and listen to J. Hillis Miller (as pointed out in the essays in this book as well) and would require revisiting everything that has been said and seen. This context, the rough seas and the rising waters around this film, have been captivated in the already mentioned title of one of Miller's lectures and essays which encapsulates his entire opus: *the critical climate change*, to which the present film and book are an attempted performative response. This should be heard in all its transformative

---

6   Hillis Miller's *The Conflagration of Community* profoundly motivates my essay "Expiration, Conflagration: the Jews in the Work of Aleksandar Tišma." The essay is part of the thematic collection I edited, together with the essay on Kertesz from Miller's book, and Emmanuel Levinas' essay "The Name of a Dog, or the Natural Right," *Interculturality* 7, Summer 2014 (in Serbian).

7   J. Hillis Miller, *Reading for Our Time*. Adam Bede *and* Middlemarch *Revisited*. (Edinburgh: Edinburgh University Press), 2012.

theoretical, political, educational, and environmental urgency. I can easily imagine a film sequel where those questions would be asked anew and new answers given in the new world-wide situation, such as almost daily new evidence of global warming.

But there is another reason why I can imagine a sequel to this film or book, a reason which animated them in the first place. It would be to participate, again, with the viewer and reader, around and dedicated to J. Hillis Miller's person and work, in an unqualified and never ending, affirmation, and perpetuation of this *limitless yes*.

*Introduction*

# Documenting Ourselves: Miller's "First Sail" and the Critical Community

HENRY SUSSMAN

*What matters to the dialectician is having the winds of world history in his sails. Thinking for him means: setting the sails. What is important is how they are set. Words are his sails. The way they are set makes them into concepts.*
—Walter Benjamin, *The Arcades Project* [N9, 6]

Dragan Kujundžić's "The First Sail," a documentary lovingly devoted to the life, times, publications, friendships, career, and mind of J. Hillis Miller, was not nominated for any Academy Awards, in Documentary or any other category. Some of its forays into academic colloquia do not produce high drama or technological wonderment. If the attendees at these events are in any way striking, it is in how normal-looking they are. The cinematography, meandering back to the same sail-boating sequences and Maine coastal landmarks, is in places choppy with self-authorizing integrity.

Yet the production of the film out of the close collegial collaboration between Miller and Kujundžić is indeed for the critical community, that dispersed and inchoate, increasingly interactive cadre of readers who insist on conducting and communicating their findings at the cutting-edge of theoretical discernment and rigor, a landmark happening, an *Ereignis* in the fullest sense of the word. The project not only takes on the invaluable task of documenting J. Hillis Miller and his current overviews on the critical vocation and the contemporary status of intellectual creativity within the academic and broader socio-political settings. To a significant degree, this film establishes the very same community's mindset, approach, and etiquettes—in an age of ubiquitous digital recording and storage—with respect to the broader exigency that it begin, for a range of critical exigencies, to document itself.

The media-value of the academic events that the film incorporates can only be characterized as prosaic; its extended interviews with Miller as chatty, and, with the notable exception of striking sailing scenes along the Maine coast, its visual program as decidedly *non-ambitious*. Yet is precisely by these bearings that *The First Sail* rises splendidly to the challenge of documenting what is compelling and authentic about the critical community's broader mission and quest as of the present juncture. Even while J. Hillis Miller is the exemplary, inevitable subject for this project, and Kujundžić's selecting him as its occasion is far from accidental, the demand for precisely this kind of document transcends even Miller.

Within the critical community that J. Hillis Miller has galvanized, and to which he's devoted himself with extraordinary multifaceted generosity, his ongoing role can only be characterized as first student. In order to become the dominant theoretically-motivated critic of more than half a century's standing, he's had, at all times, to be the most persistent, flexible, and resolutely creative student. He has in this sense embodied two of the crucial Buddhist aporias regarding teaching: the exemplary teacher is the first student; and, while the telling teacher *lectures at,* s/he also *attends,* and at a hyper-critical level of intensity. The listening power of a truly landmark teacher is prodigious.

In book after book, Miller demonstrates conclusively that he has absorbed more critically, attended more carefully, and thought more creatively than anyone else in sight. His latest books only intensify in these tendencies. *The First Sail* makes a powerful case that this sustained achievement, on the highest level of critical processing, results from Miller's provenance and calling as an American original, this in multiple senses. In view of high-powered theory's pitched skepticism vis à vis biographical criticism and argumentation, the film goes to unexpected lengths to trace J. Hillis Miller's achievement and body of interventions against the backdrop of his father, of the same name, who, among other things, presided over the formation of the SUNY system in the mid-1940's and was in service as president of the University of Florida in

1953, the untimely moment of his death. This formation separates our J. Hillis Miller from being yet another towering academic figure who haphazardly found his way. It suggests that a coherent, radically democratic educational philosophy was at play even during the undergraduate years at Oberlin, where as a sophomore he switched from a scientific orientation (fully at play in some of Miller' most daring contributions, on telepathy in literature, the "fractal" Proust) to a critical one.

I vividly recall being introduced to figures including Charles du Bos and Georges Poulet in a graduate criticism seminar of Miller's for the English Department at Johns Hopkins in Spring, 1969. These were hardly household names to a recent English B.A. from Brandeis whose erudition still left everything to be desired. It was clear at the time that Miller had accessed these memorable readers completely on his own. Their "influence" consisted in the degree that they played into a hermeneutic "platform" that Miller had, with striking deliberation, already constructed. Being made in the U.S.A. had abetted Miller in his gumption to scour the very *world* of letters for the materials that he needed in order to align his brand of reading with the prevailing formats in the field, stylistic as well as philosophical. Miller is still unearthing unexpected and utterly compelling nodes of literary programming and wonderment as he continues his watch, as the pivotal position of Imre Kertéz, and his novel, *Fatelessness*, in the recent *The Conflagration of Community* attests.

Miller has accessed and assembled the polymorphous materials that he has synthesized into a "golden braid" of landmark readings completely on his own. While *The First Sail* duly notes his close friendships and collaborations with other powerful figures, notably Paul de Man, Jacques Derrida, and Harold Bloom, Miller relied on himself to know what was important, what moat urgently demanded rereading and recasting. As he recounts in the film, his earliest U.S. ancestor emigrated as a Hessian Revolutionary War soldier in service to the British. He traces his oldest-native-born ancestor to 1786. Among the families to which the Millers—and the maternal Critzers—were linked over time was the Hopkins family (as in Johns Hopkins), only a chance linkage to his eventually teaching there. Miller's omnivorous literary and methodological appetite not only had a distinctly American cast; so did the utterly democratic rapport he maintained with his students, resolutely refusing to rank, "filter," "manage" or "administer" them in any way. Their fate would be to settle into the niche, as into the virtual reading archive, of their own devising.

*The First Sail* indeed documents that Miller is as assiduous a reader of social sub-systems and the universities with which he's been affiliated as of literary texts and theoretical exposition. Yet he has never allowed himself to become the fixture of a particular institution, wherever it ranks in the pantheon of academies, to take on its institutional idiom, attitude, and invective. It was with striking fluidity that he was able to leave first Johns Hopkins and then Yale behind when it became clear that his overarching critical mission, his interactive and self-referential critical "beat" over time and reading, would be better served in a different environment. He is renowned for the pains he has taken, as a mentor and as an information-broker, to assure that his charges could thrive in whichever institutional settings that housed them. Yet the rigor with which he has refused to practice institutional operations on his students may well be the crown jewel of the overall radical democracy in which he has cast his activities as a teacher, literary and theoretical authority, and force in the academic profession. This is: absolutely unbiased and unrestricted equality with respect to the classroom, reading, and productive interchange with students and colleagues. This educational bearing is a collaborative project with J. Hillis Miller the elder that has persisted more than six decades after his death. Floating unpowered over the smooth space of water with one's intellectual soulmates is a particularly tangible, touching form that radical democracy assumes. In the imagery of "The First Sail," a love of sailing shared by father and son translates into the very best that the amalgam of American colleges and universities can achieve. As we sail along the poetically dense thought-patterns communicated by Hillis's unforgettable voice, we are reminded that for all that public higher education in particular may be impacted, at least in the short-run, a stunningly open-access commitment to excellence is still within the U.S. system's reach.

It is perforce that *The First Sail* highlights Miller's resolutely constructive long-term collaboration with Jacques Derrida and his globe-trotting participation at the most "happening" of world-wide symposia, wherever they have happened to take place. A disproportion of Miller's public profile of the past three or so decades is taken up by these roles. Yet a long personal and intellectual history were already under way, the accretion of a unique mindset and readerly practice, well in advance of these familiar images. In tracking Miller back to Maine, site of the home he made with his lifetime partner, Dorothy, the constant home-base amid notable moves and constant travel, and where he keeps his books, Kujundžić admirably opens up the broader panorama on Miller's biography and achievement.

Ironically, from a "down East" point of view, and in spite of half a century's residence on Deer Isle and then also in Sedgwick, Maine, he is still regarded as "from elsewhere." Although truly the mainstay of a virtual community of readers and critics who depend on his relentless sanity as his inventiveness, the itinerant critic Miller is, ultimately, as homeless as the rest of us. He is homeless in the sense of that composite rebus Odradek, in Kafka's "Die Sorge des Hausvaters," whose specific address is "no fixed abode." Miller is himself a creature of the open-ended fluid movement figured best of all in the random plying of a sailboat along the Maine coast. Punctuating this flow are the haunting, dissonant chords of Natalia Pschenichnikova's carefully composed soundtrack for the film. The music reminds us aurally that abodes are not as "fixed" as they may appear; that sailing on board the dialectical sailboat of Benjamin's pivotal Convolute N of *The Arcades Project* is almost never smooth.

The Miller who is never quite at home, whose constant updating and reformulation of his own critical output pushes back against the architecture of any established corpus others might attribute to him, subtends the image the documentary offers us of Miller comfortably ensconced among a substantial home-library of publications that he has self-fashioned. Pamela Gilbert, MC of a University of Florida conference dedicated to Miller's work spliced in early in the documentary, properly reminds us of the full panoply of theoretical discourses to which Miller has productively contributed: queer and environmental theories prominent recent entries in a group of long-standing methodological idioms; formal criticism, narratology, deconstruction, and speech-act theory chief among these latter. Yet in my own futile efforts to keep up with Miller's productivity, setting my ongoing readings in Miller on a parallel but completely distinct track with my readings in Derrida, it is Miller's ongoing recursion to speech-act theory, the study of where the "tread" of open-ended linguistic ambiguity and play meets the "road" of actions implemented as well as programmed by words, that claims a special privilege. Going back even before his 2001 *Speech Acts in Literature*, Miller has elucidated speech acts convincingly and demonstrated their relevance, indeed their indispensability, to the literary and theoretical works under discussion every time he has broached the topic. What, I found myself asking at one juncture, drives Miller back to this particular "scene of the critical crime."

I was only fully prepared to take in yet another mind-boggling lesson from my teacher when treated to his recent work on communities in and around literature: their possibility, their constitution, their "wiring," and their duration. In his forthcoming *Communities in Fiction*, Miller brings us back to some of the most compelling "virtual" landscapes that have made him who he is. Among the ports of call in this landmark study: Trollope, Hardy, Conrad, Woolf, and Pynchon. This is, on multiple levels, a work of "homing." Miller's credo, in his capacity as "first reader" within the rhizomatic community of scholars, readers, and writers that has homesteaded around him for all these decades, is that these texts, more than any geographical locale or academic institution, are his true home. With an intellectual generosity surpassing itself with each successive study, Miller once again, in *Communities in Fiction*, brings us "home," to the home that most matters.

Now the social code lending this virtual literary topography any order or coherence it can claim is the code (or program) of speech acts. For Miller, these tropes, both substantive and operative, exercise a relevance and exigency that is inexhaustible. Speech acts are what his remarkable watch on the literature of the 19th and 20th centuries, a vast library of philosophical and critical thinkers, and edifying acuity to political and technological developments has brought him: this as a compelling means of addressing intangibles also encountered in such fields as depth psychology and Cognitive Science. Particularly in the long chapter on Hardy, Miller appeals to speech acts as the social and linguistic operating system of communities, virtual and otherwise. Yet as he concedes near the end of the Hardy section, speech acts are the software of social systems as thinkers from Max Weber and Simmel to Luhmann adumbrate them. Speech acts may abound and flourish in virtual fictive environments, but as Miller acknowledges, in real-world social systems, they not only serve as edifying instruments of striving and reality-testing, as they do in the world of Trollope. They can also be used for purposes of deliberate falsification, misinformation, libel, profiling, filtration, exclusion, and persecution (even when a "civil face" is applied to these functions).

It is no small measure of Miller's devotion to his students, one membership I haven't allowed to lapse, that he has insisted upon their full literacy and facility in the language of speech acts. This is a strategy as much of self-protection as of advancement. Speech acts not only share crucial structural features with embedded cybernetic operating languages (notably, isomorphism); in object-relations theory, they are the very instrument of manifestly non-empathic (in this sense, anti-communal) "acting out." Speech acts are very acute instruments that can cut both ways. While amid the virtual domains of cultural fascination, speech acts can be studied with impunity to their fundamentally controlling and self-interested cast; in the world of institutional actuality, as a tangible phenomenon, they demand ongoing and pitched vigilance. It even makes practical sense for any of us in the critical community, those of us whose true home is somewhere in VR—to hone in on the embedded codes of the "operative" communities with which we are affiliated—at whatever remove of affiliation or alienation we are situated. Through fluency in this action-language, one might attain something like social mastery—whose only liability in turn would be, under conditions of sedateness or an exaggerated sense of "social ownership" or entitlement, critical blindness to new and potentially fruitful "lines of thought." It's not by accident that Derrida initiated the storied trajectory of deconstruction with a questioning of "propriety" as concerted and deliberate as the one regarding "presence."

*The First Sail* is an invitation to and a celebration of the critical community that Miller has configured as much out of his politics of education as through his exegetical and theoretical creativity. Its visual vocabulary is spare but striking. Even in setting out, Kujundžić is fully aware that the centerpiece of the document has to be Miller's conversation, his verbal discourse itself. Miller's conversation is an artwork and a legend on our times in its own right. The flow in this remarkable commentary, which ranges across the field of theoretical influences, memorable works of poetry and fiction, and reminiscences of friends and colleagues, is the accretion not only of Miller's encounters with artworks, conceptual models, and significant others, but of conversations that his projects have struck up, both with themselves and with others of his projects. Among many of Miller's critical distinctions, his relentless insistence on revising and upgrading, substantively and methodologically, his "takes" looms particularly large.

Miller's conversational voice is the synthesis of *all* the signature intellectual interchanges, transpiring in a milieu of empathy and *ouverture* to the other, with which we have ever been blessed. While delivered in the real time of filming and in this sense seemingly off-hand, Miller's comments are in fact the result of loops of "second-order processing" that have taken place under his watch, in an unbroken stream of critical mindfulness, for six decades as of this writing. Dragan Kujundžić, in understanding that the stream of Miller's elaborated conversation is what we, the critical community, particularly need to *hear* from Miller, is what readers and cultural participants at a further remove need to *take in* of Miller, sets the agenda for further efforts at academic documentation in the wake of *The First Sail* with discerning prescience.

It may well be that our richest property as critics is seemingly what is most readily to hand and mundane: the "strange loops" of imagery, articulation, and theoretical savvy that have become inextricably embedded into our conversation. We are capable of spinning out this oral-discursive fabric almost on demand. Yet as the palimpsest of lifetime engagements with cultural artifacts, colleagues, and mentors, and in courses, both taken and given, lectures, and at other public events, our conversation may well be, even if we don't match up to Miller, the best of us that can be recorded and archived. As the supplement to our writings, that is.

Everything in *The First Sail* is strategically, aesthetically, and didactically gauged to highlight Miller's conversation, whether to a receptive audience in Gainesville, Florida or in a sailboat with Richard Eaton, a friend. It is in framing Miller's oral-textual achievement as a conversationalist that *The First Sail* succeeds most admirably and consistently.

Kujundžić deftly splices three parallel frames to Miller's utterly singular and original conversation together: public appearances at major conferences, the 2003 "J" Conference at UC-Irvine, at which Derrida rendered touching tribute to a friendship with Hillis approaching four decades' duration (Derrrida's last U.S. appearance before learning of his own fatal malady), and in Gainsville; ambient scenes (sailing, walking) in the coastal Maine environment; and extended discussions in Miller's Sedgwick study. This conversation is, literally, the admission-ticket to the film. As it pursues its trajectory from Miller's ancestral roots and partnership with Dorothy to the succession of his career, to his particularly meaningful exchanges with de Man and Derrida, to his deepest personal stakes in reading and in cultural inscription, this chat never wavers in its intensity, precision, humanity, and empathy. Miller lauds Derrida in particular for his "extraordinary ability to play in language," and cites the latter's construction, "auto-co-immunity," as a telling late instance of a verbal facility enabling the latter, in short shrift, to extract the *social* significance of auto-immune deficiency while "working through" his highly ambivalent rapport to communities, both on the large scale and in the immediate vicinity. Performing a brief gloss of Yeats's "The Cold Heaven" on camera, Miller attests to finding it still "immensely moving," to being compelled by "the linguistic concentration and complexity." Through Kujundžić's lens, we see that the renowned teacher and critic is still driven by primal cultural instinct, one enabling him to freely cross, as few of us do, the frontier between literary and cultural wonderment and expressed political disenchantment. Miller's musings on current environmental disaster and a bottom-line economic policy that has given us derivatives and the financial meltdown of 2008 are as informed by his facility with concepts and his unerring readerly intuition as his masterful recent books. His utterly unabashed taking a stand is a timely reminder and incentive for us all.

It is these turns of a conversation itself synthesized out of self-referential and autopoietic critical oversight that are the rich reward of viewing "The First Sail." To whatever degree *The First Sail* was produced amid the gorgeous landscape and intimate trappings of Miller's long-time home, his performance is a public one, with its own constraints and demands. When Miller converses, it is *on the record,* if on no other record, the transcript of his unbroken string of eventful cultural engagements and syntheses. Miller has worked hard by the end of the extended discussion late in the film. Intimate and personal though the conversation may be, it is *not* a casual matter.

Dragan Kujundžić has subtended this documentary of J. Hillis Miller's life, times, and sensibility with a profound understanding of the weft and warp of critical thinking and text. He has thereby remembered to record, at many levels of reference and detail, what is of most importance about a mind of luminescent aesthetic taste, theoretical originality, and ethical sensibility. He has undertaken this vital project both in the service of Miller's "immediate" but vast critical community *and* for those who have not been fortunate enough to interact with him directly. These values, of aesthetics and ethics as well as of production, will serve further projects of documenting ourselves—and I fervently hope they ensue—exceptionally well indeed.

These are but a few of the considerations awakened in me by viewing "The First Sail." They are of course modulated by the particular circumstances of the long-standing relationship with my teacher with which I've been blessed. What follows in the present volume is a series of responses to the film and explanations of far greater precision and ingenuity than anything that I have been able to muster. Additional materials, including an interview with the director, and consistently incisive commentaries, touching the film's circumstances, imagery, composition, rhythms, moods, its broader theoretical context, and its signature images, follow. The critical receptions have been rendered by Sarah Dillon, Éamonn Dunne, Charlie Gere, Michael O'Rourke, Nicholas Royle, and Julian Wolfreys, as well as by the director himself. Readers will unmistakably note that these responses speak eloquently for themselves. They are written at a level of detail and with a wit and precision that J. Hillis Miller has infused into his ongoing pedagogy and exemplified throughout every dimension of his work and public service.

# Part 1

*Film Transcript*

# The First Sail: J. Hillis Miller.

Video. Deer Isle Productions, 2011.

Sound of waves and of foghorn in darkness.

                                                                               00:30

Opening shot, the Deer Isle Stonington Lighthouse in daytime.

On screen title:

The First Sail

J Hillis Miller

A film by Dragan Kujundžić

                                                                               01:03

Benjamin River, Maine, establishing shots. Hillis entering a dinghy, talking to his sailing mate Richard Eaton.

On screen title: Deer Isle, Main, June 12, 2010

                                                                               01:18

> Are we ready?
>
> We are ready!

Richard Eaton starts rowing towards the sailboat. The camera is hand held, wavers, and moves with the waves of the floating platform, trying to get Hillis into focus of the long shot.

                                                                               01:47

### PAMELA GILBERT (OFF CAMERA):

J. Hillis Miller has cast a long shadow over literary criticism and theory in the second half of the Twentieth Century. He began publishing in 1952, in the *Harvard Advocate*.

Pamela Gilbert now on screen, with on screen title:

"Dr. Pamela Gilbert, University of Florida, October 12, 2006. 'Who or What?— Jacques Derrida,' Academic Conference."

### PAMELA GILBERT:

Since that time he has published (I am sure I am shorting him on this) well over one hundred articles and chapters and twenty some odd books.

### HILLIS FROM THE AUDIENCE:

Sounds about right.

### PAMELA GILBERT:

Sounds about right (laughs).

02:12

### HILLIS AND RICHARD ROWING, PAMELA GILBERT CONTINUES OFF SCREEN:

He was educated at Oberlin, and Harvard University, he taught at Johns Hopkins and Yale, and his most recent appointment was and is as UCI Distinguished Research Professor in the Department of Comparative Literature and English, where he taught until recently, since 1986. He is a Fellow of the American Arts and Sciences, past president of the MLA, and a *doctor honoris causa* of numerous universities, including of course the University of Florida. Hillis work spans 19$^{th}$ and 20$^{th}$ century English, American and Comparative Literature, and of course literary theory. His interests included phenomenological criticism, speech act theory, deconstruction, cultural studies, and queer theory… His most recent books include *Topographies*, *On Literature: Thinking in Action*, *Literature as Conduct: Speech Acts in Henry James*, (this is a very abbreviated list), and he is currently working on a book on later Derrida and his work recently has focused mostly on communities in literature.

Miller's influence simply cannot be overestimated. Prolific and original critic and theorist, he was a popularizer of Derrida's ideas at the time when they seemed very opaque to many literary critics (and that is how I first encountered his [Derrida'] work struggling with these exciting ideas).

PAMELA GILBERT ON SCREEN:

James Kinkaid accurately said that 'Hillis brought to the field an intelligence so deft and at the same time so generous that he made us all feel smarter.'
And I think that's accurate.

03: 52

HILLIS IN THE SAILBOAT, SAILING
TOWARDS THE CAMERA, VOICEOVER:

Why do I like sailing as opposed to motorboats? I think it's pretty clear, it's a kind of flight fantasy—flight not in the sense of running away but in the sense of flying—it's the fact that it doesn't involve a motor. So there's something kind of magic about it. You're harnessing the wind and making use of the wind to move across the water and it takes a lot of skill to learn how to do that.

DRAGAN:

You also told me that you like to throw airplanes, model planes.

HILLIS:

Yes, it's related to the interest I had not in motorized model planes but in gliders, same thing. They're called gliders, no motor; you just throw them up in the air and if you do it right they circle around and come down. In fact, I used to design and make my own, from my own designs. This was all the way up until I was married, until I was twenty-one I was doing that. It obviously had an important role in my fantasy life, because of the idea of being free of the earth, floating around up there.

### HILLIS SAILING, SPEAKING TO THE CAMERA:

We are going to sail off into the distance.
Everything has been put together wrong!
So it took us longer than I promised you.
But we'll sail out here and sail back.

The boat sails into the distance, fade out.

06:01

### PAMELA GILBERT, ON SCREEN:

Let us now put everything in question:
Professor J. Hillis Miller.

### HILLIS, ON CAMERA:

I wore the jacket so you could see me take it off… But that's all I'm going to take off… (Laughter) It's really too warm. Can I be heard in the back? Raise your hand if I get inaudible or if I start talking to myself. Which may be the case anyway. (Laughter).

I once heard a reading by Wallace Stevens where I happened to be near the front. As the hour went on Stevens got more and more carried away by his own poetry and his voice got softer and softer, people in the back started getting out of the room and leaving, he paid no attention… he went on reading… But I could hear, I was near the front, he read "Large Red Man Reading " and "Credences of Summer," "Now in the midsummer come and all fools slaughtered…" It was a wonderful experience. But I remember him… He was an insurance executive, I remember him quite falsely, as wearing high button shoes and a celluloid collar. That's not true, but he was, like his "Jar in Tennessee," "tall and of a port in air." He was a big man.

Hillis and Dragan leafing through a book by Jacques Derrida; zoom to the handwritten book dedication to Hillis and Dorothy, briefly discernible. Hillis continues off camera:

> This is a very light-hearted lecture, unlike the more serious ones that we've had.
>
> It's called "Derrida's Politics of Autoimmunity," but it has a subtitle which I did not share with my introducer, which is "Horror Autotoxicus" (laughter).

07:56

```
          BACK TO HILLIS ON CAMERA, LECTURE:
```

> "Horror autotoxicus" was the name as you'll see, I'll come back to this, given a century ago by the visionary bacteriologist Paul Erhlich, to autoimmunity. He called it "horror autotoxicus." So this is really a lecture about "horror autotoxicus."

Fadeout.

08:18

Sailing, Benjamin River.

Cut to Gainesville, establishing shot, on screen title:

"President's House, University of Florida, March 23, 2010."

```
          INTERIOR OF THE HOUSE, DRAGAN OFF
          CAMERA, HANDING HILLIS A PICTURE:
```

> Let me just show this picture to Hillis, it is in the Spring of 1953. (The picture of Hillis' father and mother). I would like to ask Hillis what he remembers, if he has any memory of this.

```
                    HILLIS:
```

Well that would've been nearby, certainly. That's my parents in their early 50s, in 1953. They were born either in 1899 or 1900; I'm not quite sure. So that would've been about when they were about fifty-three. My father died when he was fifty-three. And they would've been standing right out here, right in front of the house.

Right out front, yes.

Intertitle:

Hillis' father, J. Hillis Miller Sr., served as President of the University of Florida from 1947 to 1953. He oversaw the first years of co-educational enrollment and made seminal steps in establishing the university's now prestigious medical college.

09:31

Back on camera

> HILLIS:
>
> He's giving her a flower. (*laughing*)
>
> DRAGAN:
>
> A flower, yes. You said he had a runner's heart?
>
> HILLIS:
>
> Yes, he was a marathon runner.
>
> DRAGAN:
>
> He was a runner?
>
> HILLIS:
>
> Oh yes, he was a very good marathon runner. I've inherited from him my father's lungs.

A photograph of "Hillis age 11 with his father," the father giving Hillis a sailboat as a gift.

> ...and legs because I found it easy to learn how to run; I was up to ten kilometers

every other day for quite a long time. Not anymore, I can't run that far. But he had rheumatic fever in his teenage years before he did the running. That damages the heart. The running probably didn't help any.

DRAGAN:

He didn't know that probably?

HILLIS:

He didn't know that it didn't help? Well he might not have cared. He was among other things, and I haven't heard anybody mention this, a great sportsman. Fishing—he loved fishing, and camping.

10:30

Before he came here, my father was Associate Commissioner for Higher and Professional Education for the State of New York. So he was in charge... He presided over the decision not to have one huge central state university, but to create the SUNY system. Doesn't mean he did it single handed, but as the Associate Commissioner for Higher and Professional Education, he was the Chair of the committee that had to decide—after the war, like Florida, there was a huge increase of the number of students, and they had to do something. And they decided, I think correctly, because the alternative would have been to have one huge campus somewhere. Whereas I think New York State is probably served better by having Binghamton and Albany and Buffalo.

So that was a hard decision for my father to leave what was important work in Albany, as Associate Commissioner. He had supervised the accreditation of new places. Yeshiva—I remember the whole process of giving them accreditation, allowing them to give advanced degrees, and so on. So it was not unimportant work. And Florida, the University of Florida, 2500 students? In the middle of a bunch of palmettos, etcetera.

He saw this as a risky but very challenging opportunity, because he was a daring, courageous administrator. And he'd never been President of a big university, only of a small college. And he realized that there was going to be expansion, big expansion, so they must have sold it to him on those grounds.

The promise was that he could build buildings, develop programs, and that's what he did. He appointed deans, lots of deans; he brought a guy that he had known before as the Vice President. He appointed a whole lot of other people. He built a lot of buildings, and presided over the transformation of the University of Florida into a major research university.

And he foresaw that this would give him lots of opportunity actually to do things and he enjoyed that immensely. That's how he got his jollies; it was building a new building, persuading the legislature to do the medical school, helping the law school become a major law school, all of those things he really liked.

DRAGAN:

If he saw this now with 50,000 students he would be proud. But this would be something he anticipated.

HILLIS:

Yes. And all this was in the name of educating of people and in the name of the academic freedom that he talks about in that quotation [you gave yesterday in your introduction to my lecture], freedom to think, freedom to write, freedom to teach, and so on.

Intertitle:

From 1953 to 1972 Hillis Jr. taught at The Johns Hopkins University where he forged a lifelong friendship with Jacques Derrida,

one of the most celebrated philosophers
and critical theorists of our time.

In 1972, Miller joined the faculty at Yale
University alongside many other renowned
literary critics including Paul de Man,
Harold Bloom, and Geoffrey Hartman.

Fadeout.

14:02

HILLIS ON CAMERA IN THE UF
PRESIDENT'S HOUSE, CONTINUES:

No, I went there in '72, so it would've been
1972. And I've always remembered this, as Paul
went up the stairs to his bedroom, because
we lived in a fair sized Victorian house, he
turned around and said, "you're in," and then
he hesitated and typical de Man, "If you want
to be." And it was the next day that I got the
call from the Chair offering me a job at Yale.

And I should finish this by saying that
Bloom and I became very close colleagues
and friends, later, thereafter.

DRAGAN OFF CAMERA:

Was he the one, you told me, who
wrote, "Be bold, be very bold"?

HILLIS:

Oh yes, when I was Chair he had the privilege
of using the little corner bathroom.
And he would come rolling by when I was
running some committee meeting around the
table, muttering under this breath but
loud enough for everybody to hear:

"*Oh, I must void the Bloomian bladder.*" He
would disappear into this little room. And then
sometimes when I wasn't there I would come back
and find this little note on my desk that would
say, "be bold, be very bold!" signed, *Ignoto*. I
could tell that this was Bloomian handwriting.

He was a boy from the Bronx, who had never been in the country. Ithaca as you know is in the boondocks; it's a pretty small place. So Bloom was out walking with somebody, I don't think it was his room-mate Schneewind (who became a distinguished philosopher, specializing in nineteenth-century British philosophy), but again I'm sure this is a true story. Suddenly he draws himself up and says 'what is that enormous hairy animal?' And his friend says, 'Harold, that's a cow.' (*laughing*) He had never seen a cow.

DRAGAN, OFF CAMERA:

That turned out later to be quite a school, right? When Jacques came a few years later …

HILLIS:

That was Paul and I who managed to put that over on the Provost because it was provostial money, completely free money, that it was not a real appointment, he was appointed simply to come once a year. And it was run out of whatever department Paul de Man was Chair of at the point, so it was run out of French when he was still Chair of French, and then when he moved to be Chair of Comp Lit—I mean the bureaucratic side of it, getting him paid and all that sort of thing; getting him a room to lecture in. It was typical Derrida, the size of the class got bigger and bigger from year to year as people began to hear about this.

DRAGAN:

How come his name was first mentioned…
Paul de Man knew him probably? …

HILLIS:

Oh Derrida? I know what you're asking. It probably was Paul's idea because de Man probably knew Derrida personally. Well … it's not quite that simple because I used to have lunch with Derrida at Hopkins long before I went to Yale, so we knew one another pretty well. And I think when I followed de Man from Hopkins to Yale, then we said 'oh, maybe we can get Derrida to shift from Hopkins to Yale.'

Fadeout.

18:02

### HILLIS' LECTURE AT UF CONTINUES:

"I am not one of the family," says Derrida, in general, "I do not define myself on the basis of my belonging to the family, or to civil society, or to the state, I do not define myself on the basis of elementary forms of kinship"—so much for Lévi-Strauss—

"but it also means more figuratively that I am not part of any group, that I do not identify myself with linguistic community, a national community, a political party, or with any group or clique whatsoever, with any philosophical or literary school."[1] So much for the "Yale School" or any idea that Derrida thought himself as part of it (laughter).

Sailing, Benjamin River.

Fadeout.

Establishing shot, Hillis' winter residence house. Title on screen, "Sedgwick, Maine, June 5th, 2010"

Close up on water stream running nearby.

Zoom on Hillis' eye, wound and scar over his eye in slow motion.

Inside the house.

19:00

### DRAGAN (OFF CAMERA THROUGHOUT):

---

[1] Jacques Derrida and Maurizio Ferraris, *A Taste for the Secret*, trans. Giacomo Donis, ed. Giacomo Donis and David Webb (Cambridge, England: Polity Press, 2001), 27.

Hillis, how did you get this scar? Did
you get into a fight or something?
What did you do to the other guy?

HILLIS:

Yes, you should see the other guy, right. No, I tripped in California on the campus. Just stepped aside, and tripped and fell down. I think the cut was caused by the glass, because the glasses were broken, and the lens came out. Because it's a very neat cut, but it was very deep. Deep enough to require some stitches. ...

Video set-up with Dragan and Hillis; video of Derrida played on a laptop computer;

Close up on Hillis' reactions to the lecture.

20:00

JACQUES DERRIDA OFF SCREEN, CAMERA
TRAINED ON HILLIS WATCHING:

"*Je me suis si souvent demandé*, I have so often asked myself, perhaps for more than thirty-five years, from the depths of my friendship and admiration for him, how one could be J. Hillis Miller. (Hillis laughs). *Quel est son 'je' à lui?* What is his own 'je, his own 'I'? And what taste could this *je*, this 'I' have?

The taste I have for him or the taste he has for others and for me, is it the same?"

Hillis dissolves into Jacques Derrida's lecture, seen on a MacBook Pro laptop:

"Is it the same as the one he has for himself?"

On screen title:

"Jacques Derrida, 'J': Around the Work of J. Hillis Miller," Academic Conference,

University of California, Irvine, April 18, 2003"

JACQUES DERRIDA LECTURE ON THE LAPTOP, CONT.:

"One may very well doubt that it is. This doubt likewise takes on a very perceptible flavor in me, an obscurely immediate sense. We are moving here in that strange geometry where the nearest and the most distant are but one and the same. The most similar and the infinitely other return in a circle to each other. How does J. Hillis Miller *himself* feel when he says 'je,' 'I' or when he has the feeling of 'himself'"?

The computer dissolves, close up of Jacques Derrida at the lectern:

"Now, with your permission, I confess and make public my original sin, namely, the first wrong I committed against J. as against the hidden God of this first name. In 1969, I had known Hillis for a year; we were already linked by friendship, thanks to another Hopkins, this time Johns Hopkins. We were then teaching together and we already had our Tuesday lunches, a tradition that continued from Hopkins to Yale and still continues at Irvine thirty years later. Well, I was at the time foolish enough and thought myself clever enough to believe I was capable of deciphering on my own the hidden first name behind the J. I was also ignorant enough of American customs to exhibit presumptuously the result of my supposed discovery. I thus wrote to Hillis, no doubt more than once (I have no archive of this), letters whose envelopes bore the address: John Hillis Miller. I probably committed this wrong very many times, to Hillis's amusement or irritation, when I received from him, on June $2^{nd}$, 1969, a long, beautiful, and richly detailed letter.

Then, in two lines, came a postscript. Here it is, you will see it, I am not lying to you (laughter): 'By the way, my first name is "Joseph," not "John," not that it matters in the least, since I've never used that name in any case!'"

Jacques Derrida turns to an assistant helping with the overhead projector:

"You can now show the letter."

23:28

Close up to the letter. Jacques Derrida off screen and in darkness while the letter is being projected:

"I've never used that name in any case! Exclamation point. By saying that he had 'never used' it, he meant that no one, no one in the world (except me, in sum, and then wrongly!) had ever used it to call him, in the performative, vocative, and apostrophizing mode of address. No one had ever addressed him by calling him 'Hi, J. Hillis!' or 'Hi, Joseph Hillis!'

Here then is the initial of a name before the name, here is the initial of a hidden first name that, by a sort of sacred proscription or sacred prescription, it is forbidden to approach or pronounce in ordinary life and every day. Something like a divine first name hidden in the name."

"You should now turn the projector off"

JACQUES DERRIDA, ON SCREEN, CONT.:

"This will be in the Archive …"

Fadeout.

24:00

J. Hillis Miller on screen.

DRAGAN:

What comes to your mind when you see this picture?

HILLIS:

Well, I was thinking about that. Several things: very moving, of course. And one thing that I noticed seeing this picture was that he was already looking old and not all that well.

So it was only a couple of years before he died.

The other thing, I said it was very moving to see, but it is like the return of a ghost, and it makes you think of the possibilities of new technologies, which allow the survival in such a strikingly immediate kind of way of somebody who is now dead. Just as we can now—I talk about this in *The Medium is the Maker*—you can now hear Glenn Gould playing "The Goldberg Variations," even though those fingers that were so amazing on the keyboard aren't around anymore. So I'm very much aware of that.

The other thing that I noticed as you were playing it backwards, trying to find your way, playing it a second time so it could be filmed, is the, you might say, de-naturing effect of the possibility of repetition. You know that you can play this over and over again. You did this, just now. And the effect of that doubling is uncanny, and in a sense it reinforces this ghost, this ghost keeps coming, this uncanny ghost can be brought back at any time. On the other hand it distances it, because it reminds you—it reminded me at any rate—this is only an artifact, it's not really Jacques Derrida, it's just the product of an enormously complicated digital means of reproduction. So that means that I'm moved but not—let's put it this way—not to tears, because it doesn't really come through to me as the return of Jacques Derrida.

26:51

The other thing that is pretty obvious is his command of what he was saying is fantastic. You know, by the time he's got through the first minute you're completely in his hands, and you know that there's something absolutely original going on, that nobody has ever said in that way before. And you are—this is the thing that would be lost in the transcription—you realize how much of this depended on facial expression, timing, hesitations, sense of humor, smiles, and on the play of the two languages—the accent, the irrepressible way in which he would say it in French, have to say some of these things in French, and then in English.

So I think what Derrida has is an extraordinary sensibility to play in language, and what you can make that do. That was certainly true of those pages. The other memory that I have, an early Derrida memory, when Derrida was then hired by Hopkins to come every third year and give two seminars, he'd be there for a whole semester. It was different from the arrangement at Yale or Irvine, where he came every year. At Hopkins he came every third year.

So he came. So I went around to hear the first seminar, which was on Plato, on *Mimesis*. Just to see whether I could still understand spoken French. It was that trivial. And the first seminar was the one on Mallarmé's *Mimique*, and Plato on *Mimesis*. And I thought it was fantastic! I had never heard a seminar like that, anywhere. So I started a lifetime of listening to Derrida's seminars, because you never knew what they were going to be like.

But I really ask myself what is going on in Derrida that's so fascinating, it's a continuous ... there's a passage in Valéry, somewhere, which is always stuck in my mind.

Where Valéry says, language ... words like "time" are not at all problematic, as when you say, "What time is it?" or "Hurry up please, it's time," or something. They only become enigmatic when you ask questions like "What is time?" And the image he gives is a narrow plank over an abyss. If you just walk briskly across that plank, no problem. If you stop in the middle and start jumping up and down on the plank, big problem! *(laughing)* And asking yourself, "What is time?" "Do I understand what time is?" is like jumping up and down on the plank. And that's what Derrida does, all of the time...

DRAGAN:

A lot of jumping up and down over the abyss.

HILLIS:

A lot of jumping on narrow planks over the abyss.

Crossfade.

….

30:35

HILLIS, CONT.:

He used to talk about the office hours at Irvine; he was very good at holding office hours. And he would say these people would often come a long way, to show up at his office hours, they would come in and sit across his desk from him, over there in the French department. And then they would be so anxious and frightened that they wouldn't say anything, they would just sit there (*laughing*). And Derrida said this was very difficult, he would sit there waiting for them to say something. And they would just sit silently, looking across, totally tongue-tied. You know, here I am in the presence of the great Jacques Derrida and what could I say to him that would be at all commensurate with the greatness … And he said this was very difficult, apparently it happened all the time. He never knew what to do, what to say next.

Crossfade.

….

HILLIS, CONT.:

"There is a feature of the Derrida book which is not simply praise and mourning, but there is another side of Derrida which most people I think would not go along with. There is a dark side and I wanted to bring that side out, not necessarily to agree with it, perhaps to disagree with it, but also to bring out what I see is heterogeneity in his work. You already mentioned one place where this exists. And that is this idea of autoimmunity. That's a very interesting claim. He claims, Derrida, very powerfully, in the quite late essays on religion and other places, that not individual human beings, but collectivities, such as a nation-state, are inhabited by, what he calls an "auto-co-immunity," playing on "community," and "auto-immunity." That is like the autoimmune disease that, by the way, killed him, because pancreatic cancer is, one explanation of it, it that it is an autoimmune disease. The notion of immunity, and also of auto-immunity, is taken from the social realm, because *"munus"*—it's the same as in the word community—*munus* meant somebody who was authorized by the state in some way, some kind of leader, in a community. Somebody who was immune would be somebody who was protected in some way, ... the *"munus"* was the money that you had to pay, that you owed, roughly speaking.

For example, if I'm a thief or something, and make it into the church, I'm immune. You can't arrest me. So that language was then taken by scientists to describe the immune system. It's an interesting metaphorical transfer. And then they discovered auto-immunity, that is to say, this dangerous situation in which the immune system protects the body from itself, and can begin destroying organs, like the pancreas.

What Derrida does is take that concept of auto-immunity, and put it back into the social realm where it originally came from. And he makes a kind of law of this; what's interesting about it is that the immune system is not within our control, so it's not something that you can cure by thinking about it. It just goes on doing its thing. The endocrine system does this, the various hormones travel around, etcetera. And when something goes wrong with it, you can't cure it by thinking about it. It's a part of the body that's mechanical, one might say. "Machine-al." The immune system just goes on doing its thing.

And Derrida wants to transfer that aspect to society. And it's frightening. It says that every, he's saying, every, any, community or nation, or group that's organized politically in some way, has an inevitable tendency to destroy itself. Like an autoimmune disease, which is lethal, in the end.

36:08

Cut to Hillis' lecture on autoimmunity at UF:

"It's funny, during the Vietnam War I was against the Vietnam War, strongly and totally, unhappy about it, but I was not what I am now, which is frightened… Not so much frightened by the war on terror, but…. our own government.

Cut to Hillis, Sedgwick:

However nice these people are, however much devoted they are to liberal ideas, etcetera, etcetera. So you'd have to say there's a real contradiction there. So to stress too much the positive political hopefulness, etcetera, the idea that you can always begin again, the notion of a performative as an inaugural moment, etcetera all of those are there in Derrida, but it's interesting that at the end of his life, that auto-immunity thing appears and it's not very hopeful.

The phone rings off camera. Hillis reaches to it.

Crossfade.

…

Hillis, cont.:

DRAGAN:

Let me ask you what Marc Redfield asked you, he prefaced it by saying, "if you dare," that is, if I dare. To which I responded, "It's your question!"

**HILLIS:**

Don't blame me. (*laughing*) Don't blame the messenger.

**DRAGAN:**

So he says, "ask him—if you dare—whether he ever felt jealous or competitive with Paul and Jacques?"

**HILLIS:**

Oh sure. Yes, of course. There's a part of me that's somewhat annoyed by the fact that we've spent so much time talking about Derrida (*winks; laughs*). Sure. For every person who reads my stuff, there are a hundred people who read Derrida. Yes, I'm a competitive person. But I'm happy to have such success as I have had.

Fadeout.

Intertitle:

"That is my last word. At least for now. It is the end of what have to say 'For Derrida,' in the double sense of 'In memory of Derrida, dedicated to Derrida,' and 'on behalf of Derrida.' As though he needed my defense! Are these chapters 'works of mourning'? Probably, they have also been my way of discovering that Derrida was right when he said that mourning is 'impossible,' 'absolute,' 'endless,' and in the end only with difficulty to be distinguished from melancholy. If these essays are works of mourning, they have not worked."

—J. Hillis Miller, "Absolute Mourning," *For Derrida*, (2009).

Fadeout.

Photograph of Hillis and Derrida in 2002.

VOICE OF JACQUES DERRIDA, OFF:

"For nothing in the world would I have passed up the chance to recall publicly that it has been given to me, like a benediction, to know Joseph Hillis Miller for more than thirty-five years, to have had the honor of teaching at his side … the honor also of having shared with him more than with any other, through I don't know how many countries, colloquia, meetings of all sorts, the intellectual adventure that signs and seals our lives."

Fadeout

39:29

Exterior shot of (the front of) home.

Shot of the driveway going out into a wooded area. In the distance Hillis has just put a letter in the mailbox and is walking into the scene along the driveway. Sound of feet on gravel. Fade in and out photograph of the mailbox and home driveway street sign: "Hungry Deer Dr. 697"

HILLIS WALKS PAST THE CAMERA
AND OUT OF THE FRAME:

Am I on camera?

Cut to sailing, Benjamin River.

Cut to home interior, Sedgwick.

DRAGAN:

Tell us a little about where we are now, what brought you here, and then I will have some follow-up questions about Maine.

HILLIS:

We're in our winter house in Sedgwick, Maine, which is on the mainland across from Deer Isle, which means that the water nearby is the Eggemoggin Reach, which separates the mainland from Deer Isle. But we're overlooking the harbor where my sailboat is kept, which is called the Benjamin River.

**DRAGAN:**

How did you choose Maine for your home?

**HILLIS:**

Well, that's a long story because essentially my wife's family had a summer place here, and we used to come here in the summer time, and then eventually when that house got too full of three generations: my sister-in-law and her family, and our family, Dorothy's brother and his family, we decided we needed to have a separate house so we bought the one in Deer Isle, which, that was in the 1960s.

So, we've owned that house longer than any house we've ever owned, so it's really home for us. And I may have told you this story, when we decided some years ago that we could imagine that people do die in California, but we couldn't imagine, for us, being buried there, so we decided that we would see about being buried. It was time to begin worrying about this to make things simpler for our children.

So we went to the town office in Deer Isle, where the person I pay taxes to and have for now forty years, is named Weed, "Weed" is a local name, Twyla Weed.

So I said, Ms. Weed, can an off-islander be buried on the Island? And she said, I don't see why not. And I said, where? We don't go to church here, etc. So she named two graveyards: one in Deer Isle, which is the Deer Isle town cemetery; and then one down the road from us in Deer Isle, across the Sunshine Bar, which is a small cemetery. We went to the big one in Deer Isle, this seemed entirely too fancy to us. So, we went to the other one, which was run by … originally was a Haskell—Haskell is another local name like Weed—and we called one of the Haskells who'd come around to show us.

You have to take the next lot, the next plot down the hill, up at the end of the graveyard, which is only probably two, three acres, very small, surrounded by woods. You have to take the next one down the hill that's available. He showed us the plot that we would have, and I said, how much? And he said, $100, and I said, we'll take two! (*Laughs*).

So we own two cemetery plots that are about a mile and a half down the road from us. And that shows that we really … This is really home for us now. We thought about being buried on the property, the Deer Isle property, which there's a tradition in Maine of doing, little family cemeteries which are on the farm. But Dorothy thought it would be very awkward for our children if they decided to sell the house, what do you do—our grandchildren—with grand-papa, grand-mama, who are buried down at the end of the … How do you explain this to the people who are buying your house?

Fade in/out photograph from Deer Isle, view south of Sunshine Bar Road to the Sunshine Peninsula, towards the Jericho Bay and Isle au Haut in the far distance.

### HILLIS, OFF:

This was home, this is where Dorothy wanted to be, and me too.

44:57

….

### HILLIS BACK ON CAMERA, CONT.:

Well we always thought from the beginning, when I first visited Dorothy here, which goes back to when we were both in college, I always thought Maine was a wonderfully beautiful place. Everybody else does too. And we like the winters, the austerity. We like weather. That was one of the problems with California: no weather. Day after day, it's early morning low clouds and fog, burn-off and the temperature is going to be seventy-five, and next day it's exactly the same. I noticed this when I was back there a month ago, same, same weather. Here you never know.

When we used to cross the bridge from New Hampshire into Maine, which is 250 miles Southwest of here, we would, there's a folk tradition—do you know this? That when you go across a bridge, its bad luck to have your feet on the ground, so you'd lift your feet up—You didn't know that?—(Dragan: No.)—So we would lift our feet up, except the person who was driving the car, and cheer, the whole family would say, "Here we are in Maine, we're entering, we're coming to Maine!"

DRAGAN:

How does Maine as a place where you work, differ from these urban spaces where you were attached to a University?

HILLIS:

That's not at all an easy question. I think that my memory of this would be that when I was at Hopkins at Baltimore, or New Haven at Yale. Well in New Haven we lived out in the country too, in Bethany, eight miles away from New Haven. And in the case of that experience, when I'd drive home at night, when I crossed the Wilbur Cross Parkway and I got near the woods in our house in Bethany, I would begin to relax. So almost, almost all of my actual writing has been done at home, unlike some people who work at the university. And Maine was that way even more so, it was like a weight being lifted from my shoulders.

47:33

Establishing shot and on screen title, "Miller Summer Home, Deer Isle, Maine, June 7th, 2010." Hillis in the distance walking away and disappears behind the house. Pan to the right to Deer Isle Sound.

Cut to close up of seagulls and ducks bobbing in the ocean. Fog horn audible.

> HILLIS OFF CAMERA:
>
> My own family on both sides, were mostly Pennsylvania Dutch, from … in the case of the Miller side, I know a little bit more about it.
>
> HILLIS ON SCREEN, INTERIOR:
>
> He was a soldier in the British army from Hesse, and King George had a little deal with the King of Hesse, or whatever he's called, and then went and rounded up farm boys in Hesse—part of Germany—and put red coats on them, and sent them to the colony to fight in the Revolutionary War. A lot of them, it wasn't just a few.
>
> They were smart enough to surrender, a whole lot of them, at the battle of Saratoga, which is way up in New York State. They were allowed to settle in the United States after the war, and marry local women, on condition that they never again bear arms, they were forbidden to do that. And then a lot of them moved down the valley, the Shenandoah Valley on one side or the other of the Blue Ridge Mountains, to become farmers in Virginia. And on both sides, that's my ancestors.
>
> This ancestor of mine, my great-great-great-great grandfather, I think of him as blonde, blue eyed, speaking German like anything: Corporal Mueller. But the name is Miller, because Miller is also a German name, but let's say he was Corporal Mueller, from some farm or another. He named his son who was born in 1786, that is after the Revolution and after the establishment of the United States, he named his son, George Washington Miller, to show what a patriot he was. And they remained small farmers on both sides.
>
> My mother's maiden name was Critzer which was probably Kreitzer or something, but that's another German name. And it shows the hostility

to Germans in the United States because of the
first World War, that my mother brought me up
to believe that I was Scotch-Irish and English
with a small mixture of German. Because I have
family names like Hopkins, as I mentioned
yesterday, and Rodes, which is a lowland
Scottish name. There's no doubt that those
are family names. But my mother's mother, my
grandmother Critzer's maiden name, was Minnie
Schultz (actually Minta Hopkins Schultz).
That doesn't sound to me like a Scotch-Irish
or English name. The surname is a German,
Pennsylvania Dutch name, through and through.

Crossfade.

......

### HILLIS, CONT.:

There's a reference to Johns Hopkins. It
would be the same family. And actually it's a
family name, it's one of my family names. My
brother's middle name is, he's William Hopkins
Miller. And our son is Matthew Hopkins. So
Hopkins is one of my family names. Which we're
all, and I had a cousin named Minta Hopkins.
So this would be on my mother's side. There
was a man named Stephen Hopkins, who signed
the Declaration of Independence. He was from
Rhode Island, one of my direct ancestors.

Johns Hopkins was a wealthy merchant who
established the Johns Hopkins University
with his gift of money. My side of the
family was the poor, Virginia, farmer
side. But we're all descended from Stephen
Hopkins. So if you look at the Declaration
of Independence, way down at the right,
in a very spidery, shaky handwriting,
it says Stephen H. ... Steven Hopkins.

Facsimile of Declaration of Independence, Ken
Burns effect, close up to the signature.

### HILLIS:

I'm not sure there's a middle name.

HILLIS CONT.:

I have two, three theories about this. It's obvious that the other people have already signed. Remember, signing the Declaration of Independence took a lot of courage. If we had lost, they would have hung them all. They would have lined them all up and hanged them. So one explanation is that he was scared to death, that's why his handwriting is so shaky. Second explanation is that he was drunk. They had given him a lot of wine to drink and brought him in, and said, 'Come on Steve, you can sign. It's just a piece of paper.' (*Laughs*).

The third explanation would be probably the truthful one, was that he was kind of old. But I'm very proud of this ancestor. This courageous ancestor of mine. [I've now looked him up. He had palsy, and had to hold one hand with the other to write. (JHM)]

Exterior shot of (side of) Deer Isle home, through the deer fence. Hillis walks past camera. Camera follows him into his garden, entering the house. Hillis off camera:

53:13

You remember I went to Oberlin College, and then to a very traditional PhD program in English at Harvard, where all of my teachers were very hostile to Theory.

I was a Physics major for the first year and a half at Oberlin. And then in the middle of my sophomore year I decided that I really wanted to do literature.

HILLIS, INTERIOR, CONT.:

And I've often told the story of how Dorothy—that I was what they called, "going with" Dorothy all very innocent, drinking Coca—Cola, going to the movies, etcetera, together. I said, Dorothy, I think I'm thinking of changing my major and I want you to understand that this means poverty, life long poverty. And Dorothy said, oh she would live in a cottage with me, etcetera. I'm making a joke of this, but it's serious. It was very important for me, that she said you should do what your vocation tells you to do. And my father was the same way. I went back at Christmas and I had lunch with my Papa, who was the Associate Commissioner for Higher and Professional Education for the State of New York. And we went out to lunch and I said, Dad, I'm thinking of changing my major. And again he supported me in doing this. He said if that's really what you want to do, you should do it.

But what really interested me about literature, was its very peculiar use of language. It struck me as something like when a physicist gets some anomalous set of signals from outer space: the problem is to explain why. But this is really weird. And it struck me that the language of English literature was weird in the same way, and it took some explaining.

And I remember exactly the poem that struck me as paradigmatic for this. And this was Tennyson's *Tears, Idle Tears*. There's Ricks' edition of Tennyson poetry, and there's *Tears, Idle Tears*, which is part of *The Princess*, it's one of the songs in *The Princess*. It's a poem everybody reads. It struck me as really strange. Really strange. "Tears, idle tears, I know not what they mean. Tears from the depths of some divine despair, something, something … Gather in the heart, and rise to eyes. And thinking of the days that are no more." What the hell does that mean? What does it mean, "tears from the depths of some divine despair"? And what does it mean to say, "idle tears"? Why are they idle if they are motivated? And in what sense do these tears rise from some divine despair, which must be down, it can't be up! Because they rise in the heart and gather to the eyes. And what does this have to do with thinking of the days that are no more? I mean, it really does, did seem to me to take some explaining. In those days you were given *Tears, Idle Tears* to read and nobody saw this as a problem.

And I think ... I can ... explain ... just the
other day, going back to *Alice in Wonderland*,
looking up a passage. And I think the *Alice*
books may be the source of this, blame it all
on Lewis Carroll. Because I taught myself
to read at the age of five in order to
read the *Alice* books so my mother wouldn't
have to read them to me. So I obviously
thought *Alice in Wonderland* was terrific.

When I go back ... what I remember from *Alice
in Wonderful* and when I go back to look at
it, it's the linguistic stuff. ... And then I
remembered the question of mouse, and the
mouse-tail, and the passage in the *Alice*
books where the mouse is telling, is reciting
a poem but it appears on the page of *Alice
in Wonderland* as a kind of tail. And Alice
says, yes, it is a long tail, certainly.
But she means, the mouse's tail, and the
mouse then, on the next page, says, let's
see, well where was I? And she says, I think
you got to the fourth bend. (*laughing*)

58:19

And the mouse is very offended. I had not!
Says the mouse. And Alice then says, oh,
a knot! I really like to undo knots. So
you have this dazzling series of puns from
page to page. For some reason (it's not an
explanation), but for some reason I found
at the age of five these puns—the wordplay—
in the *Alice* books, absolutely fascinating
and you could say that's still the case.

...

And you can carry this too far, in the sense
that literature is not just made of linguistic
jokes. For example, I find that the other
side of it, even for *Tears, Idle Tears*, but
also for—after all, my dissertation was not
on poetry but about Dickens' novels—the other
side of it is I've always found literature
immensely moving, in its ability to create
a kind of imaginary place that I could go

to where things happened. Where, you say, why should I care about what happens to these totally fictional characters? But I do care. And I find, for example, Kertész's *Fatelessness* is an absolutely marvelous novel. Not because it's full of wordplay, but because it tells an almost unbearable story of somebody who survived the camps. So there would be a mistake to say that my interest in literature is purely in jokes and wordplay. So there's a double side to it.

...

The other thing that I remember reading as a sophomore at Oberlin—again, it was not a course but it was just something that I came upon or somebody said, why don't you read this—it was Dostoyevsky's *Notes from the Underground*. I remember this in typical sophomoric fashion, I remember it begins, "I'm a sick man, I'm a spiteful man, I think my liver is diseased ..." And I read this and I said, here at last, there's somebody like me! (*laughing*) Somebody ... I've encountered a soul mate for the first time in my life! So, that book was very important for me, because it led me to believe...

DRAGAN:

"I am not a piano key!" [DK: a quote from the *Notes from Underground*].

HILLIS (LAUGHING):

"I am not a piano key!" Here at last, I've found somebody who's like me.

01:01:22

It must have been very difficult for Dorothy, because I met her, as I may have mentioned—no, I haven't mentioned. I met her during freshmen week.

I was walking ... there's a square with walkways that go across, a sort of park. And I was walking across this park, coming this way, and I saw ahead a sort of at the center of the park: this young woman. And I'm not joking; it was love at first sight.

Fade in/out photograph, "Hillis and Dorothy with Daughter Robin, 1952."

And it has remained now, we've been married for over sixty years, it's remained exactly the same. I looked at Dorothy and I said, 'that's the person.' And I had to pursue her quite a bit. I was only sixteen years old. I'm not all that socially adroit now, but you should've seen me at the age of sixteen.

For example … I happened to be assigned to the same … well, the freshmen all ate in the freshmen women's dormitory, and the men ate their meals there. This was supposed to socialize you, because the tables were with linen, believe it or not, and you were served by other students, and so on, so that you were supposed to be taught how to be polite. But I was such a clown that at some point I had stretched myself out on the floor, below Dorothy, for some reason or other. And the house lady, whatever her name is, came and found me in this posture, making an absolute fool of myself on the floor. So it must have been very difficult for Dorothy to have this totally callow youth. So it took quite a lot of doing to persuade Dorothy that I was the person that she should spend the rest of her life with. And she periodically, I think, still asks herself whether this was a great idea.

Hillis in his office pointing at a bookcase, voice off camera, then followed, by hand held camera around the office:

01:03:53

This is all my stuff. That behind there is more of my stuff. And these are mine. Often they are multiple copies. This is all the stuff that I have not put in my CV. And there are bunch more over here… And all of these are fairly recent things. There are a lot of duplicates. Here is *Conrad in the 21st Century*, here is *Conrad in the 21st Century* again. And a fair number of these are translations, which I cannot read.

I've been worrying about the utility of my vocation, and particularly the utility of reading literature, in the old-fashioned sense. And I don't think it's all that easy to answer that question.

Cut.

......

### HILLIS, SEDGWICK HOME INTERIOR:

Why read literature today? I'm not quite sure it's all that easy a question to answer.

Partly because reading literature has always been pointless in the sense that it's an end in itself. So its very hard with a straight face to say, 'you ought to read *Hamlet*!' Why? And secondly, there's no doubt I think, the role of reading literature these days is diminished. It's got to be. Most people spend something like eight or nine hours a day online, one way or another. They are not reading Shakespeare during that time.

### DRAGAN:

And actually I have another question from England, from John Schad, which is "Could literature ever save us?"

### HILLIS:

(*laughing*) I'm afraid we're going to have to save ourselves, John. But I do have some things to say—that could be one answer to the question, why read literature: because it will save us.

Cut.

01:06:19

Sailing.

Fadeout.

Hillis, interior.

DRAGAN:

So why read literature?

HILLIS:

Well that, I'm still thinking about this.

I'd like to pin these things down to particular examples, and I have an example, which is a poem that I have talked about, written about before, but I would … So you say, what do you mean by literature? Well, we know in general. But this is a poem by Yeats, very short. That has always seemed to me immensely moving. So I ask this question in a concrete way, should people read Yeats' *The Cold Heaven*? And if so, why? And how would you go about teaching the poem? How would you justify this?

It's not very long. May I read it?

DRAGAN:

Of course.

HILLIS:

Anyway, here's the poem. It's a fairly early poem, by Yeats. Here it goes: it's called *The Cold Heaven*.

01:07:56

"Suddenly I saw the cold and
rook-delighting heaven

That seemed as though ice burned
and was but the more ice,

And thereupon imagination and heart were driven

So wild that every casual
thought of that and this

Vanished, and left but memories,
that should be out of season

With the hot blood of youth, of
love crossed long ago;

And I took all the blame out
of all sense and reason,

Until I cried and trembled
and rocked to and fro,

Riddled with light. Ah! when the
ghost begins to quicken,

Confusion of the death-bed over, is it sent

Out naked on the roads, as the
books say, and stricken

By the injustice of the skies for punishment?"

Now I find that poem immensely moving, and if I'm asked why I think other people should read it, I really think my answer is, it's up to you. That is to say, I can't really tell you that this is going to save you, or that this is going to give you the right kind of aesthetic ideology. Or the right set of ideas. Or that it's just a good thing to know the poems of that great Irish poet, W.B. Yeats. You say, "why should I care about this guy?"

You might say that this comes back around to saying that what I really cherish about literature and would say I find it worth a lifetime to study it, is the linguistic concentration and complexity. This is twelve lines—1-2-3-4-5-6. Yes, it's not a sonnet. It's made of four quatrains that more or less rhyme in very other line: heaven/driven, ice/this, season/reason, ago/fro, so that it's alternating rhymes, and that's important in the poem.

But who but Yeats could have put that "Ah!" into a poem? "Ah! When the ghost begins to quicken."

01:10:35

Cut to sailing.

Fadeout.

### HILLIS, INTERIOR:

As you know there are three or four areas where we're in big trouble: one of them is in the health care system; one is in the financial system; one is in climate change; the fourth one is in what's happened to our educational system.

Cut to Hillis UF lecture:

Now my question is: how did this suicidal situation come about? What possible explanation for such auto-destructive behavior on so many fronts at once?

### HILLIS, INTERIOR, CONT.:

History—American History—certainly only survives for most people in the United States now by way of textbooks.

So that those Texas people are also leaving Thomas Jefferson out of American History and they want to be sure that they get in the conservative, Reagan period, and we ought to know about that. But ... and history of course, is always problematic. Nevertheless, that's a diabolical thing to do, particularly because the state of Texas, next to California, is the biggest buyer of textbooks.

...

But if you just take climate change: we've had fifteen years to recognize that this was happening. And we've had plenty of time to recognize, that if you go on doing offshore oil drilling, sooner or later…

Fade in/out picture of a burning oil well in the Gulf of Mexico, "Deepwater Horizon Oil Spill, April 2010."

01:13:04

You don't have to be a prophet or a big scientist to know that sooner or later, something catastrophic is going to happen to one of those. So it was foreseeable. And it was not sufficiently anticipated.

So it's exactly parallel, as many commentators have said, to the financial situation. Which again, was foreseeable. Anybody with half a wit could see that if you're going to do these credit default swaps and derivatives, sooner or later something very bad was going to happen if you didn't regulate them. So they were not regulated, just as BP was not sufficiently regulated—partly because of the failure of the minerals management people, etcetera. But I'm not surprised by that, because it's staffed by people who come from the oil industry. Just as the financial regulators are from Goldman Sachs, etc., so it's not a surprise, but it is self-destructive. Even for them! I mean in the long run, they're putting themselves out of business, because if you have no more middleclass, nobody with money to buy cars, they're not going to be able to buy gasoline to put in the cars, etcetera, etcetera.

So that even, from the most narrow financial consideration, it was stupid. So the question is how could this have happened? And what should we do now? And I must say not all that much is being done.

It may be enough to make some outcry. It's in our hands! It's in the hands of the people. How we vote. There are huge obstacles with all sorts of lies told by the media, and so on, nevertheless, if people get angry enough they might force some events. And I think they are angry both about the banks and about BP. It upsets a lot of people. And you are right. As we were saying earlier, it would be laughable if it weren't so sad.

01:15:24

Hillis and Richard in the dinghy, rowing back towards the camera.

Cut to Hillis:

> I've had some experience over the years, not so much with cameras as with tape, audio recordings, and you try to forget about it as much as possible and be yourself. And I'm pretty good at that. On the other hand I am aware of this camera eye over here looking at me, very impassive, single eye.

DRAGAN:

> Like Polyphemus.

Cut to photograph, Hillis in his office, looking petrified. The Ken Burns effect slowly pulls back and pans slightly to the left to reveal a gloved hand holding a camera.

HILLIS OFF:

> Yes, it's like Polyphemus, and this eye is not blinking. There's no face with any expression. It's absolutely neutral and impassive…

HILLIS, INTERIOR, CONT.:

> …and I know that it's recording everything. And we've learned that this recording is at a very high level of fidelity, and that's anxious-making. It's the impersonality of the recording that it doesn't respond in any way. So it is a little bit like the—I've never been psychoanalyzed—but it is a little bit like it must be like for the analyst who is not supposed to do anything but sit there and ask very neutral kind of questions. Or to rephrase what you've said, as a kind of question, and lead you on. So I have a feeling, I have a very uncomfortable feeling before this piece of apparatus. I'm afraid of it.

01:17:31

**DRAGAN:**

What fascinates you the most now?

**HILLIS:**

Now? Well a pretty good answer would be to say the effect of what happens when my work is read in China or Iran, or some place like that. But I am also I think fascinated by the—to be serious for a moment—by this question of utility of reading literature anymore at all, in the period of critical climate change, that does interest me.

When every day I open the New York Times online and find some new disaster, or learn something about people who are learning to grow their own vegetables because they think—I think probably correctly—that if the oil runs out too fast there are going to be big problems and we're making no effort to prepare for this; anymore than we're making an effort … — well, we have to make an effort, because if the water goes up by about a meter, the Deer Isle house would be caput. Because there's no part of that land which is more than a few feet above sea level and this bank is already eroding. That is one of the reasons why—George or someone asked—why did we buy this house in Sedgwick? One of the reasons is that this house would still be here, when the Deer Isle house, sooner or later, will become clam-flats. And that's great sadness to me, but we can just live here [in Sedgwick]. So …

01:19:25

**DRAGAN:**

Hillis, since this is a film, I will give you a chance to give a parting shot, or an adieu. Or a parting shot.

**HILLIS:**

(*Laughing*) Parting shot. (*laughing*). All hail to anybody who actually ever sees this, I greet you from this ghostly cinematic realm that's been ... I will ... my parting shot is my story about Matthew, which has to do with talking, since I've been talking now for hours. Years ago when I was at Hopkins, in my late twenties, I got virus pneumonia; it was then I stopped smoking, because you can't smoke. And I had a low fever for a long time so I had to stay at home. Matthew was about four years old, or so. And a friend of mine named Cliff Cherpak came to visit me in my bed of pain, which was not so painful because it was just a low fever by then; nobody dies of virus pneumonia, but there's no ... antibiotics don't really cure it.

So he knocked on the door, and Matthew answered the door, and Cherpak said, "I'd like to talk to your father." And Matthew said, "there's been too much talking already," and closed the door. (*laughing*)

Cherpak thought this was so funny that he went home. And he called up and said "I tried to come and see you, but Matthew said there's been too much talking already." So this is my parting shot, to say after so many hours, I feel there's been too much talking already.

Camera pulls from close up to medium shot; Hillis sits for a moment, takes off the microphone.

01:21:39

Fadeout to black. Sound of waves, and foghorn at regular intervals. Footage of Hillis selected from the film, extra footage and B rolls. Hillis entering the house. Zoom over Hillis' shoulder on the doorknocker shaped as lighthouse. Dissolve into the Stonington Deer Isle lighthouse in daytime. Fade to black.

01:23:02

The Stonington Deer Isle lighthouse light at night blinks continuously on the dark screen, only the light visible in intervals, the foghorn heard, and the last chord of

Natalia Pschenichnikova's sound score punctuates the scroll and the Deer Isle Productions title. The credits roll over:

*

Written and Directed by

Dragan Kujundžić

*

Camera operated by

Georg Koszulinsky

*

Edited by

Dave Rodriguez

*

Additional Camera Work

Dave Rodriguez

J. Hillis Miller Medical Center Complex, University of Florida, May 2011

*

Photography

Barbara Cohen

Jacques Derrida and J. Hillis Miller, University of California, Irvine, April 2002

Georg Koszulinski, Dragan Kujundžić

Deer Isle, Maine, June 2010

*

Original Music

Natalia Pschenichnikova

*

Music Recording

Torsten Ottersberg

gogh surround

musik production gmbh

Berlin, Germany

*

Transcript

Taryn Devereux

**

Archival Footage

Jacques Derrida, "Justices," conference on
"'J': Around the Work of J. Hillis Miller,"
University of California, Irvine, April 2003

Special permission by Marguerite Derrida gratefully
acknowledged. © Succession Derrida 2011

*

Archival Footage

Pamela Gilbert, "Introduction to J. Hillis Miller"
and J. Hillis Miller, "Derrida's Politics of
Autoimmunity," conference on "Who or What—Jacques
Derrida," University of Florida, October 2006

*

Additional Interview Questions

Derek Attridge, Rachel Bowlby, Barbara Cohen, Tom
Cohen, Shan Dan, John Leavey, Akira Lippit, Marc
Redfield, Haun Saussy, John Schad, Henry Sussman,
Greg Ulmer, Ning Yizhong and Julian Wolfreys

*

68  Film Transcript

Financial and material support
gratefully acknowledged:

University of Florida

The Office of the President J. Bernard Machen

The Office of the Provost Joe Glover

College of the Liberal Arts and
Sciences, Dean Paul D'Anieri

College of Medicine, Dean Michael L. Good

Medical Humanities Program, College of
Medicine, Director Nina Stoyan-Rosenzweig

College of Journalism and Telecommunications,
Department of Telecommunication,
Chair David H. Ostroff

*

Financial and Material Support
Gratefully Acknowledged:

University of Florida

The Center for the Humanities and the
Public Sphere, Director Bonnie Effros

Alexander Grass Endowment in Jewish
History, Chair Mitchell Hart

Department of Languages, Literatures
and Cultures, Chair Mary Watt

Department of English, and Program in Film
and Media Studies, Chair Pamela Gilbert

France Florida Research Institute,
Director Carol Murphy

Center for Jewish Studies, Director Jack Kugelmass

Center for Women's Studies and Gender
Research, Director Judith Page

\*

The First Sail rough cut was screened at the University of California, Berkeley, April 2011. Special thanks to Anne Nesbet, Eric Naiman, Olga Matich, M. P. Desmond, Wendy L. Garfield, Xiaojuan Shu, David Simon, and the Department of Comparative Literature

\*

Thanks to all who put wind in the sails of this film, in particular:

Shifra Armon, Roger Beebe, Nina Caputo, Barbara Cohen, Tom Cohen, Bliss Cua Lim, Joanna Delorme, Sigi Jottkandt, Akira Lippit, William Little, Brian Mann, Ginete Michaud, Gerardo Munoz, Gabriele Schwab, Ronald Sundstrom, Henry Sussman, Samuel Weber, Phillip Wegner and Brigitte Weltman-Aron

\*

My utmost gratitude to J. Hillis Miller and Dorothy Miller

\*

Filmed on location in Gainesville, Florida, March 2010; and Deer Isle and Sedgwick, Maine, June, 2010

\*

Cut to photograph of a deer taken on Deer Isle, on screen title:

© Deer Isle Productions, 2011

\*

01:25:20

Cut to Hillis, sailing, talking to the camera:

Everything has been put together wrong!

Cut to intertitle:

The First Sail: J. Hillis Miller

©2011

01:25:28

Fadeout to black

*Interview*

# The First Sail: J. Hillis Miller – An Interview With Dragan Kujundžić

TARYN DEVEREUX

*"Deconstruction attempts to resist the totalizing and totalitarian tendencies of criticism. It attempts to resist its own tendencies to come to rest in some sense of mastery over the work. It resists these in the name of an uneasy joy of interpretation, beyond nihilism, always in movement, a going beyond which remains in place, as the parasite is outside the door but also always already within, uncanniest of guests."*

—J. Hillis Miller, "The Critic as Host"

What was Hillis' initial reaction to your proposal for this project?[1] Did he set any guidelines or stipulations? How long has the project been in the works? Describe its trajectory: throughout the process, were there any major changes in method, focus, structure, etc.? If so, did they arise organically or were they the result of any challenges or ideas you had?

J. Hillis Miller is a person of tremendous generosity. Without him giving his time this would not have been possible. His initial reaction? In an email: "You will have to make a purse silk out of a sow's ear." As with everything he does, Hillis downplayed his importance. His genuine and profound modesty was something I had to take into account starting this

---

1   This interview first appeared as "The First Sail: J. Hillis Miller," interview, *Sin Frontera*, April 2011, published by Department of Spanish and Portuguese, University of Florida, at https://ufsinfronteradotcom.files.wordpress.com/2011/04/dragan-kujundzic-first-sail-interview.pdf.

project. There were no limitations to what I ask, and no questions were sent beforehand.

The project is an extension of my involvement with Hillis' work, most recently by organizing a conference in his honor with my colleague and friend Barbara Cohen, which was called "J." That was seven years ago. The proceedings of this conference were published in two academic venues, by *Critical Inquiry* (The University of Chicago Press) and by Fordham University Press. Jacques Derrida served as a plenary speaker at this conference and wrote an invaluable essay called "Justices" assessing Hillis' work. This project also stems from my desire to find new ways to talk to Hillis at length. It started as a work in progress called "Flights of Fancy: J. Hillis Miller and Friends." I wanted from the start to film Hillis sailing (he is an avid sailor on boats powered by sails), and to include Hillis' friends around the world. Everything else stemmed from that first flight of fancy. His friends sent me questions for this project, and their enthusiasm kept me going and convinced me that this is a worthwhile project. Hillis has friends from China to England and all around the world. These questions were part of interviews that took place during the ten or twelve filmed interview sessions at the University of Florida in March 2010 and on Deer Isle, Maine, in June 2010. I also added of course many more of my own, pertaining to Hillis' work.

This film belongs to the genre of fan cinema. Another (it has been so far) secret, title, of this project, but I reveal it here, is *J'aime JHM*. Which pronounced in French gives a repetition and may be heard as *J'aime, j'aime*. Kind of love without borders, *sin frontera*, in two languages, *en deux langues*. With this project I want to show how much I love J. Hillis Miller.

*In The Medium is the Maker, Hillis contrasts "communicating with the dead" with "receiving telepathic communications from those who are still alive though at a distance," rooting them both in the occult and observing that "death is never far away either in telepathic experiences or in spiritualism" (16). Your interview footage with him ultimately will be defined as both, and Hillis notes that he is aware of this.*

*How do you suppose he would respond upon viewing himself in video? Do you think that the 'video' as a medium for Hillis has a different sort of influence than it does for Derrida?*

*You are producing both a book and a film from this project: how will these respective mediums differ in their treatment of Hillis? What do you make of the irony of filming a man who describes television, in the words of Derrida, as a "sham, a simulacrum," that which "was there, at some distance here and now, reaches us, in another here and now on the screen, through elaborate delays, relays, and message-shaping filters" (13)? Did your consciousness of such alter the way you developed the project?*

Deconstruction has taught us that every sign is testamentary. Hillis is of course aware that his filmed interview deposits a memory onto the substrate of film (digital tape) and allows for a spectral recurrence and returns. There is an inscription of death and finitude in any giving of inter-view. Including this one I am involved in right now. As I tell my students in the course called Vampire Cinema, playing on the title of *Interview With a Vampire*, every inter-view is also an intra-vein. It draws blood. In the *Medium is the Maker* quoted, Hillis has a yet again innovative analysis pertaining to the question of finitude in Heidegger and Derrida. For Heidegger, the finitude of being (*da-sein*) partakes in the movement of general Being, it "holds," Hillis says, "all the horizons of time with one mobile unit.... Heidegger's time is grounded in *Sein*, Being with a capital B. Derrida's time is created out of performative media, the media as makers… On each occasion a given medium is used that use creates its own ground and its own *différance*." What this means is that each time we use a technical apparatus, flip a cell phone, type on the computer, make a film, watch a TV, we are opening a new temporal ground in which our finitude is both confirmed and traversed and overcome. By using technical apparatuses, we partake in our own survival. And that happens every time we speak, teach or touch someone. But it is most discernible in the usage of the technical apparatuses like recording live or life.

However, the chance of any inscription, anything deposited to memory is also that it partakes in the possibility of survival. It allows that which is recorded to have an afterlife. Like something Walter Benjamin saw in translation, a *Nachreifen*, a late ripening in the afterlife. It encodes into the process of recording a possibility of return to come from the future and in the future. It will come in the future as an affirmation of what has come to pass, whether the protagonists of this particular film called *The*

*First Sail* are around or not (I certainly hope for the former, I have some selfish interests in being around for many more years, and wish the same for Hillis!). So it is also a joyous occasion, do not touch that dial, we shall return after these messages! Our absence is from the start implied in the process of recording; the finitude of our *da-sein*, being here, is a condition of filming, even though we are around well and alive. But the repetition encoded by this film (of the great on camera time shared with Hillis during this project) and of the possibility of coming back, is also a cause for rejoicing. Both Derrida and Hillis teach us the importance of this performative aspect of media, at work any time we use a prosthetic apparatus to confine something to memory. It is both sad and joyous. It confronts him with the finitude of his friend's demise, but is also somewhat soothing. It is a sham simulacrum, this thing called film or television, nothing replaces the singular live being, but it also gives the memory of life a chance to live on in this spectral manner. And that spectrality is at work in life itself.

Any archive, Derrida said in *Archive Fever*, actually comes from the future, from the time yet to come, *a-venir*.

The book will contain the filmed material in transcript; the film of course will be about 85 minutes long. But the venue of publication is most fortunate. It will appear as a book with the Open Humanities Press. In the book version, I will be able to include all the anecdotes surrounding the filming, the work of some of my collaborators will be included, and I am particularly pleased that it will have an introduction by Henry Sussman. "The Cinema of J. Hillis Miller" will be the title I am toying with for my own essay to introduce the project. The book may also contain excerpts from recent essays by J. Hillis Miller. The online version will allow the inclusion of some streamed visual material from the interviews instead of just photographs. That multimediality fits this project perfectly.

As for telepathy. This project is a product (if one could employ the logic of causality here) of a number of coincidences. Starting with the first one that I met Derrida first as a signature on a guest book page in 1983 at Cornell University. He signed a blank page of a guest book in the Telluride House at Cornell, and I came two weeks later (I was then an undergraduate student from Belgrade, the former Yugoslavia, invited to stay there by Jonathan Culler), and signed at the first next available place, right below him! First we met telepathically, as signatures! On my way back home to Belgrade I carried two essays with me I made while at Cornell, J. Hillis Miller's "The Critic as Host," which you have (telepathically?) reproduced at the beginning of this interview, and Jacques Derrida's "Living On/Border Lines"—incidentally another essay on borders. Then there was an incredible coincidence that later on I worked with Derrida and Hillis at the University of California, Irvine, we became colleagues, I organized events with them, a conference in Hillis' honor, etc. And then when I moved to the University of Florida, it turned out that Hillis' father was the first post WW 2 president of the University, J. Hillis Miller Senior, that Hillis grew up here, frequently visits, is a *doctor honoris causa* of the University of Florida and has spent part of his life as young adult here! All the reasons for making a film about Hillis were right there! The latest one happened only three month ago. I was in Los Angeles when I was handed the tapes I believed lost I had commissioned of the Derrida conference ("Who or What—Jacques Derrida") that I organized at the University of Florida in October of 2006, with Hillis' keynote address! Something that took place five years ago and three thousand miles away resurfaced in California. I thought that was Hillis' and Derrida's way of telling me, "do not worry Dragan, the film will turn out ok, take these home, and welcome to California!" The footage from that conference in 2006 (Hillis' plenary talk) now actually opens the film in its rough cuts (the film should be finished by end of May 2011). I see in this a work of telepathy, an unfolding of an unwritten program, like an affirmation from a distance I am receiving (like a message) from these two great thinkers and protagonists of this film. Without borders indeed!

*During one of the interview sessions, you take the opportunity to mention your "own being swept away by [Hillis'] writing;" in particular, your encounter with The Critic as Host, which you describe as one of those "moments of absolute fascination." Many other scholars and students have also cited Hillis as a major source of inspiration and challenge for their work.*

*In the present academic climate, the trenchant glare of Deconstructive thought has waned, and many scholars have been left to wonder, where does criticism go from here. Do you think that in today's university's system, Hillis' work is still relevant? Appreciated? Not only through the works that emerged* in debt to his ingenuity, but in terms of contemporary applicability and usage? Certainly many students continue to encounter Derrida, or at the very least can identify him, but does this hold true for J. Hillis Miller? Why or why not?

I discovered "deconstruction" at the age of 19 in Belgrade, then Yugoslavia. I was writing my first term paper, called "Plato's Concept of Literature." For that paper I read some of the classic assessments of Plato's work by A.E.Taylor, etc. The works like Taylor's assessed in an exemplary scholarly way Plato's ideas but told me nothing about why exactly this is relevant today. Then I stumbled on a paragraph from Derrida's *Plato's Pharmacy* which took my breath away. No one told me to read this, this imposed itself onto me on its own at a very young age. Just like no one told me to copy these two essays (at a great expense then, for a student from Yugoslavia budget in 1983, to bring them with me back to Belgrade, they just powerfully imposed themselves on me). Since then, I have heard about "deconstruction" that this was all premature, the time for this has not come yet, this is all only fashion, etc. And now the trend is to say, oh, deconstruction, it is passé! So it never quite took place! It was too early and now too late, too bad for it! Which is probably something that Derrida would agree with, deconstruction may be that which gives place but is never at one with itself, but for different reasons than those who assess it in bad faith. For me deconstruction was never a question of a "trend." What I sensed spoke to me about the great achievements of the Western literary and philosophical tradition, and made them alive, relevant, vibrant, lively! That moment of encountering the work of Derrida and Hillis (in my introduction to the "J" section in *Critical Inquiry* I likened their texts working on me from a distance like letters, sealed with a kiss) is now thirty years behind me. That is when I first read the pages from Hillis' seminal essay "The Critic as Host." But the fascination is new as always. In two hundred years our epoch will be known as the epoch of deconstruction.

And I urge you if you have not yet read Jacques Derrida's essay about "9/11," to do so; I consider it to be the most lucid essay written about what is happening to the world and to the U.S. at the current moment. No one has given a better political analysis of our own time, of the most pressing matters related to this event, than Jacques Derrida. And maybe that is why many who have vested interests in keeping the status quo, perpetuating certain securitarian measures in this country are afraid of it. Or read what Samuel Weber, another thinker close to Derrida and "deconstruction" has to say about "9/11" in his *Theatricality as Medium*, or what J. Hillis Miller writes about the current crisis in the United States in his recent essays, and you will see why for many a deconstructive intervention with probing political insights represents a threat. These writings challenge some very powerful interests in politics, society and academia while reaffirming others. These thinkers are reworking the political or historical and theoretical ground on which we stand.

This film is in itself a testament to the vibrancy of J. Hillis Miller. A year ago I approached David Rodriguez to serve as editor to the film. He was so infatuated with the material (no doubt due to Hillis' magnetic on camera influence though he never met in person) that he chose to write his MA Thesis about the making of this film in the light of J. Hillis Miller's work! And he wrote an amazing document. So I say, Hillis is going strong in his ability to attract and inspire any scholar who stumbles upon his work!

*Who is the intended audience for this project? Does the intended audience for the book differ from that of the film in any way? In what spheres do you see this film and accompanying book to be utilized? Where will they be made available? From the interview, Hillis seems enthusiastic and supportive of the movement to create online collections and libraries; will this project be available in this format?*

This has been an object of extended discussion with my editor, David Rodriguez. We of course have no clue who will in fact watch the film in the end. But some calculation is part of the decision process: what to put in the film, what to cut, in what order, etc. We want the film to be "accessible" to the "lay" audience. Hillis comes from a long family tree of Virginians, his great great grandfather is one of the signatories of the Declaration of Independence. Hillis talks about that in the film. His father was a commissioner for higher education and as such a founder of the State University of New York system, and then moved on to found the great Medical School at the University of Florida. Hillis' father passed away at an early age of 53 while still in the office. Hillis had a difficult life at times (I've read in his archive his letters requesting financial support from various institutions where he was a graduate student), before becoming one of the greatest American minds of our time. This is a biography of an exceptional man by any standards. I am carefully weighing my words. It is worth telling on its own. In addition, Hillis has had an outstanding career, of a kind that is less and less possible at an American University. This is also a film on the background of the decline of a great system of higher education in the U.S.. We discuss numerous topics which should be of concern to everyone, there is no "ivory tower" discussion in these interviews (or for that matter in Hillis' later works): climate change, health insurance, US securitarian policies, Homeland Security, wars, the reactionary politics of the Republican (Tea) Party and the Bush years, etc. This film and the topics raised are of concern to anyone who wants to hear a wise man reflecting on the current state of the world, and that will be featured prominently. In addition, these reflections show the power of deconstructive thinking and will show that Hillis' work has always had this potential. He is using it now when it politically matters the most, and when such interventions have the greatest political value and effect. In any case, when they are terribly needed.

We want all of this to be visible in the film. However, there are aspects of this interview for which one needs to be receptive to intellectual topics. But true intellectual cinema will also have the power to go across cultural borders. Hillis does all the work!

There is another aspect of the film, related to the possibility of engaging strategies of deconstruction in making this film. David and I have had long discussions related to both the ethics and aesthetics of representation, both in terms of content and in terms of the film material. For example, the following sequence: It starts with the establishing shot of Hillis' house in Sedgwick. Then there is a flow of the nearby brook for fifteen seconds (passage of time? of life?). Followed by a slow motion close up of Hillis' one eye and a cut in his skin visible above it, without any explanation. Followed by a question, Where did you get this cut? In Irvine, California, I fell, the glass lens cut above the eye. Then we go on and discuss Jacques Derrida's lecture in Irvine dedicated to Hillis work. Here is briefly the thinking that went into that sequence: a cut above the eye (a cut in the skin, *pelicula*, the little skin of cinema), a wounded gaze, related to California (where Hillis last saw Derrida, discussed in the segment), an eye almost cut by a lens (which should bring to mind the modernist tradition, the broken eye glasses in Eisenstein's Odessa steps from *Battleship Potemkin* as well as the split eyeball in *Un Chien Andalou* by Louis Bunuel and Salvador Dali). Followed by the question of mourning and the discussion of the relationship between and image and the specter, etc. I am mentioning these greats of cinema not to compare myself to them, but to show the theoretical and historical knowledge I have as an academic, which has gone into the making of the film. I hope some of these procedures will be visible and make sense even to those who do not know Derrida's work on the testamentary logic of the sign, or Hillis' on performativity. I hope that this knowledge put to work (as well as the great camera work by Georg Koszulinsky) will be visible to all without any prior knowledge and that it adds to the intertextual and other effects of this film.

*You have hours of footage of Hillis—interviews both in Gainesville and at his house in Maine, on his boat, in his office, etc. How do you plan on condensing this material into a documentary film? Is there a specific theme or topic you want to focus on?*

Indeed this is a vast amount of material. The standard ratio in documentaries is 20 or 25 hours to one hour minimum. For each hour of the documentary, you have to make 25 hours of filming. The ratio of all the material I have is one to one. Everything filmed is filmworthy, I practically have no on camera time that cannot be put into the film. And then there are several lectures: Hillis on Derrida's notion of autoimmunity from the 2006 conference at the University of Florida; his lecture on the critical climate change from 2010 at the University of Florida. There is an abundance of material that has to be condensed in a bit of over an hour. We have our work cut out for us.

I am pleased to say that the interest in this project has been very encouraging. I have already held a projection of the rough cuts at the University of California, Berkeley in the Comparative Literature Department two weeks ago (April 1, 2011).

*The full interview with Hillis is vast. Through anecdotes and analyses, we learn of everything from Hillis' childhood to the politics behind the tenure of his colleagues. He is prompted by questions that are well-developed and thoughtful, as contributed by yourself and the colleagues, friends, and students of his you contacted. However, I was surprised that a question regarding the controversy surrounding the anti-Semitic, wartime writings of the late Paul de Man never arose. Hillis has indeed written about it, but it seems to be an odd omission. In fact, some of the submitted questions you received listed this as a question to ask Hillis. It seems likely intentional? Otherwise an anomalous accident or act of the unconscious? If it was, in fact, intentionally excluded, why?*

I have actually had the chance to ask only a fraction of the questions asked of Hillis by his friends. I had to make choices, often made by the course of the interviews. And when it concerned Hillis' published work, I concentrated on his current writings, not what he wrote in the past. Apart from a discussion of Victorian Literature, most if not all of the theoretical discussion is concentrated on the critical climate change, Hillis' relationship with Derrida (several friends asked him that in fact, and it is something I have been engaged with in my work), the current state of the university, the media, the oil spill in the Gulf of Mexico, etc. So I focused on the most recent writings and on current issues. And I would have wanted to ask Hillis about many other books of his, he wrote some 40 of them, and hundreds of articles! The Paul de Man "affair" simply did not come up, but that is among many other topics omitted. These omissions have not been calculated in any way. And I wish I had had 30 more hours of interview time to ask all I wanted to ask, and what his friends asked him. However, I am glad you brought this up, anti-Semitism is, in fact, the topic of his latest published book (to appear in Summer 2011 by The University of Chicago Press) called *The Conflagration of Community: Literature After Auschwitz*. The book raises the issues of literature and the Holocaust in a systematic way, from Kafka and Benjamin, to Imre Kertesz. And my work with Hillis on the film and my own book is not finished. I plan to ask him all the omitted questions when we prepare the transcript for publication. In addition, I am organizing an event in October of this year, which will be focused on this latest work on the Holocaust and literature by J. Hillis Miller, with his participation. We hope to screen for the first time *The First Sail: J. Hillis Miller* on that occasion as well and have a discussion in his presence. In preparation for that, I am in the process of writing my own interview with Hillis on the topic of anti-Semitism and literature, to be published in *Ha-tanin*, the yearbook of Jewish Studies at the University of Florida.[2] So I will have an opportunity to raise the issues you mentioned in conjunction with Hillis' recent work on literature and the Holocaust. I intend to include that new written interview as an appendix to the interview material transcribed from the film once we publish it as a book. So this omission (together with a number of other questions still pending) is only temporary and the questions and additional responses will find their way in the final version of the book. This is still a work in progress.

[Dragan's explanation is correct. I was not asked about De Man's wartime writings. If I had been asked I would have repeated what I wrote at the time they were made public: 1) The anti-Semitic essay is unforgivable, and cannot be explained away by context, even though it is important to learn about that context and important also actually to read that essay and the rest of the wartime writings. 2) The de Man I knew in the 1970's and early 1980's never uttered an anti-Semitic word or sentence. As chair of French at Yale, for example, he brought about the appointment of Shoshana Felman against opposition in that department. He was a close colleague of Geoffrey Hartman and taught a joint course in the Literature Major with him. Jacques Derrida was de Man's close friend and colleague over many years, and de Man worked with another close colleague, Harold Bloom, to contribute to *Deconstruction and Criticism*. 3) De Man never said anything to me about his wartime writings, except a vague statement at one point that he supported himself during the war by journalism. I was too naïve or incurious to follow that up and ask, "Journalism for what journals?" 4) De Man's latter writings do not reflect the anti-semitism and nationalism of the wartime writings. Quite the opposite. Nationalism was one of his constant targets in seminars, lectures, and writings. An example is his repudiation of "later Heidegger"

---

2   The interview Dragan Kujundžić conducted with Hillis Miller related to the questions of anti-Semitism did in fact subsequently take place, and may be found in *haTanin, Journal of the Center for Jewish Studies*, University of Florida, Issue 22, 2013, page 20-21. Online location: http://web.jst.ufl.edu/haTanin/2013/2014-01_HaTanin_Final.pdf

or his comments on the ideological notion that the Dutch are all phlegmatic. He lectured and wrote brilliantly about Walter Benjamin. People ought to read carefully de Man's essays and books before passing judgment on them. 4) My book, *Conflagrations of Community: Fiction Before and After Auschwitz* (Chicago: 2011), is, as Dragan says, the place to go to find out about my own attempt to confront the Holocaust by way of the topic of community, by way of Holocaust fictions, and by way of the questions about whether such fictions are possible or a good thing. JHM]

*Hillis is a very affable figure on the screen; he clearly takes immense joy in his work and his trademark "what, me worry?"—Alfred E. Neuman—attitude mitigates the darker edges of Deconstructionism.*

*What was your favorite part about working with Hillis? How do you think the audience will appreciate him?*

Let us not end on a "darker" note. This is also a good opportunity to remind us that "deconstruction" is a great philosophy of affirmation and laughter. In my own work, I have written about Jacques Derrida and laughter and have coined the word "deRIDEOlogy" (from the Latin *rideo, ridere, risi, risum*, to laugh, combining it with Derrida's name to form the name of this, to paraphrase Nietzsche, "Merry Science" that deconstruction is), to capture this force of originary affirmation, which Jacques Derrida called the "yes saying" or the "yes laughter" (*oui dire* and *oui rire*), for example, when he wrote about Joyce. His last, unfinished essay, dedicated to his friend Samuel Weber, is called, "You Must Be Joking" (*Vous voulez rire*)! Throughout his work Derrida wrote about laughter. So let us not forget that while "deconstruction" has tremendous probing interpretive powers to cut through the alienating ruling ideologies (thus while dealing with the darker side of life, it is not dark in itself), it is first and foremost a philosophical practice of transformation, and a thought of originary affirmation. Nothing "dark" about it. You gotta be joking!

And indeed, it has been a profound joy to work with J. Hillis Miller, I consider my encounter with him and his work a blessing of my life! And his on camera persona simply emanates warmth, wisdom, intelligence and humor. He mitigates not only the "darker sides of Deconstruction" but also the darker side of life! Just consider the anecdote (this will be in the film) he tells how he and his wife Dorothy decided where to be buried. "We knew that people DO die in California, but we could not think of us being buried there!" Hillis' stories are full of such anecdotes and warm memories of his friends. And since you started with the quote from "The Critic as Host," may I say how great a host that critic, J. Hillis Miller is? Both my cameraman and I were treated royally by Hillis and his wife Dorothy, and made available their homes for our filming, upward of forty or fifty hours to include the prep time, us the intruders with our cumbersome equipment, questions, imposing on their time, moving the furniture around, etc. Hillis is an exceptionally generous host. He in fact allowed us to be hosts in his own house.

Some of the decisions regarding the choice of the filming shot close up for most of the time during the interviews, were motivated by the sense that Hillis has a great cinematic presence, and that the most interesting drama in the film is the one played out on his face, all else is secondary! I had a long discussion with my cameraman, Georg Koszulinsky, before we started, regarding what kind of shot format should be used. I wanted to capture that spirit, wit, humor, and a sense of serene wisdom which he emanates in real life, so we set on a close up, at rare times extreme close up, and pulling back to medium close when we wanted to underscore some point he was making, and show him in the environment of his library. I am glad that you think we managed to make those qualities come across.

# Part 2

*Chapter 1*

SARAH DILLON

# "Talking about the same questions but at another rhythm": Deconstruction and Film

What is the relationship between deconstruction and film? How, where and when do they encounter each other? What is there intelligible to say about those encounters and how might we go about saying it? In *The Medium is the Maker* (2009), J. Hillis Miller describes Jacques Derrida's reading strategy—and thus, of course, his philosophical thought, since the two practices are simultaneous—as a process of "'micrological' attention" (70). Derrida, Miller says, "looks carefully at tiny, apparently insignificant, details of language or gesture. These are usually, in one way or another, tropes" (70). According to Miller, "it is a big mistake, Derrida believes, ever to rise above these particularities to some abstract conceptual level" (70). I want to go about answering my opening questions then, not on the level of the abstract or the theoretically general, but by focusing upon the particular: both a particular film, Dragan Kujundžić's *The First Sail* (2011); and a particular trope, that of rhythm. Rhythm serves here, as tropes so often uncannily do, in a doubled capacity: both as the foci for a particular analysis, here, of the relationship between deconstruction and film; and as the tropic signifier of the relationship between the general and the particular. Tropes invariably carry this self-referential function—in a rhythmic feedback loop the particular trope tropes the general trope of which it is, however, but one example.[1] In *Echographies of Television* (2002), Derrida asserts that "between the most general logos (the greatest predictability) and the most unpredictable singularities

---

1  See, for instance, my work with the eponymous trope in *The Palimpsest*, in particular, Chapter 4 "On Poetry and Metaphor."

comes the intermediate schema of *rhythm*" (16)—rhythm allows us to move between the general and the particular, hence my specific attention to rhythm will act as a medium for more general observations.

## Shared Spectrality

Deconstruction's explicit statements on film, and teletechnologies in general—found in the writings of both Derrida and Miller—identify the shared embededness of deconstruction and film in the logic of spectrality. The most explicit statement of this takes place, appropriately, on film, during Derrida's cameo appearance in Ken McMullen's *Ghost Dance* (1983) in which Derrida plays himself playing himself. In an improvised response to the actress Pascale Ogier's question, "Do you believe in ghosts?" Derrida observes that "the cinema is the art of ghosts, a battle of phantoms ... It's the art of allowing ghosts to come back." He gives voice to his belief that "ghosts are part of the future and that the modern technology of images, like cinematography and telecommunication, enhances the power of ghosts and their ability to haunt us. In fact, it's because I wished to tempt the ghosts out, that I agreed to appear in a film." We find similar observations throughout Derrida's work on technology, for example in "The Ghost Dance," an interview in *Public* in 1989, where Derrida reiterates that "the experience of ghosts ... is accentuated, accelerated by modern technologies like film, television, the telephone. These technologies inhabit, as it were, a phantom structure. Cinema is the art of phantoms" (61).[2] For deconstruction, the logic of spectrality—both the non-contemporaneity of the present with itself and the open possibility of the phantasmatic return of the past and arrival of the future—is an absolute necessity. As Derrida says in *Echographies of Television*, "without this possible coming-back, and if we refuse to acknowledge its irreducible originality, we are deprived of memory, heritage, justice, of everything that has value beyond life and by which the dignity of life is measured" (23). As the science of ghosts, as the medium of that spectral return, film bears an essential affinity with deconstruction. More than this, in fact, film takes its place alongside such terms as "*difference*," "parergon," "writing," "the

---

2   A further iteration of this theme can be found in *Echographies of Television* (see esp. pp. 117-20 in which he discusses the scene in *Ghost Dance* cited above).

supplement," "woman," as yet another figure or mechanism that performs Derrida's deconstruction of the phallogocentrism of Western thought. Derrida says as much to Steigler in *Echographies of Television* when he acknowledges that "the way in which I had tried to define writing implied that it was already, as you noted, a teletechnology, with all that this entails of an original expropriation" (37).

And yet, film is not writing, or at least not in the non-arche sense of speech and writing dependent on language. Rather, the uniqueness or singularity of film is that its essence is non-linguistic.[3] As Derrida remarks in an interview with Brunette and Wills entitled "The Spatial Arts" (1994),

> if there is a specificity to the cinematic medium, it is foreign to the word. That is to say that even the most talkative cinema supposes a reinscription of the word within a specific cinematic element not governed by the word. If there is something specific in cinema or video—without speaking of the differences between video and television—it is the form in which discourse is put into play, inscribed or situated, without in principle governing the work. (13)

If, as Derrida says, film puts discourse into play, but is not governed by it, what, then, is that "specific cinematic element not governed by the

---

3  This may in fact be why neither Derrida nor Miller has performed a deconstruction of a filmic text. No film has provoked these readers by its strangeness, by its otherness, by that impenetrability to which Hillis Miller refers in *The First Sail* when talking about reading literature. No film has placed that demand on them to respond, in the same way in which literary and philosophical texts have, to tease out its play and its alterity. Derrida may insist throughout his work that "the most effective deconstruction ... is one that deals with the nondiscursive, or with discursive institutions that don't have the form of a written discourse" (Brunette and Wills, "The Spatial Arts" 14), but there is no doubt that Derrida and Miller work at their best, at their most productive and insightful, when riffing off a written text. The filmic text simply does not, as we now colloquially put it, "do it for them." That does not mean, of course, that one cannot perform a deconstructive reading of a film, but rather that that task falls to those who inherit deconstruction. I venture such a reading of *The First Sail* below. For further examples see my reading of *My Life Without Me* in "Cinematic Incorporation"; the performative chapters of Peter Brunette and David Wills' *Screen/Play* (1989) and Robert Smith's brief but excellent reading of *Jurassic Park* in "Deconstruction and Film" (2000).

word"? The answer is not the image, but rhythm. The image in stasis is photography; the image in movement is film. And that movement is rhythmic, whether it be regular, flowing, progressive, or jarring; whether the film is produced with mellifluous continuity editing or discordant crosscutting.

## Rhythm

Deconstruction and film bear a joint relationship to the non-discursive rhythm that is at once essential to, but wholly other than, language. As Brian Massumi says, "rhythm carries the force of the phrase, above and beyond its structure and meaning" ("Floating the Social" 42).[4] In *Versions of Pygmalion* (1990), reading Heinreich von Kleist's essay "On the Gradual Fabrication of Thoughts While Speaking" (1805/6), Miller notes this paramount importance of rhythm to speech and writing:

> A series of syllables without rhythmical emphasis and without the articulations signaled in written language by spaces and by marks of punctuation—dashes, commas, colons, semicolons, underlinings, capitalizations, quotation marks, the period at the end—is meaningless. A series of words in a foreign language pronounced with approximate correctness but with the wrong rhythmical emphasis often conveys nothing at all when addressed to a native speaker of that language. Moreover, alteration of the punctuation of a sentence, alteration of the signals that indicate the proper rhythmical cadence of the sentence, can change the meaning drastically. (109-10)

Rhythm—whether it be the cadence of spoken speech or the graphic rhythmic denotations of grammar and syntax—is essential to the

---

4   See Massumi for an extended discussion of the fascinating electronic art installation by Rafael Lozano-Hemmers entitled *Amodal Suspension. Relational Architecture No. 8* (2003) in which text messages are translated into rhythmically pulsing beams of light: "The encoding of letter frequency into the beam attaches it genetically to culture-specific rhythms of speech. But the encoding is not visually decodable by the viewer any more than the meaning of the message can be seen in the pulse and flutter. What comes across is, simply, the rhythm. A language-like rhythm—without the actual language" ("Floating the Social" 42).

meaningfulness and comprehensibility of semantic content, whilst at the same time being entirely other to that content. As Miller further explains, "the rhythmical emphases of an oral sentence, like the marks of punctuation in a piece of written language, are without semantic meaning in themselves. A dash is without referential significance. You do not enunciate it when you read the sentence aloud. The rhythm of a spoken sentence does not alter the semantic content of the words taken separately" (110). Rather, "such elements indicate joints, hinges, articulations, spaces, or pauses, the nonsignifying and nonphenomenal syntactical aspects of language without which language could not make sense" (110). Rhythm, be it in the form of "pauses," "emphases," or "articulations" means nothing in itself but is "nevertheless necessary to the fabrication of the thought" (110).

Deconstruction, as a reading and writing practice, is peculiarly sensitive to these residual rhythms that structure language even as they do not inform its linguistic semantic content. Anyone who hears/heard Derrida lecture live knows this intuitively. Miller refers to it in his interview with Éamonn Dunne at the end of *J. Hillis Miller and the Possibilities of Reading* (2010), when he talks about the "rhythm and tempo" of "Derrida's expansive inexhaustibly inventive developments—a wonderful two hour seminar I once heard on the phrase "je t'aime," for example" (134). Just like film, deconstruction is, as Miller says in "The Critic as Host," "always in movement" (170); both are governed by the nonlinguistic rhythm that haunts language. Moreover, deconstruction is, and will increasingly be, dependent on film (and other tele-technologies) for the preservation of its rhythms.

Film's spectrality preserves the rhythms that beat at the heart of deconstruction. We see this in Miller's comments in *The First Sail* after watching Derrida lecture on him. (Here incidentally we have the technologic of spectrality *en abyme*, since we are watching a film of Miller talking about Derrida after watching him watch a film of Derrida talking about Miller.) Watching Derrida on screen, after his death, Miller makes the now expected observation regarding the uncanny return that film facilitates: "It is like the return of a ghost. It makes you think about the possibilities of new technologies which allow the survival, in such a strikingly immediate kind of way, of somebody who's now dead." But he is also careful to note that film does not bring Jacques Derrida back, in the flesh—the corporeal resurrection is a deception, a hoax, artifactual not actual.[5] What it does bring back is his speech and its rhythms, preserved "live" despite the absence of the body that gave voice to them. Derrida's command, his originality, depended, Miller says, so much on "timing," on "hesitation," that is, on rhythm. "This," he says, "is the thing that would be lost in the transcription." This is the thing that film preserves. And this is what we witness, with regard to Miller himself, in *The First Sail*.

## The Gradual Fabrication of Thoughts

*The First Sail* consists, in the main part, of material from thirty hours of interviews with Miller during March and June 2010. The interview is a paradigmatic example of, in Kleist's terminology, the gradual fabrication of thoughts whilst speaking. Miller and Kleist's comments in relation to this act, then, are directly relevant to the content of the Miller interviews. But they are also relevant to the editorial act which produces this 85 minute film from thirty hours of interview material. Cutting is the filmic equivalent of the rhythmical emphases of spoken speech or the punctuation of written notation. And the rhythm of cutting and splicing to create the interviews we witness in *The First Sail* works precisely in the dual capacity that Miller identifies in relation to the potential interruptions to Kleist's exemplary speakers. Rhythm provides the cadence that makes meaning possible, especially in an improvisatory setting such as an interview or a cutting room, but these rhythms—or their equivalent, the visibility of the digital splices in the final film—also mark the trace of the discontinuous, anacoluthic process that has created the final thought. As Miller says,

> they give the sequence of words the cadence necessary to meaning, [but] at the same time they are antirhythmical caesuras, breaks, or suspensions. These disarticulations are the

---

5   Referring to this section of the film in interview, Kujundžić calls film and television a "sham simulacra" which "confronts him [Miller] with the finitude of his friend's demise, but is also somewhat soothing": "nothing replaces the singular live being, but it also gives the memory of life a chance to live on in this spectral manner. And that spectrality is at work in life itself" (5).

> traces within the linguistically generated thought, when it is complete, of the contingencies and discontinuities that are hidden and forgotten when the achieved "period" is turned back on retrospectively, given a logical meaning, and assimilated into one or another historical narrative. (110)

The film's editing makes of many hours of interviews with Miller an achieved "period," in his own terminology, which retrospectively gives a logical meaning to his hours of discourse and which assimilates it into a historical narrative. But the rhythmic visibility of that editing in the film serves as an intratextual reminder of the process by which that retrospective "period" has been achieved.

Earlier in his discussion of Kleist, Miller explains his theory of a "specifically linguistic time," one that is generated "within the suspended and extended moment of the gradual fabrication of thoughts while speaking" (*Versions of Pygmalion* 108). According to Miller:

> This temporality reaches out toward a not yet foreseen future to come back to the beginning in the moment of a triumphant completion of the thought. The period takes time to complete. During that time the forward march of historical or narrative time is suspended. Only when the "period" is finished, only when the string of words generated by the gradual fabrication of thoughts has come to an end and makes sense, can it be turned back on retrospectively. (108)

Film adds another movement to this process. The gradual fabrication of thoughts that occurs whilst Miller speaks in interview occurs first; this is followed by the gradual fabrication of thoughts that is the editing of that material to create the ostensibly "continuous" interviews that constitute the body of the film. In that second movement of fabrication, the "forward march of historical and narrative time" is again suspended, as the editor decides which content to include and which content to exclude.[6]

---

6   See Walter Benjamin's resonant comments in "The Work of Art in the Age of Mechanical Reproduction" (1936) that the illusory nature of film is "that of the second degree, the result of cutting" (226): "That is to say, in the studio the mechanical equipment has penetrated so deeply into reality that its pure aspect freed from the foreign substance of equipment is the result of a special procedure, namely, the shooting by the specially adjusted camera and the

Here, in the cutting room, we have the filmic equivalent of Miller's "linguistic time," a suspended temporality. Only when the final cut has been made, the "period" here being the final version of the film, can one then view it retrospectively and thus reinsert it into time, into history, in this instance as an artifact: "Only then has the thought been expressed in a code that allows it to be repeated, iterated, say by being printed [or screened] therefore capable of entertaining history again each time it is read [or viewed]" (Miller, *Versions of Pygmalion* 108).[7] Every act of reading, here of viewing the film, "constitutes the reassimilation of the linguistically codified thought into historical and narrative time" (108). But each screening or viewing of *The First Sail* is a unique assimilation into a specific historical time and a singular narrative, of which the essays in this collection provide just a few examples. At this moment, *The First Sail* has only recently been launched. Who knows as yet what waves it will cause as it moves through space and time, what readings it will encounter and provoke.

## Ecotechnics

Does film preserve the rhythms of deconstruction as they would be if the camera were not there? At the end of *The First Sail*, Miller notes that he is aware of the presence of the impassive, unblinking eye of the camera and that "that's anxious making." Derrida too was uncomfortable in front of the camera, not because of its impersonality, but because it forced him into rhythms that were not natural to him, that he both learnt to accommodate and saw it as an intellectual obligation to challenge. This is clear in the rhythmic subtext of comments about rhythm that sound throughout

---

 mounting of the shot together with other similar ones. The equipment-free aspect of reality here has become the height of artifice; the sight of immediate reality has become an orchid in the land of technology" (226).

7  One might ask, of course, how this process is complicated by contemporary extra-filmic projects such as Kujundžić's decision to publish all the interview material online; or, for example, by deleted scenes and director's cuts included on DVD issues. These innovations reify Miller's observation that "the completed period is a strange kind of anacoluthon … The period appears perfectly grammatical, but it is an encrypted anacoluthon. It has barely discernible fissures where the contingencies of its original process of formation may be discerned by a sharp-eyed observer" (*Versions of Pygmalion* 111).

*Echographies*, punctuating that text's louder conversation about technology and spectrality. "Already, I have the impression that our control is very limited," Derrida says:

> I am *at home* [chez moi], but with all these machines and all these prostheses watching, surrounding, seducing us, the quote "natural" conditions of expression, discussion, reflection, deliberation are to a large extent breached, falsified, warped. One's first impulse would therefore be to at least try to reconstitute the conditions in which one would be able to say what one wants to say at the rhythm at which and in the conditions in which one wants to say it. And has a right to say it. And in the ways that would be least inappropriate. This is always difficult. It is *never* purely and simply possible, but it is *particularly* difficult in front of the camera. (Derrida and Stiegler, *Echographies* 32-33)

In both *The First Sail* and *Echographies* (a transcription of a series of filmed interviews), the camera enters the home: it intrudes into the literal home of these two men, but it also challenging the at-homeness of their discourse and its "natural" rhythms. The demand is both to attempt to preserve the "natural" in the face of, and, as we have seen, via, the technological, and, at the same time, to explore the provocation that teletechnologies make for different styles and rhythms of thought, speech and writing, of communication and exchange:

> We must consequently try both to mark the fact that we aren't able to speak here in the way that we are used to speaking and writing about these subjects, we must try not to efface this constraint, and at the same time, to respect the specificity of this situation in order to address these questions, in the moment, with another rhythm and in another style. (Derrida and Stiegler, *Echographies* 38)

In the scene entitled "Inheritances—and Rhythm," Derrida continues to explore the tension between the "natural" and the technological, between the rhythms of unrecorded speech and the rhythms of teletechnologies:

I don't speak, I don't think, I don't respond in the same way anymore, at the same rhythm as when I'm alone, daydreaming or reflecting at the wheel of my car or in front of my computer or a blank page, or as when I'm with one of you, as was the case a little while ago, as will be the case again in a moment, talking about the same questions but at another rhythm, with another relation to time and to urgency. This does not mean, at that moment, one has enough time—one never has enough time—but the relation to urgency and to rhythm would be different and now it has suddenly been transformed by this system of scenographic and technical devices. As soon as someone says "Roll tape!" a race begins, one starts not to speak, not to think in the same way anymore, almost not to think at all anymore...One's relation to words, to their way of coming or of not coming, is different... (Derrida and Stiegler, *Echographies* 70)

Film, television, radio, all teletechnologies, bring with them "a new temporality of technics...another rhythmics" (72). This new rhythmics is indissociable from the most pressing political, economic, and ethical questions of our times, but at the same time it is one from which intellectuals retreat. And "the more they are removed from this experience, the less they are accustomed to it, the less they are able to forget the artifice of the scenario" (71). Being on camera does not just alter Derrida's rhythms—he goes so far here as to say that it halts him entirely: "When the process of recording begins, I am inhibited, paralyzed, arrested, I don't 'get anywhere' [*je "fais du sur-place"*] and I don't think, I don't speak in the way I do when I'm not in this situation" (71).

How, then, might deconstruction meet the challenge of the new technological rhythmics? How might it move beyond, as it must do, this paralysis? The editorial choices behind the filming and composition of *The First Sail* provide a number of answers to these questions. In the first instance, the film helps the viewer to, as Derrida says above, "forget the artifice of the situation." *The First Sail* "naturalises" the technological through extensive continuity or invisible editing. Whilst the film includes scenes of Miller sailing, footage from a lecture at the University of Florida, images of photographs, websites, and so on, the body of the film is made up of fixed tripod camera footage of Miller sitting in one of his residences, talking to the interviewer. The camera occasionally zooms in and out, but its position and Miller's remain static. This type of cinematography creates the illusion of reality, it attempts to place you as viewer in unmediated conversation with Miller as speaker. The presence of the camera, the artifactuality of the recording, is diminished. One answer the film offers, then, is that to preserve the "natural" in opposition to the rhythms of these new technologies, one has to eliminate as much as possible the intrusion of, or at least an awareness of the presence of, these technologies.

At the same time, however, the film does not allow this sustained illusion of reality—it deconstructs it, as a film about a key figure of deconstruction must. For, as Derrida says in his film *Derrida*, "one of the gestures of deconstruction is not to naturalize what isn't natural." The film performs this deconstruction in a number of ways, affirming and exacerbating, as Nicholas Royle says of *Derrida* in "Blind Cinema" (2005), "the sense that film is never natural" (14). To give just a few examples: in the long interview scenes, regular, if slight, flickers in the image indicate that far from continuity editing, these scenes have in fact been edited. The appearance of temporal continuity has only been achieved through careful digital cutting and splicing. These rhythmic flickers, unobtrusive but apparent, remind the viewer that what we have here is not one uninterrupted linear interview but a montage of clips from many many hours of interviews. The material we are presented with may not even be in chronological order; the sentences which Miller speaks, may not even be his, as the film splices together not only his images but also his words.[8] The film, then, does not allow us to forget that what we are watching is a recording, even at its most "naturalistic" moments. As Derrida insists any encounter between deconstruction and film must, it archives "the re-marking of

---

8   Frequently, the soundtrack of Miller speaking continues seamlessly across the visual cuts (the aural splices are not "visible"), literally putting sentences, if not words, in Miller's mouth. In response to the delivery of an earlier version of this paper at *J. Hillis Miller: The Theory to Come, An International Symposium*, University of Lancaster, June 2012, Miller confirmed that he had a strong sense when watching the film that his meaning had been violated by the imposition of different rhythms on his actions and speech.

this fact that we are recording" (Derrida and Stiegler, *Echographies* 70).⁹

In this sense, the film is a performative example of *ecotechnics*, a phrase Miller takes from Jean-Luc Nancy's *Corpus* (2008) and plays with in "Ecotechnics: Ecotechnological Odradek" (2012) in a remarkable reading of Kafka's short piece, "The Worry of the Father of the Family" (1919). For Miller, the ecotechnical provides a model for understanding the world and our place in it that replaces the organic unity model which has dominated the history of Western thought. In the latter, "*Techné* is opposed to *Physis*, just as subject is opposed to object. *Techné* is a skill manipulated by subjectivities and their bodies. Technology adds something to a nature thought of as already externally out there and as organic" (Miller, "Ecotechnics"). In contrast, the ecotechnical provides a name for the deconstruction of the opposition between the natural and the artificial.¹⁰ In the characteristic deconstructive move, the natural and the artificial, *physis* and *techné*, are not separate entities, one with a purer and hierarchical value in relation to the other. Rather, each inhabits the other with a parasitic productivity to the extent that neither can be thought irrespective of the other.

A paradigmatic example of the ecotechnical would be sailing, that activity so beloved of Miller, which is only possible due to the connected ecotechnical functioning of the technical (the boat), the natural (the wind) and the human (the body and mind of the sailor). In the first of a number of sailing scenes that recur throughout *The First Sail*, Miller observes that he loves sailing because it is a "harnessing of the wind," hence also his interest in gliders. Sailing is at once technical, yet not obtrusively so; it does not subordinate the human or the natural to the brute technological, in the same way in which, for instance, motor boating does. And yet, the threat of brute technology hangs over these

---

9   See Peggy Kamuf's analysis of similar techniques and effects in *D'ailleurs, Derrida* (1999): "word and image are both held in relation and divorced from each other, they are, in other words, articulated, held together/apart. In this and other ways, the listener/viewer is kept constantly alert not only to the texture and dimension of film, but also to its artifacture as Derrida might have called it. Or simply, to its writing" ("Stunned" 110).

10  See, for instance, Derrida's discussion of the technological condition in *Points* (1995), esp. pp. 244-5. For further discussion of this see Clark's "Deconstruction and Technology" (2000).

ecotechnical scenes both in the ugly outboard motor affixed to the back of Miller's beautiful traditional sail boat, and in the noise of the motor that plays over these scenes, the motor, it is assumed, of the motorboat from which Miller's sail boat is being filmed. *The First Sail* both performs the ecotechnical but also contains within itself, not least by its very fact of being a film, stark reminders of its precarious balance, of the constant threat, in the twenty-first century, that the technical and the human might at any moment outdo, overrun, eventually destroy, the ecological.

A final example of the film's deconstructive ecotechnics is to be found in a comparative analysis of the film's opening and closing scenes. The film opens with a blank dark screen, with the soundtrack of waves lapping rhythmically on the shore, punctuated by the warning horn of a lighthouse. The image of a coast-line in daylight then fades in and the lighthouse and the sea from which the soundtrack originates become visible. We hear the lighthouse horn twice more, and then the image fades out and the film begins. At the end of the film, we find the reverse of the opening: the same coastal shot, the same lighthouse warning sound, the same soundtrack of waves, and then a fade out. But of course this iteration is a repetition that is not quite the same, for centre right on the blackout screen, even as the credits roll, the light from the lighthouse flashes intermittently. The light warns us that this is not merely a technological fade out to a blank screen. Rather, this is still active filming, but of the same scene at night time, hence the continuation also of the wave and horn soundtrack. The film preserves this coastal image even in the dark, via the night-time visual rhythm of the flashing light and the aural rhythm of the warning horn. In doing so, the film reminds the viewer of its own spectral operations since, as Derrida says, "what happens with spectrality, with phantomality … is that something becomes almost visible only insofar as it is not visible in flesh and blood. It is a night visibility. As soon as there is a technology of the image, visibility brings night. It incarnates in a night body, it radiates a night light" (Derrida and Stiegler, *Echographies* 115). The nightlight impresses on the viewer, as the credits roll, that what they have seen is not J. Hillis Miller the man, is not the natural landscape, but the technological reproduction of him and it. At the same time, as a figure of the ecotechnical, the lighthouse reminds the viewer that the natural and the technological, Miller the man, and Miller the man-on-screen, are irreducible from one another. In the twenty first century, we can no longer distinguish one from the other absolutely, but must find ever new ways of negotiating their interrelation, of understanding how the technological guides our relation with the ecological and with each other, whilst also heeding the ecotechnological warnings of the dangers of the seas on which we sail.

### Ghost Dance: A Coda

"All artifactuality," Derrida says, "take[s] place through intervention at the level of what is called framing, rhythm, borders, form, contextualization" (Derrida and Stiegler, *Echographies* 52). We visit those rhythms and borders again, rhythmic exchanges between sound and image, between the natural and the technological, between deconstruction and film at the end of the film *Ghost Dance*.[11] The opening credits of this film run against an image and sound track of waves crashing against the shore, and the tide sucking them back out. Running in and out of the water in time with the waves, a woman attempts to set sail what appears to be a large piece of paper. The waves continually wash it back in again. The scene is punctuated aurally by another lighthouse warning horn. Similar to the framing of *The First Sail*, *Ghost Dance* ends with the same woman (who we know now is one of the two actresses who play the film's doubled female lead) returning to that coastline carrying stills from the film in which she is starring. The sound of the waves on the shore returns, running over the image track of the actress framing the stills in mud on the coastal cliffs and in the shingle on the beach—images of Derrida, and of her co-stars. In the final sequence she drags a raft containing one of the film stills along the beach to the water. The punctuation of the warning horn returns and the film ends with the mesmerising, rhythmical tidal ebb and flow as another film still is eventually carried out to sea. The final sequence of *Ghost Dance* reifies Derrida's ecotechnical observation that "everything we are talking about is engaged in a transformation the very rhythm of which is determining and increasingly incalculable. For it is

---

11   A full ecotechnical reading of *Ghost Dance* which pays close attention to that film's negotiation of the relationship between the "natural" and the "technical" is yet to come.

*breaking*, it is rolling up on itself like a wave, which accumulates strength and mass as it accelerates" (Derrida and Stiegler, *Echographies* 71). Deconstruction and film. Film and deconstruction. Deconstructive film. Filmic deconstructions. The rhythms of these exchanges punctuate the ceaseless flow of discourse in our contemporary ecotechnical moment; they allow us to meet the incalculable impact of teletechnologies, to ride the wave, embracing, albeit with caution, its massive acceleration; moving forwards, moving on, always at a certain pace, whatever that might be; "talking about the same questions but at another rhythm."

## Works Cited

Benjamin, Walter. "The Work of Art in the Age of Mechanical Reproduction" (1936). *Illuminations*. Ed. Hannah Arendt. Trans. Harry Zohn. London: Fontana Press, 1992. 211-44.

Brunette, Peter and David Wills. *Screen/Play: Derrida and Film Theory*. Princeton and Oxford: Princeton University Press, 1989.

Brunette, Peter and David Wills. "The Spatial Arts: An Interview with Jacques Derrida." *Deconstruction and the Visual Arts: Art, Media and Architecture*. Ed. Peter Brunette and David Wills. Cambridge: Cambridge University Press, 1994. 9-32.

Clark, Timothy. "Deconstruction and Technology." *Deconstructions: A User's Guide*. Ed. Nicholas Royle. Basingstoke: Palgrave, 2000. 238-57.

*D'ailleurs, Derrida*. Dir. Safaa Fathy. Gloria Films, 1999.

*Derrida*. Dir. Kirby Dick and Amy Ziering Kofman. Jane Doe Films, 2002.

Derrida, Jacques. "The Ghost Dance: An Interview with Jacques Derrida." Interview with Mark Lewis and Andrew Payne. Trans. Jean-Luc Svoboda. *Public* 2 (1989): 60-74.

—. *Points ... Interviews, 1974-1994*. Ed. Elizabeth Weber. Trans. Peggy Kamuf et al. Stanford: Stanford University Press, 1995.

—. and Bernard Stiegler. *Echographies of Television: Filmed Interviews*. Trans. Jennifer Bajorek. Cambridge: Polity Press, 2002.

Dillon, Sarah. *The Palimpsest: Literature, Criticism, Theory*. London: Continuum, 2007.

—. "Cinematic Incorporation: Literature in *My Life Without Me*," *Film Philosophy* 19 (2015).

Dunne, Éamonn, *J. Hillis Miller and the Possibilities of Reading: Literature After Deconstruction*. London: Continuum, 2010.

*The First Sail*. Dir. Dragan Kujundžić. Deer Isle Productions, 2011.

*Ghost Dance*. Dir. Ken McMullen. Looseyard Productions, 1983.

Kamuf, Peggy. "Stunned: Derrida on Film." *To Follow: The Wake of Jacques Derrida*. Edinburgh: Edinburgh University Press, 2010. 108-19.

Kujundžić, Dragan. "The First Sail: J. Hillis Miller." *Sin Frontera* (Spring 2011): 1-15.

Massumi, Brian. "Floating the Social: The Electronic Art of Noise." *Reverberations: The Philosophy, Aesthetics and Politics of Noise*. Ed. Michael Goddard, Benjamin Halligan, and Paul Hegarty. London: Continuum, 2012. 40-57.

Miller, J. Hillis. "Just Reading: Kleist's "Der Findling."" *Versions of Pygmalion*. Cambridge and London: Harvard University Press, 1990. 82-140.

—. "The Critic as Host." *Theory Now and Then*. Durham: Duke University Press, 1991. 143-170.

—. *The Medium is the Maker: Browning, Freud, Derrida and the New Telepathic Ecotechnologies*. Brighton: Sussex Academic Press, 2009.

—. "Ecotechnics: Ecotechnological Odradek." *Telemorphosis: Theory in the Era of Climate Change, Vol. 1*. Ed. Tom Cohen. Ann Arbor: Open Humanities Press, 2012. 65-103. theory-in-the-era-of-climate-change-vol-1?rgn=div1;view=fulltext, accessed May 12, 2013.

Royle, Nicholas. "Blind Cinema." *Screenplay and Essays on the Film Derrida*. Ed. Kirby Dick and Amy Ziering Kofman. Manchester: Manchester University Press, 2005. 10-21.

Smith, Robert. "Deconstruction and Film." *Deconstructions: A User's Guide*. Ed. Nicholas Royle. Basingstoke: Palgrave: 2000. 119-36.

*Chapter 2*

## Just a Miracle

Charlie Gere

In this essay I engage with *The First Sail*, Dragan Kujundžić's film about the life and work of J. Hillis Miller, as a means to think through the question of the cinematic image, and what it might mean for critical thinking. I start with a kind of exemplary scene. Those present at the screening of *The First Sail* at Lancaster University in the spring of 2012, would have witnessed Miller, present in the auditorium, watching himself on the screen watching himself on another screen next to Jacques Derrida, who was in the process of giving a talk about Miller. Thus an almost parodic representation of the relation between presence and absence, between the living, the spectral and the literally dead, was staged. The scene nested at the heart of this Russian doll of a staging was Derrida's presentation of a paper about Miller, in which he describes his solecism, in their early acquaintance, of addressing Miller as "John," believing that to be the name concealed by the initial "J." He recounts how Miller, in a letter, gently pointed out both that his first name is actually Joseph, not John, and, also, that he never used his first name. At this point the actual letter from Miller to Derrida is projected behind Derrida, with this admonition diplomatically placed in a post-script beneath Miller's signature.

With the release of *The First Sail* Miller joins the short list of critical thinkers who have been the subject of a film documentary, which includes Derrida (twice), and Slavoj Žižek. Derrida has also appeared in a feature film, Ken McMullen's *Ghost Dance*, which I discuss at the end of the paper. Given both Miller's and Derrida's refusal to engage with film, and Derrida's frequent disavowals of any expertise in matters other than philosophy and literature, the question arises of whether it is legitimate to make films about them, or indeed any critical thinker. Attempts to render the ideas of such thinkers accessible through the moving image are indeed always questionable, given that their medium is text. Can films of this sort do their work justice? Can *The First Sail* do Miller's work justice? In this context the use of the term "justice" has a particular, and deliberate resonance. "Justices" is the name of the essay Jacques Derrida wrote about J. Hillis Miller and in particular his reading of Gerard Hopkins in his early work *The Disappearance of God*, Derrida's presentation of which is the very scene from *The First Sail*, described above.

The title of Derrida's essay comes from Hopkins' use of the word justice as a verb, as in "the just man justices." As Derrida defines it,

> To justice would be to produce justice, cause it to prevail, make it come about, as an event, but without instrumentalizing it in a transitive fashion, without objectifying it, but rather making it proceed from itself even as one keeps it close itself, to what one is, namely *just*, closest to what one thinks, says, does, shows, and manifests. The one who thus justices does not refer in the first or the last place to the calculable rules and norms of law. He is just by essence, just as he breathes. He does what is just, he accomplishes the just in a spontaneous manner. ("Justices" 692)

In the essay Derrida declares that he is giving the nickname "the Just" to Hillis Miller. Miller's discussion of Hopkin's notion of "selftaste" and his notions of singularity and the absence of God become the basis for Derrida's extended discussion of the univocal aloneness of both God and humans. Derrida quotes Miller quoting Hopkins,

> And [my isolation] is much more true when we consider the mind; when I consider my selfbeing, my consciousness and feeling of myself, that taste of myself, of *I* and *me* above and in all things, which is more distinctive than the taste of ale or alum, more distinctive than the smell of walnutleaf or camphor, and is incommunicable by any means to another man (as when I was a child I used to ask myself: what must it be to be someone else?). Nothing else in nature comes near to this unspeakable stress of pitch, distinctiveness, and selving,

this selfbeing of my own. Nothing explains it or resembles it ... searching nature I taste *self* but at one tankard, that of my own being. The development, refinement, condensation of nothing shews any sign of being able to match this to me or give me another taste of it, a taste even resembling it. (Miller, *Disappearance* 271)

Playing on Miller's use of the initial J, which sounds like "je" in French, Derrida writes that,

*Je me suis si souvent demande´*, I have so often asked myself, perhaps for more than thirty-five years, from the depths of my friendship and admiration for him, how one could be J. Hillis Miller. *Quel est son "je" a` lui?* What is his own *je*, his I? ("Justices" 690)

He continues,

The taste I have for him or the taste he has for others and for me, is it the same? Is it the same as the one he has for himself? One may very well doubt that it is. This doubt likewise takes on a very perceptible flavor in me, an obscurely immediate sense. We are moving here in that strange geometry where the nearest and the most distant are but one and the same. The most similar and the infinitely other return in a circle to each other. How does J. Hillis Miller *himself* feel when he says "je," "I" or when he has the feeling of "himself"? These borders of the I are vertiginous, but inevitable. We all rub up against them, make contact without contact, in particular as concerns our dearest friends. This is even what is astonishing about friendship, when it is somewhat alert. It is also vigilant friendship that startles us awake to this strange question: what does it mean, for an I *to feel itself?* "How does he *himself* feel, J. Hillis Miller? J. Hillis Miller *himself,* the other, the wholly other that he remains for me?" ("Justices" 690)

That we cannot ever know how the other feels is the basis of the "ethics of reading," the title of a book by J. Hillis Miller, published in 1987. In "Passions Performative: Derrida, Wittgenstein, Austin," Miller describes the notion, taken from Husserl, that there is "in principle no direct access to and verifiable indirect access either to the ego of another person, to his or her thoughts, memories, hopes, sensations, passions" (*Speech* 159)

This unknowability, this secrecy that determines our experience of the other, is what gives literature its force. In his essay "Passions," Derrida links democracy to literature and suggests that there is "no democracy without literature; no literature without democracy." Literature is the right to say anything, which ties it to "a certain noncensure, to the space of democratic freedom" (*On the Name* 28). But this also means that the author is not responsible to anyone for what he has written, and thus has the right of nonresponse. Thus, Derrida declares, what literature allows is that "there is a secret" (both "Il y a du secret," "there is a secret," and "Il y a là du secret," "<u>there</u> is a secret") (*On the Name* 28):

> There is in literature, in the exemplary secret of literature, a chance of saying everything without touching upon the secret. When all hypotheses are permitted, groundless and ad infinitum, about the meaning of a text, or the final intentions of an author, whose person is no more represented than nonrepresented by a character or by a narrator, by a poetic or fictional sentence, which detaches itself from its presumed source and thus remains locked away [*au secret*], when there is no longer even any sense in making decisions about some secret behind the surface of a textual manifestation (and it is this situation which I would call text or trace), when it is the call [*appel*] of this secret, however, which point back to the other or to something else, when it is this itself which keeps our passions aroused, and holds us to the other, then the secret impassions us. (*On the Name* 29)

This is also perhaps the problem when philosophers co-opt works of literature in pursuit of their philosophical arguments. Such readings often fail to do justice to the excess of any text, and the excess of reading a text. As Miller puts it in *Black Holes*:

> The phrase "excess of reading" names the way reading exceeds initial theoretical presuppositions, the use of literary works as examples of a conceptual argument, and any attempt to

encompass a work by its historical or cultural contexts. Each work gives knowledge (or nonknowledge—an experience of the limits of knowledge) that is singular and unique, attainable in no other way. If this were not the case, if the work could be accounted for by its context, then there would be no reason beyond aesthetic titillation to go to all the hard work necessary to read it. Everything it tells us could be known by studying its context. The work would be an empty placeholder for its circumambient culture. Reading the "of" in the second way, moreover, so that the "excess of reading" names what exceeds reading, gives yet another sense. It deploys the phrase to designate the "elusive something" that is the motivation of reading, its forever unattainable horizon. I have called that elusive "center on the horizon" the realm of the wholly others. This realm is always in excess of reading. (487)

To do justice to a work of literature is to do justice to its secret, to its singularity, and to acknowledge that the work of interpretation can never be final. In a sense this is also to acknowledge a miraculousness at the heart of literature.

In "Demeure," his essay written in response to "The Instant of my Death," Maurice Blanchot's short story or autobiographical testimony (which it is, is deliberately kept ambiguous), Derrida makes the following claim; "any testimony testified in essence to the miraculous and the extraordinary from the moment it must, by definition, appeal to an act of faith beyond any proof. When one testifies, even on the subject of the most ordinary and the most 'normal' event, one asks the other to believe one at one's word as if it were a matter of a miracle" ("Demeure" 75). Derrida suggests that this is why the privileged example of testimony is that concerning miracles, which is "the essential line between testimony and fiction." This is a passion that "goes hand in hand with the miraculous, the fantastic, the phantasmatic, the spectral, vision, apparition, the touch of the untouchable, the experience of the extraordinary, history without nature, the anomalous" ("Demeure" 75).

Which brings us back to film. In "Le Cinema et ses Fantomes," an interview in *Cahiers du Cinema* from 2001, Derrida describes cinema explicitly in terms of belief. "When I write about the cinema what interests me above all is its mode and regime of believing. There is in cinema a mode of belief altogether singular: For the century since its invention it has offered an unprecedented experience of believing" ("Le Cinema" 78). Even though, Derrida suggests, such an experience can be found in the theatre, in painting and in novels it is the cinema that allows one "to believe without believing, though this belief without belief is still a belief" ("Le Cinema" 78). He compares the experience of the cinema screen, with or without dialogue, to that of Plato's cave, offering a spectral dimension that is neither living nor dead, neither perception, nor hallucination, but offering an absolutely original modality of belief, a particular phenomenology impossible before the cinema came into existence ("Le Cinema" 78).

Interestingly, in the same interview, Derrida repudiates the idea that some kind of pure cinema was supplemented by sound. For Derrida the "grandeur of cinema" is the ability to integrate sound, and in particular speech, with images, and it is this that allows it to return to its origins, and to fulfill its original vocation in terms of belief. This is because speech is far more credible, believable, than the image. (Derrida cites Lanzmann's "Shoah," in which there are no documentary images of the Holocaust, only filmed interviews of the survivors giving their testimonies, as exemplary of this ["Le Cinema" 81]).

Here then one can return to the question with which this paper started, can *The First Sail*, do justice to the work of J Hillis Miller, and, by extension, can the moving image do justice to critical thinking, to the work of those who do such thinking. The answer is, miraculously, yes. In fact such films do more than merely succeed beyond expectation. They reveal something about cinema itself, and about its occulted vocation, as a vehicle for the miraculous testimony of the witness, to whom and for whom justice must be done. Despite the spectacular nature of much contemporary film the enduring focus of the cinematic gaze is the face, even in a debased genre such as pornography.

In a strange way cinema's portrayal of the face and of the talking subject is a kind of deconstruction of the metaphysics of presence. We are confronted by the presence of the speaker, apparently, miraculously alive and in front of us. But this is a specter even if the subject is still living, a specter furthermore that we cannot question. We must "take their word."

The screen on which the images are projected, whether cinematic, televisual or digital (an increasingly meaningless distinction) also act as a barrier to any illusions that we can have a privileged access to what they are thinking.

In *On Grammatology* Derrida points out how what was once described in terms of "language," is now increasingly characterized as "writing."

> Now we tend to say "writing" ... to designate not only the physical gestures of literal pictographic or ideographic inscription, but also the totality of what makes it possible; and also, beyond the signifying face the signified face itself. (9)

Among those phenomena now thought of in terms of writing Derrida cites choreography, and cinematography. Yet it would be a mistake to understand this merely as the application of the concept of writing as a means of understanding cinema. It is, rather, that cinema(tography) as well as photography, telegraphy, phonography, and all the other new media, the "tele-technologies," that emerged in the mid to late nineteenth century made possible the expanded understanding of "writing" that underpins Derrida's work.

Yet one might say that the origins of such media go back to the very beginnings of the metaphysics that Derrida sought to engage with, especially in his essay "Plato's Pharmacy" (*Dissemination*). It is not just the observation that Plato's famous metaphor of the cave in some ways resembles the cinema, but also that his entire *oeuvre* takes the form of a number of recordings of the experience of being taught by Socrates. Thus, as much as cinema can be construed as a kind of writing, long before the invention of cinema as we understand it, writing is also always haunted by a desire to be cinematic, to preserve and make available the fullness of lived experience and presence, particularly of the other, the face of the other. Of course, as Plato intuited and Derrida analysed, such a desire is not to be satisfied, which is perhaps ultimately its great strength, rather than a failing.

Finally, to return to the scene with which this paper started, that of Miller watching himself watching himself watching himself watching Derrida. This spectral mis-en-scene is strongly reminiscent of another such moment, described by Derrida in one of his interviews with Bernard

Stiegler, in the book *Echographies of Television*. Derrida recounts the experience of watching the film *Ghost Dance* in the United States with some students, two or three years after the death of the actress Pascale Ogier, with whom he had appeared in the film. Derrida is unnerved by watching a dead woman, apparently still alive on screen state that she "believes in ghosts." He points out that even when she first said this, a "spectrality was at work" and that one day it would be a dead woman up on that screen, haunting the living (*Echographies* 120).

Derrida then suggests that this is an example of what in *Specters of Marx* he calls the "visor effect," the feeling that we are watched by the specter, as if "before the law." The dead person is the wholly other, with whom there can be no symmetry of regard (*Echographies* 121). This then is what Derrida, writing about Louis Marin, calls the "force of an image," which is "hauntological," rather than ontological (*Work* 145). The image, whether in the form of a painted portrait, a photograph, a piece of film or video, does not re-present the other, make them present again. The image is always a trace and looks at us from the point of view of death, of the dead. Even if the subject of the image is living, spectrality is at work in the image. The other in the image is wholly other, and also looks at me as an image, and as wholly other, and each bears infinite responsibility for the other.

This is what one might call the "force of cinema," and the reason why it can add something to our understanding and experience of a thinker's work, why, in other words, it can do justice to Derrida or Miller or whomever else might be so portrayed. Watching Miller watching himself (watching himself watching himself) and also watching Derrida, was to see someone encounter both his dead friend and himself as spectral, and wholly other. We too are confronted by these specters, and accordingly are responsible to them and, in particular, to the memory of their work.

### Works Cited

Derrida, Jacques. "Demeure." *The Instant of My Death*. Maurice Blanchot. Stanford, Calif.: Stanford University Press, 1999.

—. *Dissemination*. London: Athlone, 1981.

—. and Bernard Steigler. *Echographies of Television.* Cambridge: Polity Press, 2002.

—. "'Justices.'" Trans. Peggy Kamuf. *J*, ed. Dragan Kujundžić. Spec. issue of *Critical Inquiry* 31, 3 (2005): 689-721.

—. "Le Cinema et ses Fantomes." *Cahiers du Cinema* 556 (April 2001): 75-85.

—. *Of Grammatology.* Baltimore: Johns Hopkins Press, 1976.

—. *On the Name.* Stanford, Calif.: Stanford University Press, 1995.

—. *The Work of Mourning.* Chicago: University of Illinois Press, 2001.

Miller, J. Hillis. *The Disappearance of God: Five Nineteenth Century Writers.* Chicago, IL: University of Illinois Press, 2000.

—. *Speech Acts in Literature.* Stanford, CA: Stanford University Press, 2001.

—. and Manuel Asensi. *Black Holes/J. Hillis Miller; or Boustrophedonic Reading.* Stanford, CA: Stanford University Press, 1999.

## Chapter 3

# Up

### Nicholas Royle

Embarrassed and embrangled I want to look up because I love him but at the same time, being very slow, I have to concentrate hard on reading quick enough in order to try to countersign him (he has read so much, just see, in *The First Sail*, all those books he has at home, and I know he says that "good reading… demands slow reading" [Miller, "How" 255] but I picture him reading—this is one of my abiding convictions—always at speed, with the wind constantly in his sails) and also to deal with feeling somewhat weighed down by the somatic memory of what happened last time I was invited to speak here in Dublin, in this very building, as those of you who were present might recall. I was not sure whether to laugh or cry. I arrived prepared to deliver a paper of around fifty minutes but was requested, just before I started, to do it in twenty-five, leading me to practise an art of oral kerning I never realised existed. So this time I have confined myself to a few remarks that really ought to take no more than twenty-five minutes and I shall do my utmost, while trying not to look up, though wanting to do so, to read neither too quickly nor too slowly despite being as I am so slow on the uptake, *on slow* in virtually every aspect of life. I pause here, for just a second, and look up, to wonder if I have not perhaps by now covered everything, a miniature triptych of questions, namely (1) the meaning of "up," (2) the time of a reading (doesn't Pascal's formulation, "When one reads too quickly or too slowly one understands nothing," undergo peculiar contortions in the context of film?[1] If the book gives you time, film screens itself off, keeps you to its

---

1   Pascal's aphorism provides the epigraph for Paul de Man's *Allegories of Reading: Figural Language in Rousseau, Nietzsche, Rilke, and Proust* (New

own regime. How can film give time? How most productively is "writing on film," in this case writing on *The First Sail*, to respect that regime, as if in accordance with the rights of inspection imposed by the linear unfolding of a single viewing, and betray it, lead it astray, show it veer?) and (3) the nature of somatic memory (what is somatic memory in oneself but, also, in the context of a film or, no doubt again very differently, poem or critical essay?)

I would like to express my heartfelt thanks to Eamonn Dunne and Michael O'Rourke for inviting me to speak. It is an honour to be here for the Irish premiere of Dragan Kujundžić's *The First Sail*, and above all to be able to celebrate this occasion with J. Hillis Miller himself.

But then I must confess to another source of embarrassment, which has to do with the topic of this brief talk, since it appears to coincide with what my hosts will be speaking of, namely "Tears, Idle Tears," the twenty-line song or lyric extracted from Tennyson's long poem *The Princess* (1847). Their title, as you will have seen, is "Miller"s Idle Tears." If I were at liberty to do so, an elaboration of coincidence *chez* Hillis Miller would, I imagine, quickly and easily fill fifty minutes: suffice to note that my friendship with him is, at least from one perspective, an intimate history of coincidences, of which the "telepathy effect" (I am never sure how many quotation marks to put around that phrase) is just one example.[2] I never read him, nor can I watch him on film, without this feeling, without a sense of what might be called, with a Stevensian inflection, *transport to coincidence*. And perhaps Eamonn Dunne and Michael O'Rourke would testify to something similar. At any rate, in my case, watching *The First Sail* I felt a strong connection with that passage in which he talks about Tennyson's poem, as well as a supposition, quite mistaken alas, that no one else would talk about it.

Perhaps the coincidence is not so remarkable, however, given the centrality that this short poem transpires to have had for Miller: it was his experience of this lyric, or more precisely his sense of bafflement and

---

Haven: Yale University Press, 1979). See Blaise Pascal, *Pensées*, trans. A. J. Krailsheimer (Harmondsworth: Penguin, 1966), 251.

2 See "The "Telepathy Effect": Notes toward a Reconsideration of Narrative Fiction," in *The Uncanny* (Manchester: Manchester University Press, 2003), 256-76, esp. 276, n43.

curiosity in the face of it, that solicited, at least according to what he says in the film, a kind of epiphany, a high moment in which he realizes he wants to change the course of his life, switching from being a Physics major to studying literature.

I have no idea what others are going to say about "Tears, Idle Tears," but in the presence of a scholar in whose work notions of origin, priority and secondariness are consistently queried and displaced, I claim no originality when I observe what is for me the weirder thing about all this. The instant I heard about the existence of this film called *The First Sail* I thought of "Tears, Idle Tears." I did not imagine the poem would figure in the film. After all, the phrase "the first sail" is not exactly a quotation from Tennyson. When I was watching it for the first time (my first sight of *The First Sail*) and came to the bit where Miller talks about the poem, I supposed that he would certainly make reference to "the first beam glittering on a sail." But he doesn't. I wrote to Dragan Kujundžić asking if he could tell me why the film was called *The First Sail* and he replied: "When we went to the Benjamin River to film it turned out it was literally Hillis' first sail of the year" (E-mail). Can this really be the origin of the title of the film? After all, the cover image of the DVD shows a young Hillis Miller, with his father, and a model sail-boat. Wouldn't that be the first sail? But then would the phrase "first sail" not be, in some sense at least, anchored in the nineteenth century, in that strange and beautiful line from "Tears, Idle Tears"? Would Hillis Miller, in agreeing to this title *The First Sail* (as I suppose he must have been invited to do), not have in mind its Tennysonic character? Or was it resonating merely in an unconscious fashion? But perhaps these questions are mistaken or wrongheaded. If there is somatic memory on film, in a film, it must be at once absolutely cryptic, unfathomable, resistant to knowledge and meaning, like Tennyson's tears ("I know not what they mean"), and spectral—what I would be tempted to call *a case of film memory*.[3]

It is an extraordinary moment where Hillis Miller reminisces about his initial encounter with this Tennyson poem: there he is, speaking from

---

[3] For more on the "case" in Hillis Miller, especially with regard to crypts and cryptonymy, and to deconstruction as "the case," permit me to refer to "Ghostly Preoccupations: Response to J. Hillis Miller, "The Ethics of Topography: Stevens" in *The J. Hillis Miller Reader*, ed. Julian Wolfreys (Edinburgh: Edinburgh University Press, 2005), 227-31.

"this ghostly cinematic realm" as he later describes it, wonderfully animated, his face in a sort of feigned amazement that is also real amazement, like the acting out of a hysteric suffering from reminiscences, reminiscing about this poem at which it remains difficult to know what adjectives to cast: poignant, plangent, anguished, ecstatic, bizarre, uncanny, disconnecting, disconnected, blinding. Miller recalls while reenacting his purported dilemma in the face of this poem, *tears, idle tears*, what does Tennyson mean by *idle*, what are *idle* tears, I know not what they mean, *tears from the depth of some divine despair*, what in hell does that mean?

> Tears, idle tears, I know not what they mean,
> Tears from the depth of some divine despair
> Rise in the heart, and gather to the eyes,
> In looking on the happy Autumn-fields,
> And thinking of the days that are no more.
>
> Fresh as the first beam glittering on a sail,
> That brings our friends up from the underworld,
> Sad as the last which reddens over one
> That sinks with all we love below the verge;
> So sad, so fresh, the days that are no more.
>
> Ah, sad and strange as in dark summer dawns
> The earliest pipe of half-awakened birds
> To dying ears, when unto dying eyes
> The casement slowly grows a glimmering square;
> So sad, so strange, the days that are no more.
>
> Dear as remembered kisses after death,
> And sweet as those by hopeless fancy feigned
> On lips that are for others; deep as love,
> Deep as first love, and wild with all regret;
> O Death in Life, the days that are no more.

You will readily note, I fear, how slowly I read this, in comparison with the rattling performance of Yeats's "The Cold Heaven" given by

Miller himself in *The First Sail*.⁴ At any event, this is for me one of the loveliest passages of the film, as he laughs over the baffling language of the opening of Tennyson's lyric, a lyric that is at once poem and song, "Tears, idle tears, I know not what they mean," he mixes the laughter and tears in a way that brings to my mind, and perhaps also to his, the words of Jacques Derrida: the time of tears, laughter and song is neither calculable nor repeatable.⁵ And it may seem that he has nothing to say, that he is rehearsing a sort of somatic memory of Tennyson's poem, a poem about the experience of a remembering body, a body remembered, the welling of the past into tears as a very embodiment of somatic memory, "[d]ear as remembered kisses after death." The poem might appear to have the same effect on him now, at this moment in the film, as it had when he first sailed into it, or it first sailed into him, as if indeed it leaves him in a state of speechlessness that coincides with the implicit absence of speech that is perhaps also the subject of Tennyson's poem. For while it is conventional to refer to the *speaker* of this poem (whether this be the maid mentioned in the immediately preceding lines in *The Princess* or, of course, Tennyson himself), in a significant and even eerie sense *there is no speech*: it is a poem about being deprived of speech, of a supervening of tears that, while eluding meaning ("I know not what they mean"), nonetheless say it all.

We might suppose that Hillis Miller has nothing to add, no further commentary or critical reflection, but of course this is not the case. J Hillis Miller loves to talk. That is clear even to his son Matthew at the age of four (that reminiscence constituting another of the most moving and funny moments in the film). This is in part what makes *The First Sail* so precious: here for our eyes and ears—but also for the eyes and ears of what Tennyson calls, in another arresting phrase (this time from *In*

---

4   For a fine close reading of Yeats's poem, see J. Hillis Miller, "Deconstruction and a Poem," in *Deconstructions: A User's Guide*, ed. Nicholas Royle (Basingstoke: Macmillan, 2000), 171-86.

5   See Jacques Derrida, "Envois," in *The Post Card: From Socrates to Freud and Beyond*, trans. Alan Bass (Chicago: Chicago University Press, 1987), 14-15, and "Passages – from Traumatism to Promise," trans. Peggy Kamuf, in *Points... Interviews, 1974-1994*, ed. Elisabeth Weber (London: Routledge, 1995), 388.

Memoriam), "the stranger's child"—is a record of Hillis Miller talking.[6] The "ghostly cinematic realm" of *The First Sail* may very likely transpire, in decades to come, to offer the clearest sense of what this great critic was like, of how he was, and even (in Jacques Derrida's phrase) of "how one could be J. Hillis Miller" ("Justices" 229).

J. Hillis Miller loves to talk, but he also loves to write. And so it would hardly be a surprise to learn that he has written about Tennyson's poem. But I must confess that, when I decided to try to write something about *The First Sail*, I had not read this text, entitled "Temporal Topographies: Tennyson's Tears," in the book *Topographies*. The essay is classic Miller—so lucid, probing, exacting, patient and exhilarating, calm and apocalyptic at the same time. "Tears are apocalyptic" (144), he remarks, in a memorable three-word sentence. "Temporal Topographies" is also marvelously illuminating of what seems to concern him in *The First Sail*, above all in foregrounding what is at the heart of this "powerful and moving poem" (135), namely a "poetic thinking" (135) of temporality that entails a sort of experience of the impossible, a sense of loss and longing that is also affirmation, an evocation of what is as much futural as past, the ghostly time, as he suggests, of a prosopopoeia that neither fails nor succeeds, that succeeds only insofar as it fails and fails insofar it succeeds. And still, as he makes clear, something happens.

Reading Miller's essay (originally delivered as a lecture in Taiwan in 1991) I discovered, as I invariably do when reading him, a wealth of ideas, new possibilities and directions that had not previously occurred to me. But I also encountered—as if by "telepathy effect" or the secret sharing of some "mental telegraphy" (in Mark Twain's phrase)—various formulations and motifs that left me thinking that Hillis Miller must have read what I had proposed to write before I had written it. In particular this had to do with how "Temporal Topographies" appeared to anticipate the image and figure that I had already specified as title for this talk, "Up." I wanted to gather these remarks under the heading of that little two-letter word for several reasons, but also for what is (as Miller might

---

6  "Till from the garden and the wild / A fresh association blow, / And year by year the landscape grow / Familiar to the stranger's child." See "In Memoriam," in *The Poems of Tennyson*, 954. Alan Hollinghurst adopts this phrase, "The Stranger's Child," for the title of his most recent novel.

say, following Yeats) "out of all sense and reason." I realize that I have chosen one of the most complex, as well as one of the shortest, words in the English language. I sense that it is a word that is waiting to trip me up. (Just try this at home yourself: write a paragraph about the word "up" without producing a single innuendo or double entendre.) I approach it here with as much wariness as the brevity of my talk and rush of thought conspire to make up.

I want simply to single out a few of the ways in which this tiny word comports with my sense of Hillis Miller, and responds to the impression of him evoked in Dragan Kujundžić's film. First and (as I might say quite literally) *above all*, Hillis Miller has always been a kind of upper in my life: whenever I read him or spend time with him he leaves me with a feeling of being up. I am inclined to connect this with what Derrida describes as Miller's "incomparable serenity" ("Justices" 229). Hillis Miller's writing has a clarity and good humour, a candidness and intelligence, a sense of graciousness and responsibility that is definitively elevating and uplifting. Seeing him in *The First Sail* sitting at home surrounded by his books or approaching the house or setting off in the rowboat or giving a lecture in Florida leaves you up. What Hillis Miller says, the way he says it, to see him saying it, leaves you up. His writing leaves you up.

Second, I think "up" for Hillis Miller because he is an upkeeper and he keeps up. He is, to my mind, one of the great keepers of keeping up. From our very first meeting (one icy cold weekend in Finland in April 1991, when I had invited him to speak at a conference at the University of Tampere on "The Ends of America") one of the most powerful impressions I recall was of the intense interest he took in what postgraduates and younger colleagues at Tampere were doing. More than twenty years later this sense of vigor and engagement persists. "It's amazing," one of my postgraduates at Sussex said to me the other day, "the only person who has really written about deconstruction and the internet seems to be J. Hillis Miller"—and that's not to mention his recent books on climate change or the conflagration of community or how reading George Eliot is connected with thinking about the current global financial meltdown. Miller's work keeps up and insists that *we* keep up with what is happening—culturally, intellectually, politically, socially, environmentally. In this sense, *The First Sail* is a forcefully topical and political film: whether he is talking about the "diabolical" change of Texan education policy on history textbooks, or the catastrophic Deepwater Horizon oil spill, or the continuing financial crisis engulfing the US and the world beyond, Hillis Miller is up with what is happening and sharply incisive about what is wrong, unjust, even disastrous, as well as about how, in critical ways, the folly at issue was foreseeable.

Finally, I wanted to try to say something about the word "up" in its singular appearance in Tennyson's poem: "Fresh as the first beam glittering on a sail, / That brings our friends up from the underworld…." The first thing I have to reckon with, regarding this encounter with the first sail, or with the first beam of morning glittering on it, is that Miller is already there; the first sail is his. For in "Temporal Topographies," with a sort of eerie foreshadowing of what I had hoped to try to explore here, I discovered that he had already isolated the fundamental importance of what he names the "up/down axis" (137) of this poem. I had been struck simply by the "up," but he quite rightly notes the pervasive significance of the word "down," not literally in the lyric itself but rather in the broader context of *The Princess*.[7] This enables him to arrive at the argument that, in "Tears, Idle Tears," "up is this present life and moment, while down is death" (138).

My time is, as the saying goes, almost up. I can only gesture towards what haunts and fascinates me here. Miller teaches us to read afresh, every time. Discreetly, tacitly, he borrows Tennyson's word "fresh" here to say that his concern in the essay is precisely to "try to read the poem afresh" (136). "Fresh as the first beam glittering on a sail, / That brings our friends up from the underworld…": these lines amaze me in a manner similar to the way in which Hillis Miller talks, in *The First Sail*, specifically about the opening lines of Tennyson's lyric. What would appear to be a standard reading of these lines is (to quote Miller) "friends returning by boat but not yet here" (140). Indeed, the OED specifically references these lines from Tennyson as an example of the use of the word "underworld" as "The Antipodes; also, the part of the earth beyond the horizon" (*OED*, "underworld," sense 3). I must say this makes me want to laugh, the *Oxford English Dictionary* in a bizarre underworld moment, as if one

---

7   See, for example, "Deconstruction and a Poem," 181.

could simply transliterate here: "Fresh as the first beam glittering on a sail that brings our friends up from Australia...."

Ironically perhaps, to follow the "straight" reading here would entail a certain veering in the sense of "up" as intimated by Miller in his classifying it as "this present life and moment." "Up" thus appears to be both "now" and "not yet." But of course what "up" here also and perhaps most powerfully does is evoke the return of the dead: the underworld here is not simply or literally the "the part of the earth beyond the horizon" but also, as Miller makes clear, the mythological underworld. Tennyson's poem can "raise a ghost" (146). As Miller puts it, linking this image of what the first beam brings with the tears that well up and constitute the unfathomable *raison d'être* of the poem: "Tennyson's tears of mourning are brought back up like Eurydice from the underworld, but their function as communicating messengers is lost along the way" (142). Tennyson's "up" is perhaps the most succinct figure of the uncanny temporality of the poem.

When will I see my friend again? When does the friend return? "Dead men tell no tales," as Miller likes to say, and this is the truth.[8] Yet there is also that sad, fresh thing called prosopopoeia—that rhetorical figure that he, with de Man and Derrida, has made and continues to make so *telling*, so strange and so enlightening for thinking about the world, about literature and the future. Given more time here I would like to have said more about how Tennyson's poem brings up the spirit of love and friendship, especially the ghostly presence of Arthur Henry Hallam (who, as Miller notes, is "buried not far from the ruins of Tintern Abbey," where "Tears, Idle Tears" was written: see 139). I would like to have elaborated on what the extraordinary intertextual waters of this poem bring up, not only with respect to Wordsworth's "Tintern Abbey" or Keats's "Ode to Autumn" or indeed, in more weirdly futural mode, Elizabeth Bowen's remarkable short stories "Tears, Idle Tears" and "The Happy Autumn Fields," but also regarding the demonic presence of Coleridge's "The Rime of the Ancient Mariner": *glittering, reddening, a sail*, from *life-in-death* to "Death in Life." The first beam glittering on a sail, the first sail, then, might bring our friends up in a sense not a thousand miles away perhaps from what is signified in the phrase "bringing up demons." (I always associate this phrase with an essay about crypts and cryptonymy, which I read with

---

8   See, for example, "Deconstruction and a Poem," 181.

great interest when it was published in 1988. I still recall the strangeness of the moment, some years afterwards, when Hillis informed me that "Bringing Up Demons" was written by his daughter [Sarah Miller, "Bringing"].)

Bill Readings (1960-94) begins his book *Introducing Lyotard: Art and Politics*—still, I think, the best critical exposition of Lyotard—with a modest acknowledgement: "I began to understand … [this] book's necessity in taking a seminar led by Hillis Miller" (p. xiv). Miller's work is a teaching and a reading, a teaching of reading. This is also the subject of *The First Sail*. What he allows us to see, sailing out of the film into his essay on "Tears, Idle Tears" and sailing back from the essay into the film, is an apprehension of the event as Readings glosses it: "The event thus marks a gap in historical time in the sense that it seems to inhabit at least two temporalities at once: an unthinkable future history and a past become uncannily present" (60). "Sing this poem and you will cry," Miller suggests in "Temporal Topographies" (143). But how and why? What is the point of this or any poem? How is it to be read? As he says in *The First Sail*: it's up to you.

## *Works Cited*

Derrida, Jacques. "Justices." Trans. Peggy Kamuf. *Provocations to Reading: J.Hillis Miller and the Democracy to Come*. Ed. Barbara Cohen and Dragan Kujundžić. New York: Fordham University Press, 2005. 228-61.

Kujundžić, Dragan. Message to Nicholas Royle. 5 April 2012. E-mail.

Miller, J. Hillis. "How to Read Literature." *The J. Hillis Miller Reader*. Ed. Julian Wolfreys. Edinburgh: Edinburgh University Press, 2005.

—."Temporal Topographies: Tennyson's Tears." *Topographies*. Stanford: Stanford University Press, 2005. 134-49.

Miller, Sarah E. "Bringing up Demons." *Diacritics* 18.1 (1988): 2-17.

Tennyson, Alfred. "Tears, Idle Tears." *The Poems of Tennyson*. Ed. Christopher Ricks. London: Longman, 1969. 784-6.

Readings, Bill. *Introducing Lyotard: Art and Politics*. London: Routledge, 1991.

*Chapter 4*

# Miller's Idle Tears

ÉAMONN DUNNE AND MICHAEL O'ROURKE

"Frippery" is an odd word. It is the name Hillis Miller has given to his Cape Dory Typhoon, the one we see him sailing out into the distance in Dragan Kujundžić's extraordinary film. That boat is of course a central metaphor in the film in many ways, as are the faint echoes of burbling waters punctuating and haunting its surroundings, pervading the serene quietude of the Miller summer home on Deer Isle, Maine, like the bee-loud glade in Innisfree, oddly and contradictorily peaceful and bustling at once. Miller's fantasy life is beautifully articulated in the recurring visual motif of him gliding through waters, and, verbally, in the opening recounts of his early interests in designing planes that likewise harness wind currents for free flight.

Though water and meditation may be wedded forever in human minds, as Melville's first-person narrator Ishmael famously suggests, those same waters are often obscure, illimitable, inviolable too (*Moby* 2). "The sea," Miller will say, "is terrifyingly inhuman ... no idea can wholly reduce this dark monster to order" (*Topographies* 273). But water has deeply moved him from an early age, a fact frequently evident in the inimitable style of his writings, themselves a seemingly effortless gliding, harnessing multifarious voices in great Victorian and modern literary works, a skill it has taken a lifetime's learning to achieve. Reading Miller is like an exercise in the free flight of the imagination, described in the film, a way of lifting off from the page and meandering through thoughts that are oddly directionless and pointed at the same time. Reading Miller reading, that is, is one way of seeing how "good reading" (by which is meant close rhetorical reading) invariably leads one away from a destination.

Fundamentally, reading Miller is the experience of *adestination*, of sailing into the unknown, an ad-venture in the strong sense of willing the arrival of some in-coming other about which one can really, positively, decisively, know nothing. Sailing out and sailing back again, past, passing and to come, coming about again, starting over again, afresh, afresh, afresh, as those monstrous waters never fully form to mind or voice.

But why be interested in the word "frippery"? Odd as it is. Surely, it is incidental. I want to argue here that that word somehow ironically, uncannily, encapsulates a central question (perhaps the central question) of the film. For, despite the laughter that pervades *The First Sail*, its light-heartedness and tenderness, a tangible poignancy surrounds it. Asked what fascinates him now, Miller responds "I am fascinated now, to be serious for a moment, by this question of the utility of reading literature any more in the period of critical climate change." Why read literature? It's not a simple question by any means, especially in our present moment of unprecedented digitized hyper-connectedness. And what is so striking is Miller's intelligent avoidance of trite, platitudinous responses. There is no reversion to I. A. Richards, F. R. Leavis, Kantian "purposiveness without purpose" or Arnoldian "sweetness and light"; nor is there, for that matter, a tidy agreement with Harold Bloom's latest focus on the enrichment of literature for our everyday lives.[1] There is only the question: "why should others read literature?" and the weakest of weak responses, "it's up to you." Why this must be the case can be glimpsed in "frippery."

The word is from Old French, stemming from the root "frepe" meaning old rags, rubbish, worn out, torn or useless old clothes. Somewhere along the way, though, through an odd metaphorical reversal, it came to mean the exact opposite of what it originally meant. In a strange semantic tale of rags to riches frippery became finery, tarnished clothing became *haute couture*. In William Congreve's *The Way of the World* (1700), for instance, Lady Wishfort is affronted by Mirabell's use of the word to describe her socially: "Frippery? Superannuated frippery? I'll frippery the villain; I'll reduce him to frippery and rags" (45). Whereas 70 years later Oliver Goldsmith's *She Stoops to Conquer* has Hardcastle reverse the valence by describing his daughter thus: "There's my pretty darling Kate!

---

[1] See Harold Bloom's recent book *The Anatomy of Influence: Literature as a Way of Life* (Yale: Yale University Press, 2011).

the fashions of the times have almost infected her too. By living a year or two in town, she is as fond of gauze and French frippery as the best of them" (3). Strange to think that in one lifetime the word becomes fully semantically inverted.

In more recent years, "frippery" is attended to in Mel Stuart's film adaptation of Roald Dahl's *Charlie and the Chocolate Factory* (1971). "Frippery" is employed here as a synonym for irresponsible behaviour that might lead to vandalism, mischievous or destructive actions. The golden ticket winners sign a contract before they enter Willy Wonka's wonderland. The contract is ludicrously long-winded and literally unreadable (reading like a Snellen eye test, trickling down to finer and finer print until finally there's nothing left, only pinpoints on the page). As far as one can make out the opening sentences of the contract read as follows: "WHEREAS For damage caused by lightning, earthquakes, floods, fire, frost or frippery of any sort, kind or condition, consequently the undersigned take responsibility."[2]

The rest is a wonderful example of "legalese," impenetrable jargon employed to confound even the most valiant attempts at decryption. Part of the joke, which will turn out to be quite serious for Charlie, is that the signatories of this document cannot possibly ever take responsibility for "lightning, earthquakes, floods, fire, frost or frippery of any sort, kind or condition." How could they? And yet, by signing the document, they do just that. These signatures are, to paraphrase Derrida, examples of a deep irresponsibility, hyperbolic examples of an everyday occurrence, the responsibilities of the name under the exorbitant duress of the language of the law, Wonka's wonky law (Derrida and Ferraris, *Taste* 85).

What Miller cherishes about literature is its linguistic concentration and complexity, the way language works to undo cold, comfortable complacencies. As far back as 1985, Miller was referring to the way in which language foregrounds itself in literature as a "linguistic moment." Something beyond language heralds it, calls attention to itself at precisely that moment when language inevitably fails to represent this "unknown X" at the very limits of the sayable/unsayable: "Beyond this boundary, though encountered only through words, the linguistic moment

---

2   See the following website for the transcription of the contract: http://home.comcast.net/~tom.brodhead/wonka.htm

dissolves before the *it*. The unknown X is beyond language, though it is what all language 'names,' in the gap which may not be closed between all words and any fixed identifiable referent, subjective, objective, natural, or supernatural" (Miller, *Linguistic* 339).

Black holes, catachreses for chaos, the unknown X, the wholly other, are all placeholders for that *it*, trembling at the borders of sense and reason. They all name without naming the altogether unknowable, insensible, unforeseeable at the secret heart of the literary. Those moments are the impossible made possible. They are frippery, radiant constructions and exuberant performative speech acts, excessive, ornate, overbearing, always missing the mark in astonishing arabesques and aerolites or falling far short in the foul rag and bone shop of the heart. That double sense of frippery, both beyond taste and below it, highlights the fleeting gap between right and wrong, response and responsibility, the good and bad reading. Indeed it is that very gap between finery and rags that unravels the question of utility: neither useful nor not useful but both at the same time; never quite one or the other, never filling the median gap of taste, self-taste or taste for the other. This is part of Wonka's wonky law, that the weight of language is never quite equal to the work it undertakes. The contract of reading never entirely binds, nor does it bind two different people in quite the same way. Miller's choice of Yeats and Tennyson is a case in point. The vicissitudes of circumstance – frost, fire or frippery – exceeds expectations (natural or supernatural), making the contract, like the sea, terrifyingly inhuman, monstrous. Why this must be the case for Wonka as well as Miller I will emphasise in three important threads.

~

**First thread**: Miller's sense of the good reader: someone upon whom nothing is lost. Genuine acts of reading in the Millerian universe are singular, *sui generis*, and occur as unforeseeable events, disqualifying, reshaping, undoing or dismantling any theoretical presuppositions we have brought with us to the text. That's why, in a very real sense, it is ludicrous to say J. Hillis Miller is a literary theorist. Nothing could really be further from the truth when you come to think about it; as if theory was something one could practice on its own: no theory without reading, no reading without theory.³ Theory now and then, not for all time, not for one time, for one time only, but when it happens, out of the blue, so to speak; falling like a benediction in multiple voices.

Indeed, this is one of Miller's laws, by his own admission. Miller's law: "The greatest critics are those whose readings exceed their theoretical presuppositions" (Miller, "Why Literature?" 414). In the event of reading, if it is an event worthy of the name, something happens to undo precritical assumptions, consensus with fellow readers (Stanley Fish's "interpretive communities" for example), predictions, conjectures. Reading the same works, works we think we already intimately know, might be the best way into seeing why the event and act of a genuine act of reading can never be predictable beforehand. Those readings in *The First Sail*, are second, third, fourth readings of works Miller has read in numerous books and essays already, notably *Others* for Yeats's "Cold Heaven" and *Topographies* for "Tennyson's Tears," but they are also always, always already, first readings, performative new starts, countersignatures. Derrida's word "iterability" incorporates even more succinctly the mutability, monstrosity, and otherness of this *contract* with reading, every other time it happens, signing, sealing, sailing.

"My law," says Derrida echoing Miller, "the one to which I try to devote myself or to respond, is the text of the other, its very singularity, its idiom, its appeal which precedes me. But I can only respond to it in a responsible way (and this goes for the law in general, ethics in particular) if I put in play, and in guarantee [*en gage*], my singularity, by signing, with another signature; for the countersignature signs by confirming the signature of the other, but also by signing in an absolutely new and inaugural way, both at once, like each time I confirm my own signature by signing once more: each time in the same way and each time differently, one more time, at another date" (Derrida, "Strange" 66).

Reading and theory are not opposed, so to speak, so much as asymmetrical, touching at a respectful distance; theory touching itself touching another in a kind of auto-hetero-affection, *se toucher toi*. A reading can

---

3   See also Chapter 12 of J. Hillis Miller's *Topographies* (Stanford: Stanford University Press, 1995), 323: "To put this another way, literary theory is always a reading of some specific work or works. The relation of theory to reading is itself a difficult theoretical question. Though there is no theory without reading, theory and reading are asymmetrical."

be touching in ways that can never be fully expressed in words or seen (as the etymology of the word "theory" implies); it can exceed the reader's, any reader's ability to say *why* it is touching, like Tennyson's "Tears idle tears" repeating the same word over in order, perhaps, to capture something of its innumerable meanings (tears, tears/ weeping, wrenching), or the catalogue of similes that are both like and unlike tears: "fresh as the first beam glittering on a sail."[4] Literature has no *why*, no theoretical formulation can justify the materiality of literature, its force without force, its phenomenality without phenomenality (Miller, *Topographies* 310). But the words themselves, heightened, pulled, forced open, disseminated, dehiscent, are part of that peculiarity which Miller claims took him to literature in the first place: "it is worth a lifetime to study it."

**Second Thread**: There is no way only wandering. *Methode ist Umweg* [method is detour] (Benjamin); which is why good reading is always a risk, the fortuitous outcome of a leap of faith in the text, what Frank Kermode called "divination."[5] Nietzsche is close to it in *Ecce Homo*: "When I picture a perfect reader, I always picture a monster of courage and curiosity, also something supple, cunning, cautious, a born adventurer and discoverer" (264). Intrinsic to Nietzsche's conception of the strong reader is the notion of movement, wandering, climbing, gliding, yes, even sailing, notable in several sentences from *Zarathustra* appearing as the conclusion of this section of *Ecce Homo*: "To you, the bold searchers, researchers, and whoever embarks with cunning sails on terrible seas – to you drunk with riddles, glad of the twilight.... because you do not want to grope along a thread with cowardly hand; and where you can *guess*, you hate to *deduce*" (264). Bold searching and monstrous devotion to a riddle, glad of the twilight, at home in the liminal space between knowledge and non-knowledge, sailing into terrible seas, the courage to err, that is Nietzsche's imperative, his demand of the philosopher of

---

4   Alfred Lord Tennyson, "Tears idle tears, I know not what they mean" in *Alfred Lord Tennyson: Selected Poems* ed. Christopher Ricks (London: Penguin, 2007), 92.

5   Benjamin's phrase appears as the first epigraph to Miller's *For Derrida* (New York: Fordham University Press, 2009), p. xv. Frank Kermode discusses this leap in interpretation in Chapter 7 of *An Appetite for Poetry: Essays in Literary Interpretation* (London: Collins, 1989), 152-171: "For every act of reading calls for some (perhaps minute) act of divination."

the future. All of these are significant for the kind of reader Miller sees in Derrida and Derrida, in turn, sees in Miller: "the intellectual adventure," as Derrida says in *The First Sail*, "that signs and seals our lives."

*Destinerrance*, we could say, is not only a key word in Derrida's vast protean lexicon; it is also *the* major initiative in Miller's. Nietzsche, patron philosopher of sailing, is the father of nomadic reading practices, of the (im)possibilities of reading. Miller's writings are yet one more example of why reading must be at once responsible and irresponsible to the call of some other or others, why it must always be at risk. It is also a plea with the "audacity of hope" that just reading might just make us Ariadnes awakening.[6]

**Third Thread**: The final thread is not a law, as such, but a movement beyond the law towards the possibility of justice, breaking the law in the name of a justice to-come. "Miller's exemplary justice," says Derrida, "consists of paying essential attention to the irreplaceability of the example" ("Justices" 234). In response to the question of the utility of reading, as I have said, Miller doesn't have an answer. He reverts to an example – Yeats's "The Cold Heaven." Why should we read that? How should we teach it? Shrugging his shoulders, Miller says "It's up to you." That's cold comfort, especially for those who've chosen to teach literature as their vocation, who've been *called* by it in the strongest sense of that term.

As Miller reiterates in one of two very recent essays he's written about the poem, and as I've suggested earlier, there is no *why*, apart from an obligation he feels to talk about what happens when he reads it. In the most rudimentary, humble, gracious manner, Miller wants you to hear what he thinks about the poem because it affects him in a way that, in a very real sense, is inexplicable. "Ah!" "Who but Yeats could have added that Ah!" says Miller in a wonderful moment in the film, a moment that catches sight of the incomparable humility and grace he has been bringing to his work, untiringly, for over six decades now. Though here again

---

6   Miller's argument in *Reading for Our Time* (Edinburgh: Edinburgh University Press, 2012) is that reading George Eliot's novels might, just might, with patience and rigorous attention to tropological detail, lead us to a better understanding of ideological lies and folly, and of how these follies might be unmasked.

Miller's laughter is at odds with the import of that great poem; laughing as his eyes moisten with tears.[7]

In his latest essay on the poem Miller lists 15 different points that the reader coming to the poem for the first time ought to know.[8] And that, he tells us, is just for starters. Miller's concern, I posit, is that this may all seem like frippery in the double sense of that term pointed out earlier – and what a disaster. On the one hand, literature's time is almost up, as he has been saying since 2001.[9] The new regime of teletechnological communications has changed literary study in such a way that close readings of literature seem outdated, outmoded, old school. That literature's role in society has diminished as a result of this in the last few decades is obvious: "it's gotta be," says Miller.

Books are now the frippery of a digital age, an age when the medium has made it so that kindles are outselling the printed page. Reading habits are changing, attention is diverting, torn. Miller's frippery, his idle tears/tears find themselves in the midst of a critical climate change and the waters are surely reaching up to our noses. In this latter sense, literary study is trivia, unnecessary, superfluous, frivolous. It divorces us from real, pressing needs. We should be "doing" something to instigate change in the world around us. It is in no way certain that literary study can help in this regard at all, despite claims (Miller's included) that it might make us better equipped at unmasking ideological follies. It is only with a faith in the task of reading, with a hope without hope that slow, patient, rigorous reading and the teaching of that as an art and a vocation worthy of its name, that we might come to realise its benefits in our lives. But it's up to

---

7  Viewers taken with this scene and who want to follow the reasoning behind Miller's statement, "it's up to you," should also read Chapter 7 of *Others* (Princeton: Princeton University Press, 2001) "Yeats: 'The Cold Heaven'": "'The Cold Heaven' violently empties itself out. It wastes itself, spends itself, cancels itself out in the final question and in the impossibility of deciding whether natural image or supernatural emblem takes precedence as the literal referent of which the other is the figure. This self-cancelling leaves the reader empty-handed, riddled with light, driven out of all sense and reason by an effort of reading," 181.

8  See J. Hillis Miller, "Globalization and World Literature" in *Neohelicon* 38. 2 (2011), 251-265.

9  See the opening pages of J. Hillis Miller's, *On Literature* (London: Routledge, 2002).

you. You alone. There comes a point when we all have to take responsibility for our own readings, a point when we must countersign our own contracts with the text. Sailing, sealing, signing, we must take responsibility for our own unknowable futures and for the (mis)readings we've already performed: "WHEREAS For damage caused by lightning, earthquakes, floods, fire, frost or frippery of any sort, kind or condition, consequently the undersigned take responsibility."

**ED**

*************************************************************************

Tears across the dotted line. Tears or tears are the thread(s) I would like to follow here. In *Specters of Marx* Derrida played on the idea of "wears" and "tears" (77), tears as ruptures, "abrupt breaches of syntax" (Derrida, "'Le Parjure'" 195-234), which render everything out of joint. The abrupt anacoluthonic tear in the text of the film of *The First Sail*, that which stops me in my tracks, puts everything out of kilter, is Miller's sadness. There are no actual tears of course and the film is punctuated by much laughter whether it is Hillis' or Dragan's. Even at those moments when Hillis is describing that which makes him sad or frightened he is laughing, albeit haltingly, as if, in these bad times, it is bad to laugh, or he is scared to even do that. Scared and scarred.

It is very difficult not to read the scar above Hillis' eye (incurred after a fall on the University of California Irvine campus) as a tear in the skin of the film, a punctum or rupture in its integument. This tear in the cloth of the film is "a neat cut, very deep" as he describes it (one is reminded of Hillis' reading of Freud's scar on the chin in *The Medium is the Maker* [66]) but one that nevertheless leaves a trace, a highly visible mark, even after it has been stitched up: the scar above the eye. In his essay "Telepathy," Derrida discusses the primal scene of Freud's falling from a stool and cutting his face in terms of "symbolic castration."[10] Freud bears a scar hidden beneath his beard which when he parts it reveals the wound:

---

10  Ibid., 66. It is interesting that Freud's scar is caused by a fall from a "stool" and that tears can be assimilated to excrement. Miller's reading of Browning poem "Mr Sludge, The Medium" picks up on the references to dung, excrement, shit (p. 31) but does not, so far as I recall, talk about the outflow of tears.

> The word *Narbe [scar]* comes twice from my pen, I know that the English had already used the word 'scar' to translate *Spur* much earlier on. This translation may have put some people on the trail [*piste*]. I like these words *Narbe*, 'scar', *Spur*, trace, *cicatrice* in French as well ... Nietzsche already spoke about the scar under Plato's beard. One can stroke and part the bristles so as to pretend to show, that is the whole of my lecture" (Derrida, "Telepathy" 251).

Miller's scar is not under his beard and there is no obvious allusion to symbolic castration (although later I will refer to his circumcised eyes, eyes swollen, torn and cut from weeping). However, we might reach a similar conclusion to Derrida that this scar which has healed over above the eye is one that is dehiscent. Miller's scar "don't you think, opens the text, holds it open" (Derrida, "Telepathy" 246).

But, how deep does this scar go? Later in the film Hillis recalls the love of a five year old boy for *Alice in Wonderland*. What drew that little boy to Carroll's novel was the word play (the same thing that would later move him toward Derrida), the linguistic choreography which he illustrates with a reference to the homophonic puns on tale/tail and not/knot. But this leads down the rabbit hole to a deeper question. The light-hearted love of word play is haunted on its underside by something that needs explaining, by the weirdness or strangeness of literature. *Alice in Wonderland* doesn't just make Hillis laugh; it always moves him (as all literature does when it calls, makes its insistent demand on him) in some way. Literature, he tells us, is something that he has "always found immensely *moving*." Why should I care, he asks, about fictional characters, about the creations of Eliot or Morrison or Kafka, about what happens to them. But "I do care" he insists. So there is this double side to Miller reading: on the bright side we have this interest in puns, jokes and wordplay, in the anasemic twists and turns of language. And, on the other hand, on the other side of the tear, we have this darkness, we have Miller's dark side (a seam which is often troubled or hinged by a mischievous wink, when he is asked if he has ever been jealous of Derrida or de Man for example). But why does he care so much about these fictional characters whom he telepathically inhabits? When he attempts to understand Tennyson's poem "Tears Idle Tears" it is because he himself is perplexed by the meaning of these strange tears. What ever could they mean? Why are they "idle" since they rise up and are in some way "motivated"? Tennyson's tears require some explanation. But so too do Miller's. If Freud's scar "pretends" to show us an absence then Miller's tears also reveal or re-veil an absence, not a presence. Why, after all, do they "rise up" from his heart but never gather to the eyes? I will try to explain what I think Miller's absent tears might mean. But we need to follow two tear-tracks through the film in order to do just that.

**Tear #1:**

As Hillis watches the archival footage of Derrida reading the "Justices" essay about him, about the (self)taste of J. Hillis Miller (the taste of his tears maybe?), he twice repeats that it is "very moving."[11] Surely the repetition is worth remarking. He is not moved once but twice. But he goes on to say, somewhat defensively, that he has indeed been moved but *"not to tears"* (recall the mouse's pun on not/knot in *Alice*). This is because, given the machinal nature of the new "eco-tele-technologies" which make the ghostly figure of Derrida speaking available to us, to him, Derrida "doesn't come through to me as the return of Jacques Derrida." No real tears then, or what Žižek would call "the fright of real tears."

But Miller is frightened by something. And again, he tells us this *twice*. In *For Derrida*, his twelve essays for his friend Derrida, his works of unworkable mourning for him, he tries, he claims, to be-tray him.[12]

---

11  Jacques Derrida, "Justices." Of course, the self-taste of tears is always the taste/tears of the other. In his notes on Derrida's (as yet unpublished) cannibalism seminars David Farrell Krell ventriloquizes Derrida: "Thus our own tears are always the tears of an other. We weep the other, who weeps us. This internal and inherent alterity is what enables Klein to speak of tears as excretions—not because they flow from us but because they flow from another within us, a phantasmatic other that could not be entirely consumed." David Farrell Krell, "All You Can't Eat: Derrida's Course, 'Rhétorique Du Cannibalisme' (1990-1991)," *Research in Phenomenology* 36.1 (2006), 169. The final lecture "Eating the Sun and Stars" (January 30, 1991) has much to say about tears, mourning, weeping, touching and taste.

12  We might compare Derrida claiming that "I liked words *in order to be-tray* (to treat, triturate, trice, in-trigue, trace, track)" (cited as an epigraph in Julian Wolfreys, "Responsibilities of J, or, Aphorism's Other: Criticism's

In this book with its wandering method, his aim, for all the aimlessness, is he says, to bring out a dark side to Derrida and he does so "not necessarily to agree with it."[13] It is not clear on which side of this tear in Derrida's work—the heterogeneity of which he is attempting to bring forth—Miller wants to be. He is frightened by something and he lets us know what that something is: Derrida's "late" turn to the figure of "autoimmunity" and in "Faith and Knowledge" to auto-co-immunity. If Miller himself confides that he is not so "socially adroit" then Derrida is someone who refrains from all community, enisles himself away from all groups, schools, families and this because, for Derrida, the "community" has an inexorable tendency to suicide itself.[14] Autoimmunity is a figure Miller finds "frightening" because it is not "very hopeful" (and he goes on shortly after to say that he is "frightened" by his own government). One recalls here the final interview between Derrida and Cixous where he reiterates that she is always on the side of life and he on the side of death. Cixous responds impatiently that Derrida has always been on the side of life, just more complicatedly so[15]. Miller too, is someone I have always thought of as being "for life." In his interview with Éamonn in *J. Hillis Miller and the Possibilities of Reading* he cheerily describes himself as a happy go lucky character: "As you can see, I'm essentially a cheerful person, like the hero of *Mad Magazine*: 'What, me worry?" (Dunne 125). This is perhaps why *The First Sail* and the "serious frivolity" of *For Derrida* pull me up short (but nowhere near as abruptly as the discussion in the film of his death and the graveyard plots). How, after all, can we think about tears without the taste of death, mourning, negativity, the frightening?

---

Transformation" in *Literature, in Theory: Tropes, Subjectivities, Responses and Responsibilities* [London: Continuum, 2010] p. 267) with Freud on the words scar, spur, cicatrice above.
13    J. Hillis Miller, *For Derrida*. Miller's earlier text on unworkability and community, "Unworked and Unavowable: Community in *The Awkward Age*" (in *Literature as Conduct: Speech Acts in Henry James* [New York: Fordham University Press, 2005], 84-150) is important here.
14    See especially the following chapters in *For Derrida*: "Derrida Enisled" (pp. 101-132) and "'Don't Count Me In': Derrida's Refraining" (174-190).
15    "You are against death and fiercely for life. But otherwise. Dis/Quietedly." Cixous in "From the Word to Life: A Dialogue between Jacques Derrida and Hélène Cixous," *New Literary History* 37.1 (2006), 7.

The "last word" of *For Derrida*—which appears as text on the screen during the film—is that "if these essays are works of mourning, they haven't worked" (326). In his eulogy for Jean-Marie Benoist in *The Work of Mourning* Derrida gives us a clue as to why Miller does not cry in this part of the film, why he is moved but not to tears:

> He [Benoist] does not teach us that we must not cry; he reminds us that we must not *taste* a tear: 'The act of tasting the tear is a desire to reannex the other'; one must not 'drink the tear and wonder about the strangeness of its taste compared to one's own'. Therefore: not to cry over oneself. (But does one ever do this? Does one ever do anything but this? That is the question that quivers in every tear, deploration or imploration itself). One should not develop a taste for mourning, and yet mourn we *must*. We *must*, but we must not like it—mourning, that is, mourning *itself*, if such a thing exists: not to like or love through one's own tear but only through the other, and every tear is from the other, the friend, the living, as long as we ourselves are living, reminding us, in holding life, to hold on to it. (110)

Miller holds on to his tears (but one notices the film soundtrack at certain moments like these where a sombre tonality intrudes and one note is held just like a tear). If he lets his tears flow then Miller will have consumed the other. If his tears are tears of mourning, then they haven't worked.

### Tear #2:

Miller worries in the film, in his recent essay on de Man and the "remains "of the archive" (Miller, "Paul" 55-88) and in his latest book on George Eliot's *Adam Bede* and *Middlemarch* about these "bad days" (Miller, *Reading* 166-171). More so, he is concerned, even frightened for, the "utility" of reading and his profession in these dark times. "Why read literature?" he asks and then repeats the question again "why *should* we read literature?" today. The answer, part playfully, half seriously, is that we read "because it will save us" but the onus is on us as readers: "it's up to you." So, in these times where the role of reading has become depleted, Miller warns us that the future of reading, its capacity to save us, is in our own hands.

What use is reading in these "bad times," this era of ominous critical climate change, which threatens us with species extinction, heralding what Claire Colebrook, Tom Cohen and Hillis Miller refer to as "the disappearing future" (even presaging the disappearance of theory and reading themselves). In the "Coda" to *Reading for Our Time*, Hillis revisits this recurring concern of his with the looming threats to the human species, to the educational system, with financial meltdown, and a healthcare system in crisis. No less than the question of acts of reading is at stake in this and Miller sees value in re-reading George Eliot's *Adam Bede* and *Middlemarch* in:

> these days of climate change, global financial meltdown, the universal diffusion of computer technology, the rapid transformation of developed countries' like the United States into third world countries, with a few super-rich and the rest living in misery and poverty, and finally, collective 'auto-co-immune' (as Jacques Derrida calls it) self-destruction of the human species through fossil fuel use, environment destruction, and Co2 emissions. (Miller, *Reading* 166.)

As always with Miller he accords a strange power to language, literary language in particular, and in Eliot, in his "rhetorical readings" of Eliot (whose fictional characters we ought to care about), he finds potential for veering (Nicholas Royle's word) away from the ideologies of politicians and economists who don't want us to read in the era of critical climate change.

But, we might ask again, why should we care about reading now in these bleak times? And, more crucially, why should we care about reading J. Hillis Miller? Because, in his own words, at the conclusion of *Reading for our Time*, insight into the way auto-co-immunity, trying to understand why we act self-destructively can help us (it won't stop climate change or financial implosion but it will help us to understand them and why we believe what we hear and read even though the truth is right in front of our noses). He writes:

Such insight can help us today, has helped me at least, to glimpse some explanation for why we (I mean the global 'we', all 6.946 billions of us and counting) have done practically nothing globally, too little and too late, to confront the reality of climate change (human use of fossil fuels) or the causes of the global financial meltdown (unregulated greed of bankers and financiers) and to do anything about them. I doubt if understanding will lead to action in time, but quasi-understanding would never the less be of benefit as the ocean waters rise. (Miller, *Reading* 169)

It bears repeating again: in these catastrophic times, times of downturn, you can learn a lot about reading from J. Hillis Miller. But as the waters rise, as the utility of reading falters in the face of the four pronged threat of health care reforms, financial meltdown, climate change and the decline in the educational system, why do actual tears not rise up to Miller's eyes? It is made very clear in the film that Miller thinks we are all in "big trouble." This is a "suicidal situation" as we engage in auto-destructive behaviour on so many fronts. As Claire Colebrook argues the more we know about impending ecocatastrophe and species extinction the less we seem to care, the less inclined we are to act (45). For Miller, this hypo-affective disorder is due, in large measure, to a failure to read. For "fifteen years" we have realized that climate change is going to get us into big trouble and that "sooner or later something catastrophic is going to happen." So, the disaster is foreseeable, Miller argues, but not anticipated. We know very well that something bad is going to happen but yet nothing is being done. This affect fatigue again explains, in a way, Miller's lack of *real* tears. But yet again, in making the link between the utility of reading and inactivity in the face of global crisis palpable, Miller repeats that "it is in our hands."[16]

---

16 The double-sidedness of Miller is revealed here too: "it would be laughable if it wasn't so sad" he tells Dragan and the real sadness for him, about rising water levels, is that his house at Deer Isle might end up submerged ("this is a great sadness to me"). We might think further about the way Hillis tells Éamonn that "the poem just happens to fall under your eye, but it feels like a happy accident, and you make the best of what befalls you" (*J. Hillis Miller and The Possibilities of Reading*, 125). The text is a benediction and the obligations of reading are "happy" ones. The taste of tears, as Derrida would tell us, can run from the bitter to the sweet.

Despite the despondent situation, *Reading for Our Time* boldly argues that reading "in these bad times" is justified, even urgent, in the face of critical climate change. Our auto-destructive behaviour, "throwing ourselves over the cliff," could lead to hopelessness and despair (or the anxiety and discomfort Miller feels before the camera "eye"). Tears might blur the eyes, might blind our attempts to see the truth. But as John Caputo argues in *The Prayers and Tears of Jacques Derrida*, "our eyes are always, structurally veiled, and above all veiled with tears" (313). Tears are always already there then and blindness is inescapable (Caputo here quotes Marvell's poem "Eyes and Tears" where he alludes to "these weeping eyes, those seeing tears" [310]). Miller does not, as I have repeatedly said, cry in *The First Sail* but perhaps those tears are *always already* there and he, like Derrida, prays through those tears. Miller's limitless, blind yes, yes to reading in and for our time has a jussive structuration (Éamonn would call it one of Miller's laws) as he implores what is to-come and prays and hopes for the justice to-come. As Caputo might put it, Miller's look is

> cast not toward heaven but toward the future. He looks to what is coming but coming precisely as unforeseeable, unpro-visional, unpro-vidential, unable to see a thing, lacking divine foresight, divested of the foreknowledge of some omniscient, all-foreseeing God or *savoir absolue*. So he looks to what is coming but without the eyes to see, with circumcised eyes. He looks to what is coming through his tears, with eyes swollen and sore from weeping, with imploring and beseeching eyes, with prophetic tears, tears of hope and love. (328-329)

Such loving tears, borne of a faith in something in-coming that will save us, tears that place all their hope in sailing on the crest of the future to-come, such tears that rise from our hearts and fall from our eyes into our hands, are hardly idle.

**MOR**

## Works Cited

Caputo, John D. *The Prayers and Tears of Jacques Derrida: Religion Without Religion.* Bloomington: Indiana University Press, 1997.

Colebrook, Claire. "Earth Felt the Wound: The Affective Divide." *Identities: Journal for Politics, Gender and Culture* 8.1 (2011): 45-58.

Congreve, William. *The Way of the World.* Greensboro: Empire Books, 2012.

Derrida, Jacques. "Jean-Marie Benoist (1942-1990): The Taste of Tears." *The Work of Mourning.* Trans. Pascale-Anne Brault and Michael Naas. Chicago: University of Chicago Press, 2001.

—. "Justices." *Provocations to Reading: J. Hillis Miller and the Democracy to Come.* Ed. Barbara Cohen and Dragan Kujundžić. New York: Fordham University Press, 2005.

—. "'Le Parjure', Perhaps: Storytelling and Lying ('abrupt breaches of syntax')." *Without Alibi.* Ed. and trans. Peggy Kamuf. Stanford, California: Stanford University Press, 2002. 195-234.

—. *Specters of Marx: The State of the Debt, The Work of Mourning and The New International.* Trans. Peggy Kamuf. New York: Routledge, 1994.

—. "Telepathy." Trans. Nicholas Royle. *Psyche: Inventions of the Other, Vol. 1.* Ed. Peggy Kamuf and Elizabeth Rottenburg. Stanford, California: Stanford University Press, 2007.

—. "This Strange Institution Called Literature: An Interview with Jacques Derrida." *Acts of Literature.* Ed. Derek Attridge. London: Routledge, 1992.

—. and Maurizio Ferraris. *A Taste for the Secret.* Trans. Giacomo Donis. Cambridge: Polity, 2002.

Dunne, Éamonn. "Interview: For the Reader To-Come." *J. Hillis Miller and the Possibilities of Reading: Literature After Deconstruction.* London: Continuum, 2010.

Goldsmith, Oliver. *She Stoops to Conquer.* New York: Dover, 1991.

Melville, Herman. *Moby Dick.* New York: Barnes & Noble Classics, 1993.

Miller, J. Hillis. *For Derrida.* New York: Fordham University Press, 2009.

—. *The Linguistic Moment: From Wordsworth to Stevens.* Princeton: Princeton University Press, 1985.

—. *The Medium is The Maker: Browning, Freud, Derrida and the New Telepathic Ecotechnologies.* Brighton: Sussex Academic Press, 2009.

—. "Paul de Man at work: In these bad days, what good is an archive?" *Theory and the Disappearing Future: On de Man, On Benjamin.* Eds. Tom Cohen, Claire Colebrook and J. Hillis Miller. New York: Routledge, 2012. 55-88.

—. *Reading for Our Time.* Edinburgh: Edinburgh University Press, 2012.

—. *Topographies.* Stanford, California: Stanford University Press, 1995.

—. "Why Literature? A Profession: An Interview with J. Hillis Miller." *The J. Hillis Miller Reader.* Ed. Julian Wolfreys. Edinburgh: Edinburgh University Press, 2005.

Nietzsche, Friedrich. *On the Genealogy of Morals* and *Ecce Homo.* Trans. Walter Kaufmann. New York: Vintage, 1969.

Royle, Nicholas. *Veering: A Theory of Literature.* Edinburgh: Edinburgh University Press, 2011.

Žižek, Slavoj. *The Fright of Real Tears: Krzystof Kieślowski Between Theory and Post-Theory.* London: BFI, 2001.

*Chapter 5*

# En*voiles* (Post It)

Dragan Kujundžić

That the relationship between J. Hillis Miller and Jacques Derrida occupies a unique place in the landscape of contemporary criticism is no secret. They have played as well a significant role in my intellectual building, having encountered them some thirty years ago. I have written about that in my "Journey With J on the Jour J," an introduction to Derrida's essay "'Justices'" on J. Hillis Miller, and Miller's "Isabelle's Kiss" published in *Critical Inquiry* in 2005. There, I have likened these two essays to letters on the way "to further destinations of as yet uncharted parts. Like letters, sealed with a kiss" (Kujundžić, "Journey" 688). Derrida's essay "'Justices'" includes a description of the scene in which he receives a letter from Miller ("Hillis" when referring to the film character, "J. Hillis Miller" or "Miller" when referring to Miller as author in further text), regarding the real name behind the "J" which has received extensive treatment in my film *The First Sail: J. Hillis Miller*.

In my film, *The First Sail: J. Hillis Miller*, the first thing Hillis comments upon when discussing the scene at the lecture when Derrida shows the letter, is Derrida's death, already presaged by his not looking too healthy to Hillis' eye in the filmed footage screened by Hillis in the film. The counter-time of mourning Derrida is inscribed in my own desire to film J. Hillis Miller. Derrida's specter haunts me and it haunts the film, as much as it haunts J. Hillis Miller. But not necessarily in ways that are visible or re-presentable. The ways the spectral divides the frame of the cinematic representation, what I call the effects of division and devision (a *destinerrance* of the cinematic image in fact), pose interesting and urgent questions about the modes and ethic of representation. They go from the phenomenological to the political in a heartbeat. Thus, the question of the frame, or the letter (be it a single letter, the initial of the first name, "J."), the letter which does or does not arrive, to the cinematic which does or does nor "represent" the Other, imposes itself as the burning issue pertaining to the very core of what is a tradition, history, and what our response and responsibility to it are or should be. Who writes what and who writes whom, how or whether we allow the Other to leave an imprint, what or who arrives, those are the issues which haunt the text below, in the film on J. Hillis Miller, and in Derrida's "Justices" episode reproduced in the film.

The reflections below are also marked, truly haunted, by a telepathic encounter with the Other. Someone else, Julian Wolfreys (his text follows mine in this volume), dictated this text telepathically to me, as it were. I read Wolfrey's essay after I finished mine. Thus, I realize, from an infinitely distant telepathic proximity, his own essay taught me, unbeknownst to me, how to write my own essay even before it had been written, as well as taught me how to watch my film. What is really uncanny, is that at the same time I decided to write on the scene from the film where Jacques Derrida discusses the letters he mis-addressed, in relation to *La Carte Postale* (in an email I sent to Michael O'Rourke on Wednesday, 14 March, 2012, 3:14), Julian Wolfreys wrote about the same scene in *The First Sail*, starting with the description of his visit, on the day of his lecture about *The First Sail*, to the Bodleian library at Oxford University, in search for, as he says, "that" post card which is on the cover of *La Carte Postale* (Plato teaches Socrates how to write, shown initially to Jacques Derrida by Cynthia Chase and Jonathan Culler). And thus Wolfreys' relating the whole analysis of the letters sent to Miller with an erroneous appellation (John for Joseph), and Miller's response that Derrida quotes in the film, to the analysis of *destinerrance* in *La Carte Postale*. Which I proposed to do in my email as well! But the uncanny ghosts haunting these essays proliferate, with Julian Wolfreys' conclusion of his conference presentation (delivered at Oxford University on April 13, 2012 as one of the keynotes at the conference on "Giving up the Ghost: the Haunting of Modern Culture") with a reference and analysis of *Ulysses' Gaze* by Theo Angelopoulos, which is exactly the ending of my own essay which I had already planned to relate to sailing in all senses of the term, to *Ulysses* and *Ulysses Gaze*, the destinerrant sailing of the tradition itself. In advance, I have followed Wolfrey's text blow for blow, my writing from the very start already sealed by this distant proximity and affinity which taught me how to write, in a scene of writing where I cannot tell anymore who or what came first. On occasion, our analyses reverberate with a gentle dissonance, like a counterpunctual musical motif, thus all the more underscoring the mutual affinity. "It is impossible not to believe that each of us has an internal television screen by means of which we have visions of what distant friends and relations are thinking, or not to believe that whatever we think is broadcast to the internal television screen of others," says Miller in *The Medium is the Maker* (15). This essay is exactly a product of such tele-vised encounter with Julian Wolfreys (whom I never met in person, except online, even though we overlapped for a while in the same University of Florida where we had arranged but missed encounters, tormented, like letters, with an "internal drifting").

Derrida's death has also entailed the darkening of register of some of Miller's recent writing, the dark Derrida a darkening in Miller of a wound that does not heal. I tried to exemplify this relationship in the scene where Hillis watches Derrida read a letter he had received from Miller. Relating the scene in the film about the *destinerrance* of the postal regarding J. Hillis Miller and Derrida with Joyce is justified on many levels, not least of all because of the entry in *La Carte Postale* on "20 June, 1978. I had not come back to Zurich since spring 1972. You accompany: CHECK me everywhere. Hillis, who was waiting for me at the airport (the de Mans arrive only this afternoon,) drove me to the cemetery, near to Joyce's tomb, I should say funerary monument..." (Derrida, *Post Card* 148). In his *The Medium is the Maker* Miller (just after his description of how he took Derrida sailing on his boat, *The Frippery*, featured extensively in *The First Sail*, on a day when there was a "small craft warnings" and "look what happened to Shelley when he went sailing on a day when there was too much wind!" [49-50]), claims that he has no memory of that ever happening, not "having a car in Zurich." However, "Derrida and I did go together, as the "Envois" report, on another occasion, to visit Joyce's tomb in the Zurich cemetery near the zoo. The animal cries from that zoo appear in *Finnegans Wake*. We did stand laughing before the tomb of Egon Zoller, "*Erfinder des Telephonographe*," with its engraved ticker tape machine and its carved Alpha and Omega. Derrida, as we stood looking at the tomb, connected it to his then current project about telecommunication networks, that is, the 'Envois'" (Miller *Medium*, 50). From this scene I'd just like to retain the inscription of *La Carte Postale* in the neighborhood of the telegraph, tele-technology, the uncanny repetitions of uncertain memories, the sailing on Miller's boat ("6. October 1978. ... Tomorrow, return to Yale, day after tomorrow excursion in Hillis's sailboat" [*Post Card*, 166]) and Joyce, in the cemetery, thus the relation of the letter with death.

In *The First Sail*, Derrida describes in the episode how he had once (or many times in the past) written to J. Hillis Miller addressing him, erroneously, as "*John* Hillis Miller." To which Miller responded in a letter, and that is the film scene, "My name is 'Joseph,' not 'John.' Not that it matters in the least, since I've never used that name in any case."

In the film, Hillis minimizes the video tape of Derrida, as not "really the return of Jacques Derrida," something that I sense is also at work in Hillis' description of Derrida's book on touching and J.L. Nancy as "a book I find wonderful but exceedingly difficult" (Dunne, 134) as he said in an interview to Eamonn Dunne in Dunne's *J. Hillis Miller and the Possibilities of Reading*, and I wonder if it also means difficult to touch, to behold?

This subtle tone of positioning vis-à-vis Derrida comes across, at least to me, as an attempt to ward off Derrida's return, precisely as the return of the ghost. If he came back as a ghost, it would mean that Derrida died. That is, as J. Hillis Miller says in *The Medium* is the maker, he cannot listen to Derrida's lectures on tape, because that would mean that he is really dead. But Miller knows better! We always return as ghosts, even in real life. As soon as there is a return, there is a ghost, I learned that form *The Medium is the Maker*. And from Miller's analysis of *On Touching*. And from his writing about "Absolute Mourning." And from all those other writings on zero, on the empty core of literature, on living on, etc.

What I sense in these subtle strategies of evasion to see Derrida as a ghost is a certain tenderness for Derrida which Hillis is trying to protect from opening or precisely from bringing into present or presence, like a wound which refuses to heal and which cannot or should not be touched. But not just because Hillis is protecting himself from the exposure to the death of the other, which would be understandable, anxiety ridden, an anxiety quite human and easy to explain. In this way, I would claim, Hillis is protecting Derrida's passing away from being worked though, obliterated, diminished, "properly mourned" and thus done away with. Geoffrey Bennington recently wrote about this as "militant melancholia," which I think describes Hillis in the film scene: "Who or what, in these still dark days of an ongoing melancholia I began by declaring 'militant,' militantly melancholic, something that wanted to affirm, with Jacques himself, a certain refusal of the 'normal' work of mourning and its 'normal' dealings with the death of the other—a proudly militant melancholia that soon however settled into something much less glorious, much less proud, much *more* melancholic, in fact—who or what, then, might come to open something again that might lay some claim, however modest, to the sometimes very minimal dignity of what often bears the probably misleading name of 'thought'?" (Bennington 2008, 191-2). The music in the film, composed and performed by Natalia Pschenichnikova, to whom I left complete discretion as to the placement of chords, punctuates this countertemporality of a loss splitting the scene but refusing representation, as explicitly avowed by Hillis, and so subtending the whole set of representational, framing divisions and devisions.

Hillis is protecting, in a sense, the wound or the loss from healing, by not allowing it to be touched, exposed, revealed, talked about, worked through, by not allowing Derrida to come back as a visible ghost in short.... To do that would probably be admitting to the visibility of appropriation, an apparatic appropriation of an apparition, which I sense Hillis wants to avoid or ward off. In a sense, this subtle refusal of the programmed mediatic return is precisely the work of ethics in mourning which does not appropriate, which refuses a "revealed" and visualized ghost tele-programmed by manipulation, controlled videographic and prosthetic repetition. And thus is more faithful to Derrida and his "return," predicated on the possibility of a missed encounter and a nonreturn, thus allowing a return not only of an Other, but of every other, wholly other as well.

What does it mean to be "really dead," which listening to Derrida's tapes would reveal or bring?

Seeing the "real" visible return of Derrida in the video clip would be nothing but the possibility of such an appropriation, of a completely controlled and programmed prosthetic substitute. In order to keep Derrida alive as much as possible, alive in memory, at least, one must not touch the dead or let the dead return in the exact, programmed form. Thus allowing it in this scene to return them or him more vividly in invisible forms of displacements configuring the singular scaping and escaping ("the queer inscape"—[Royle, 126], or where more generally, "To be is to be queer"—[*Derrida*, "'Justices'" 703]), of the experience of being J. Hillis Miller/Hillis. In any case, that is what I tried to edit "into" this film and the sequence (often very much blind to its effects), but the sequence operates here the displaced a- and ana-chronistic temporality whereby what comes before or after is scrambled, non-linear, in-visible and di-visible. In a word, the scene is constructed or deconstructed as a counter-time in which one waits for or comes in the wake (the trace, the mourning) of the death of the non-appropriated other. "Each is already in mourning for the other. ... It takes place every time I love" (Derrida "Aphorism," 422).

These scenes are strewn throughout Miller's recent responses about Derrida. In the film, Hillis also speaks about the "dark side" of Derrida, the nocturnal Derrida, with which Hillis wants to "maybe disagree" but which I cannot but interpret as the nocturnal Derrida in Hillis, a counter-time of mourning which Hillis preserves as he keeps it at a distance, "*The sun for sorrow will not show his head.*" The conclusion of his *For Derrida* which was quoted in the film as an intertitle states as much: "That is my last word, at least for now. ... If these essays are works of mourning, they have not worked." A certain absent core seems to open in Miller's work of late (and it is a question of coming too late, as we shall see), or seems to be the work of his writing itself, something like a touch that cannot be touched, a vacant center opened by Derrida's demise.

This has left inscriptions or inscryptions, encrypted, sometimes unconscious marks in J. Hillis Miller's *The Medium is the Maker*, for example, when he discusses Derrida on telepathy. Referring to Derrida Miller describes something that "turned up again, close at hand, at a time when it was too late…," a description of a ghost if there is any, creeping in this seemingly innocuous analytic formula. And then goes on: "This present fake lecture [note the apotropaic, "fake" protective irony here], already far too long to be read in one séance [note again the protective irony, but also the scene of writing as a conjuring up of the ghost as well as an intrusion of the French] ought to have been part of my *For Derrida*, but has been written too late for inclusion there."

In a word, such experience comes too late, to use Miller's words, there is a *decalage*, or a counter-temporality at work there, my words *For Derrida* come too late for Derrida. And right after this sentence, "my *For Derrida*," "too late for inclusion there," Hillis writes: "The Fort/Da sequence of his losing and then refinding 'Telepathy,' says Derrida, 'remains inexplicable for me even to this day....'" (Miller, *For Derrida* 44). Just after *For Derrida*, seconds later, a heartbeat later, a *Fort/Da, for Derrida*, an inscription of *Todestrieb*, of a death drive, Derrida Fort but not Da, not anymore, left to haunt Miller's work like a vacant center, a touch he cannot touch. An impossible touch of Derrida (a dubious genitive here, *je me touche toi*) which comes too late, written too late, always already too late for Derrida, but also for Miller. We will not have mourned the ghost, the spectral, in the living, never enough. And by missing the other so much he comes to the truth.

Hillis is here far from "Hillis le Mal," the rugged Virginian, the almost demonic force with an untouchable, so to speak, imperturbable serenity, which Tom Cohen justly or unjustly but humorously discerns in him, "Hillis le Mal," so not Hillis le Mal, but Hillis *l'Animal*, the animal looking for the lines of escape, the evading animal frightened by the death of the other, "l'animal que *J.* suit." "I am, he is," you will notice, a confusion engulfs the writing here in a difference which cannot be heard, or touched, but which animates the scene of writing but also of filming, like an animal que je suis/t. *L'animal*, also, *qui est mal*, the wounded, hurting animal which I follow, in me, in the other, there where we wait for each other at the limit of each other's finitude and death, at the limit of truth, there where I is the other, Je (J) *est un autre*.

This countertemporality and spectrality which cannot be seen is precisely what I tried to convey or to allow to appear without appearing (not visible to me either), then, in editing with the cascading frames, but can we *see* how many? I am the one who is probably the most blind. Let's try to enumerate some of them. The scene of Derrida on the computer is preceded by the slow motion close up of the cut on Hillis' eye made by the glass frame. And where? Hillis explains, in Irvine (which will appear shortly in Derrida's explicit mention of "the Archive") after the fall on the stairs leading to the Humanities Hall where Derrida held his seminars! The eye itself as frame; Hillis' eye held by the metonymy of the prosthetic camera eye, thus the viewer's eye, seeing the wound and the cut as frame, from which the scene flows (the water stream, the video stream....); thus, the framed, wounded lachrymose eye (seen in the slow motion, the eye/I wading anamorphically through the ocular water), the eye wounded by the loss larger than the camera, the frame and the scene, beholding the viewer, including the "director," the "I-eye" filming it in the grip of interminable blinding melancholia. In the film, I told Hillis, jokingly: "what about that scar, what did you do to the other guy?" to which Hillis responded: "Yes, you should see the other guy." And then I proceeded to edit the entire sequence about Derrida and mourning, yes, go and see the other guy who wounded Hillis' eye, go and see the mourning as the other that wounds the eye/I. But I only myself saw it (I finally myself saw the other guy!) in the end, on a big screen at the first public screening, blinded by my own wounded and lachrymose gaze and refusal to see the demise of Derrida. And Barbara Cohen's picture afterwards, framing a friendship, with J and J touching each other, the haptic in the cinematic, the ultimate ghost, and there they are both.... touching each other and by that touch creating a counter-time "at the heart of the syncope, between touching and untouchable," and thus also already a prosthetic mourning, "the ageless intrusion of technics, which is to say the transplantation of the prosthesis" (Derrida, *On Touching* 112). With the voiceover and the punctuation of the piano chord: "For nothing in the world would I have passed up the chance to recall, publicly that it has been given to me, like a benediction, to know Joseph Hillis Miller for more than thirty five years, to have had the honor of teaching at his side ... the honor also of having shared with him more than with any other, through I don't know how many countries, colloquia, meetings of all sorts, the intellectual adventure that signs and seals our lives" (Derrida, "'Justices'" 712). And then, Hillis, "Am I on camera?" walking alone (Derrida's *I Will Now Have to Walk Alone*, Deleuze's obituary, another mournful frame, was my reference here) after posting a letter, creating the counter time of mourning, they miss each other, do they miss each other, how they miss each other! Like Romeo and Juliet, the counter time of mourning as the impossibility of *being with* is put on display or on replay here,—Derrida in Hillis' solitude, (the crunching of the gravel also a sound frame, the *Mittagsgespenst* of the archive fever leaving the traces in stone) more "visible" and "in picture" than ever. Where? There.

The scene of Hillis walking back to "us," to the camera ("Am I on camera?"), when he sends the letter, comes right after the analysis of the letter sent from that very same mail box on Deer Isle, the address clearly visible in the corner of the letter which Derrida reproduced moments earlier. The letter Hillis sent in that scene of posting the letter went to Derrida... When? Then!

When is this letter, where is this letter? The letter sent by Hillis (the scene of Hillis sending the letter) in the film from Deer Isle arrived in time to follow Derrida's lecture eight years before the scene of sending; only to announce that Derrida's letters to Miller (John instead of Joseph) were not arriving to the right addressee. The letter described by Derrida seemed, in turn, "to forecast today's lecture and keynote, from more than thirty years distance" (Derrida, "Justices'" 706). Thus, the missive announces the miss and the missing, always already, from the time immemorial. I missed you, says Derrida in his lecture and in his letter, but when, where? Am I missing something here? This *destinerrance* of the letter, however, which is displayed in the film as coming after (after the long history of friendship), also comes before the film, as the traumatic space of memory of this lecture at which both Hillis and I were present. And in which scene in the film Hillis sees Derrida's demise, "he already looked old and not that well."

The memory of a loss, to which Miller's writing, his postings, have subsequently tried to respond, like in the scene of mailing the letter, but also in *For Derrida*, are profoundly informed or imprinted by this spectral but non-representable division, of "the lack which does not have a place in dissemination" (Derrida, *Post Card* 441). The letter is thus fully (un) accounted for, both before and after, here and there, but never in the right place: "The letter might not be found, or could always possibly not be found" (Derrida, *Post Card* 442) dividing the scene of representation as the infinitely divisible specter haunting the frame of "representation," but also, I would claim, informing the very scene of writing in works like *The Medium is the Maker*.

In the *Medium is the Maker* Miller has an innovative analysis pertaining to the question of finitude in Heidegger and Derrida. For Heidegger, the finitude of being (*da-sein*) partakes in the movement of general Being, it "holds," Hillis says, "all the horizons of time with one mobile unit.... Heidegger's time is grounded in *Sein*, Being with a capital B. Derrida's time is created out of performative media, the media as makers... On each occasion a given medium is used that use creates its own ground and its own differance" (Miller, *Medium* 25). What this means is that each time we use a technical apparatus, flip a cell phone, type on a computer, make a film, watch a TV, we are opening a new temporal ground in which our finitude is both confirmed and traversed and overcome. By using technical apparatuses, we partake in our own survival. And that happens every time I speak, teach or touch someone. "As if the word 'I' were inaugurating, in the first person, the very grammar of all spectrality, like a mask, 'I' of a revenant" (Derrida, "'Justices'" 714). But it is most discernible in the usage of the technical apparatuses like recording live or life. Just like Derrida's notion of the letter in *La Carte Postale*, which from "the first stroke divides itself, and must indeed support partition in order to identify itself," thus "there are nothing but post cards, anonymous morsels without fixed domicile, without legitimate addressee, letters opened, but like crypts" (Derrida, *Post Card* 53). And, just like in the scene with the letter, Derrida displays, posts a post it for all to see, a piece of an open letter but also a crypt. An inscription, the pieces (*morceaux*) of which are little bites (*morsures*) of death (*mort*). "Soon everyone will be there, and me, I will have to leave" (Derrida, *Post Card* 61).

"This too will be in the archive": the film as epitaph, cenotaph and *cine*taph.

The letter sent many years ago never quite arrives, it arrives erroneously, too late, it misses its addressee. The division of the address that Derrida tried to discern in the "J" of "J. Hillis Miller" is divided between "John" and "Joseph," thus between the Old and the New Testaments. "And one of the sins that I must have committed at the origin, by substituting John for Joseph, will have been to risk evangelizing and Christianizing a name that hovered between the Old and the New Testaments" (Derrida, "'Justices'" 718).

It is not hard to see how bemused in the film Derrida is by this originary confusion, and his mistake. Precisely, by a mistake of "revealing" the secret name, the name of the "secret God," and thus giving visibility to what must remain hidden. But by this mistaking Joseph for John, Derrida in fact enacts what he in *Ulysses Gramophone, the Yes Saying of Joyce* sees as an affirmative yet disruptive force of alterity in the messianic without the Messiah. Without this possibility of the non-arrival of the letter, of the wrong arrival of the letter already divided by this errant "sailing, sealing, signing," without this intrusion of the Jewish other in the Greek tradition, everything would be just the repetition of the same, it would lead to the non-arrival of Greek onto-theology to itself, and Ulysses (but not the novel, *Ulysses*), thus returning to himself/itself/themselves as the arrival of a dead letter. (The danger of such "Greek" return to itself is made evident in Heidegger's Danube, *Der Ister*, flowing *ruekwertz*, from Greece, towards Schwarzwald, as to its proper destination, the origin flowing to itself, as he writes in 1942; and just like Greece itself, in a Europe programmed by the exclusion of the Greek other, by the exclusion of economic justice, which is coming back to haunt Germany, in 2012, returns to Germany as the origin coming back and imploding Europe and Germany like the return of the repressed. The danger against which Miller's *Topographies* is one of the most emphatic warnings ever written, particularly regarding Heidegger, in "Slipping, Vaulting, Crossing").

Could we hear in Derrida's bemused laughter the "eschatological tone of the yes-laughter" which is "traversed by the vowels of a completely different song," that broke out in Dublin in Joyce's *Ulysses*, in the body of Molly Bloom, "necessary in order to contrive the breach necessary for the coming of the other," whom "one can always call an Elijah, if Elijah is the name of the unforeseeable other for whom a place must be kept: ... Elijah, the Other" (Derrida, "Ulysses" 294-295). The amused, contagious laughter which broke out in the lecture hall with Derrida upon the revelation of this confusion, announced, in this erroneous attribution of the letter address and the name (Christian for Jewish), a laughing recognition and affirmation, yes, yes, that the non-arrival of the other is the very condition of something happening, taking place, as a difference or diffe*ra*nce.

The possibility of this destinerrance is the very condition of the arrival of the Other. This is the lesson that the "protestant" J. teaches the "Jewish" J., in a chiasmatic reversal, in the letter in which Miller teaches Derrida how to write.

Keep the place at the table for J, the Other, "the uncanniest of guests" (J. Hillis Miller, "Critic as Host," 253).[1]

## Works Cited

Bennington, Geoffrey. "For Better or for Worse (There Again...)." *"Who or What"—Jacques Derrida*, ed. Dragan Kujunžić. Spec. issue of *Discourse* 30, 1-2 (2008): 191-207.

Derrida, Jacques. "'Justices.'" Trans. Peggy Kamuf. *J*, ed. Dragan Kujundžić. Spec. issue of *Critical Inquiry* 31, 3 (2005): 689-721.

—. *On Touching—Jean-Luc Nancy*. Trans. Christine Irizarry. Stanford: Stanford University Press, 2005.

—. "Ulysses Gramophone: Hear Say Yes in Joyce." Trans. Tina Kendall and revised by Shari Benstock. *Acts of Literature*. Ed. Derek Attridge. New York: Routledge, 1992. 253-310.

—. "Aphorism Countertime." Trans. Nicholas Royle. *Acts of Literature*. Ed. Derek Attridge. New York: Routledge, 1992. 414-35.

—. *The Post Card: From Socrates to Freud and Beyond*. Trans. Allan Bass. Chicago: The University of Chicago Press, 1987.

—. "Violence and Metaphysics." *Writing and Difference*. Trans. Alan Baas. Chicago: The University of Chicago Press, 1978.

---

[1] The film thus performs in cinematic terms a displacement and chiasmatic reversal that my essay "Journey With J on the Jour J" analyzed in theoretical terms long before the film: "It is as if the very cores of the texts by J. Hillis Miller and Jacques Derrida find their centers (the questions of the very nature and identity of the argument posed by each: "What is a kiss?" by Miller, "'*What* is J. Hillis Miller?' or '*Who* is J. Hillis Miller'" by Derrida) by welcoming each other, rupturing each other at the very moment or at the very center where the argument forms a question about itself, casts a glance at itself in a narcissistic turn towards itself, only to find that the other, J, has already occupied the place of J," Kujundžić, in "*J*," (2005).

Dunn, Eamonn. *J. Hillis Miller and the Possibilities of Reading: Literatur After Deconstruction*. New York: Continuum, 2010.

Kujundžić, Dragan. "Journey With J on the Jour J," *J*, ed. Dragan Kujundžić. Spec. issue of *Critical Inquiry* 31, 3 (2005): 684-688.

—. *The First Sail: J. Hillis Miller*. Deer Isle Productions, 2011. DVD.

Levinas, Emannuel. *Time and the Other*. Trans. Richard A. Cohen. Pittsburgh: Duquesne University Press, 1987.

Miller, J. Hillis. *The Medium Is the Maker. Browning, Freud, Derrida and the New Telepathic Ecotechnologies*. Eastborne: Sussex Academic Press, 2009.

—. *For Derrida*. New York: Fordam University Press, 2009.

—. *Topographies*. Stanford: Stanford University Press, 1995.

—. "Critic as Host." *Deconstruction & Criticism*. New York: Continuum, 1979.

Royle, Nicholas. *In Memory of Jacques Derrida*. Edinburgh: Edinburgh University Press, 2009.

Wolfreys, Julian. *Memory to come (tba) or, towards a poetics of the spectral*. An authorized conference presentation. "Giving up the Ghost: the Haunting of Modern Culture," a symposium at New College, University of Oxford, Oxford, England, Friday 13th April, 2012.

*Chapter 6*

# Memory to come (tba) or, towards a poetics of the spectral

JULIAN WOLFREYS

Having arrived earlier this morning, and thinking about ghosts, the ghosts of Oxford, and, in particular, one shade, whose disturbing motions here I like to call to mind, I took a walk to the Bodleian, its gift shop at least. I was in search of a post card. I was less interested in what it represented or who was represented than the memory of another who had, in purchasing an untold number of these cards, had made it visible to the academic world in a rather provocative way. The post card, a post card you understand, a "real" an "actual" post card, not a book about post cards, a book titled either *The Post Card* or *la carte postale*; this post card was, is, irrelevant as to its representation, or what it claims to represent to me, to us, directly. What was behind the post card though, what remains for me behind this particular card, what—or who—remains invisibly there, authorising me, giving me *carte blanche* to write, and speak of ghosts, has greater relevance. However, even this shadowy figure I feel or imagine to be there is not as significant as a distinction I have introduced, a distinction to do with representation and what cannot be represented, and which distinction therefore admits the possibility of speaking about haunting beyond representation, where the visible fails, and haunting takes place all the more forcefully through memory and that which countersigns memory, always, already: loss.

This is wonderfully illustrated in *Fanny och Alexander*, Ingmar Bergman's meditation on passing generations, the transition or dialogue between theatre and film, memory, the porous membrane between illusion and reality, and, of course ghosts. Ghosts in the film are associated with guilt, with what one cannot leave behind, but the ghosts that appear, appear chiefly to one just person, Alexander, who, like Hamlet, "sees" where others can only imagine or fail to imagine. The question is raised and maintained throughout the film as to what constitutes haunting, individually, culturally, and historically. Bergman's movie also asks, without answering, if there is an appropriate medium for the ghost, if there is a poetics of spectrality. Quite early on in the film though, on the night following the Christmas party, Bergman throws the audience something of a curve ball, in a comic moment of Grand Guignol, Gothic reference (**Clip**). This short incident, seemingly apropos of nothing so much as the pleasures of haunting, the power of illusion and the imagination, the willingness or desire to believe in ghost stories, signals nothing so much, I think, than that a certain epoch of spectrality is coming to an end, passing away, to be supplanted with another. What is being exorcised here? Perhaps nothing so much as the idea that the spectre or phantom can be represented, is representable, for everyone in the same way.

If the phantom epoch is passing, one manifestation at least, it appears to be giving way, *Fanny och Alexander* tells us, to other epochs of the ghost, or just one epoch, which today we have not yet left behind; this epoch is one which, has become markedly divided, sundered, the one incapable of speaking to the other. Bergman's film, in looking back, anticipates the advent, the coming from the future in a cinematic, narrative and temporal sleight of hand, of the new double epoch: for, on the one hand, there is, from the arrival of cinema—which itself is not an origin, merely an increasingly technologized mode itself prefigured in the phantasmagoria or magic lantern show—the technologization and mediatisation of the spectral; with this comes the proliferation of spectrality made manifest through the internet and its related virtual modalities. On the other hand, there is the retreat, the unstoppable interiorization of ghosts, announced if not first then certainly most audibly by Freud and Henry James. The ghost retreats inside us; withdrawing from the visible, from direct modes of representation, appearing barely, if at all, only here and there, to one or the other. Bergman shows us this through the film's narrative. Phantoms of the father appear, mostly to Alexander alone, though there is a significant interruption by the dead father, who appears at a moment of crisis to his own mother. By the end of the movie however, in its final scene, the ghost become ever more invisible save through cinematic technology and illusion, Alexander no longer sees his future approaching, a future always already haunted. As he walks the corridor of grandmother's apartment, a hand unexpectedly, shockingly, slaps his head. Though he had seen nothing, he does feel the force of the slap coming from his dead step-father, who in life was also a "father" symbolically, a Lutheran Bishop, the death of this father for Bergman indicating perhaps another passing, but persistently ghostly epoch, that involving the ghost stories of religion and theology. Everything to do with ghosts comes down, in the end, but also from the start, with representation, its limits, and what Edmund Husserl distinguishes as re-presentation.

Memory for Husserl is a realm not of representations but of re-presentation. The hyphen that you hear is graphic testimony to the trace in memory that I want to suggest signifies the work of spectrality. You hear it, but do not see it as I speak. It cannot be figured, and so "represented" directly. It is only ever a second order *trait*. Husserl argues that whatever the initial image recalled in memory for the subject, once the figure perceived becomes reflected on—and thereby synthesized or mediated through "memorial consciousness" in some fashion in order that the "perception of the event" or experience comes to correspond, or be analogous with, "an (actual or possible) memory of this perception" (Husserl 248) —; once it returns it comes to us to be apprehended as constellated phantasmic figures projected by the work of memory. We do not "see" directly, whatever it is we believe to be in "the mind's eye" as the phrase has it. In this way, the past returns, indirectly, as apparition, as spectral or virtual presence or present, and this is before, or aside from any psychological or psychoanalytic interpretation or filter. In turn, perception, "somehow" to cite Husserl, "becomes modified into re-presentation of what was received" (248). Not representation, never simple or direct mimetic manifestation therefore, but re-presentation, memory as the mediated trace, trace of a trace already transferred, transcribed, through which past becomes temporalized space, spaced temporality, and the subject's relation to, and apprehension of thing, to place and event, to the other is structured. In following Husserl here, what I am seeking to pursue is a reduction of haunting, phenomenologically, to begin to come to terms with the taking place of the spectral through memory, and to apprehend this in relation to questions of loss.

Despite reservations that Jean-Luc Nancy has regarding phenomenology's being closed off, or attempting to close itself off, from an unconditional hospitality or a "letting-come" as he puts it, and with that a concomitant "surprising of sense, and also…its letting-go" (Nancy 36), there is the possibility of understanding the work of the ghost, the poetics that informs that work in a manner that abandons any investment in direct representation or its adequacy. For, even though Nancy would see phenomenology as too programmed, no one can be mindful of everything that arrives from a future that is unpredictable, and which can always arrive to address us, each of us, at different times, in any moment, at different moments for any of us. We cannot be prepared for what can always come, always haunt us, or hit us with the force of a dead man's hand. That unprogrammable future, distinguished by Derrida as *l'avenir*, the to-come, as opposed to *la future*, the certain future of the sun's rising, the 14th of April following the 13th, is where we cannot be prepared to "let go." The ghost makes us let go.

To extend briefly though this consideration of Husserlian re-presentation: the image I receive as memory of my past subjectivity and the site that gives ground to my memory of my past self in relation to the other is, in its apprehension, what he calls a "phantasy presentation." It is this "'image' appearance," according to Husserl, which returns to me the earlier perception of an experience. In the distinction made here between perception—I perceive at a given moment, which is the *now* of my perception—and memory, the image of that perception returns as what the philosopher describes as "'image' re-presentation of the earlier perception" and which, in turn, is doubly constituted: on the one hand, it is the constellated image of particular phenomena, events and experiences; on the other hand, "its appearance is the image of the earlier perceptual appearance" (Husserl 233). In the temporal distinction between perception and re-presentation, memory and the constitution of the subject take on—perhaps *make visible* is the more appropriate phrase—the poetics of re-presentation; that is to say, specifically a form, an architectonic construct or invention, of the *there is* arrives, and, with that, the subject for whom there is the *there is*, both *in* the re-presentation and to the subject who has consciousness of, and therefore narrates (if only to him- or herself), the memory in particular form, with particular effects and modes of apprehension.

As a result, "the appearance of the event in memory is an 'image' of the appearance of the same event in the earlier perception" (Husserl 236). Concomitantly, the two times of perception and memory remain articulated through the spatial and temporal play, even as they threaten to engulf one another, through the inscription of difference—and, additionally, the *différance*—that informs re-presentation and the being of the subject whose presence is always caused to differ and defer itself from itself, divided by the haunting arrival between itself and its other selves. I am, therefore, always at a loss with myself. I find myself at a loss, constituted through this loss, by loss itself. In any consideration of Being, re-presentation has always already taken place. Re-presentation is opened in *and* to the subject, and from which there is no retreat, or before which there is, and can be, no sense of the world. All reading / writing amounts to such re-presentation: a "memorial presentation," which, formulated as "intuitive presentation of the event" (Husserl 236) through the place of the subject, takes the reader as if by surprise, as if for a first time—and thus, with the power of that authentic and originary revelation of the spectral, that touches one most closely.

A question informs all I have just said and will remain at work throughout: how am I going to talk about the ghost? The question assumes I know what—or who—a ghost is, indeed, *that* it is; that to speak of "ghost," "apparition," "spectre," "phantom," "phantasm," "revenant," "spook," "shade," "poltergeist," "eidolon"; to enumerate the various non-synonymous substitutions in the family of names by which we identify the effects of haunting; to assume haunting itself, spectrality in general—all such gestures begin with presumption and so avoidance. In each remark, commentary or statement, I avoid the condition of the ghost, of ghosting, haunting and the spectral by presuming that there is "ghost," there is haunting. The assumption is that such "things" take place, and that they are easily defined. An ontology is in place, a structure erected, a fortress to keep at bay unwelcome guests through a cordial behaviour founded on the pretence of a knowledge of the being of a thing which is not a thing, which is nothing as such; or rather say, which is neither something nor nothing, and which is, or appears to be.

Appearance is everything here, as Bergman gives us to see. Everything comes down to what is between representation and re-presentation, what is given to be seen and what cannot be seen directly, beyond that threshold by which representation's powers are defeated, and it must, as it were recursively, fall back on figurality, metaphor, analogy, substitution, mimesis in ruins. Appearance, apparition: these are words that name, tracing in themselves, that which comes into view. *Parere* signifies the visible; it tells us of that which comes into view; as with so many of our words for haunting, spectrality comes down, or seems to come down to the visible. The prefix, "ap-," an intensifier signifying "towards," emphasises the spatial and temporal dimensions of spectrality. This is important, for we predicate our apprehension of ghosts on what comes to us, what arrives, comes to pass, and which in this differential work in space and time, gives itself to be seen, to be visible. In this assumed visibility, there is equally an assumption of ontology. Concomitantly, with the presumption of ontology there is also another presumption that maintains our avoidance of asking more fundamental questions, and so learning to distrust our visual sense. Optical evidence plus empiricism, we might say, equals stupidity or, at least a wilful suppression, stupefaction of the other senses. Sight, far from being reasonable, a basis for reasoning or logic, is in fact a narcotic; it causes the sleep of reason that produces monsters, and all those nightmares of history from which we might like to awaken. All of this visibility should be distrusted however, at least when dealing with ghosts, revenants, and anything of their ilk. The presumption of ontology, grounded in the visible world, has to do with representation, mimesis, and, therefore, adequation. Less to do with what we see, more to do with us and how we wish to understand. For each of these terms—representation, mimesis, adequation—assume, once again, a puissance involving control, desire, and conjuration: I desire the ghost but only on my terms; I want the ghost to appear directly to me, but only on the condition of a certain form; I, little God (to use John Banville's happy phrase), make the ghost in my own image, thereby avoiding the more troubling questions.

Representation, mimesis, adequation: all have to do, when thought in relation to control, desire and conjuration, with a mistaken investment in presence. We want to have it both ways, we want the presence of what is absent, we want the simulacrum of an immediacy, but only if we can keep that simulacrum at arm's length—on the screen, say, where a remote control (what a phrase, what an idea) pauses, plays, rewinds, fast forwards, ends, begins the play of ghosts, all reduced to our spectral puppets; or on the internet, on a computer—another screen, screens of all sizes then and, therefore, representation, mimesis, presence, adequation, imitation of life. With such technology, I create the illusion that I have sovereignty over the realm of ghosts, an empire of the spectral, and I do so, fooling myself in the process, by manipulating fake presences; we all do this, each of us a latter day Faustus.

I want to step back therefore, to disappear for a moment, and give way to a ghost or two, in the visual, technological senses, which I have addressed in brief. What follows is a clip from a film by Dragan Kujundžić, *The First Sail: J. Hillis Miller.* [**Clip**] What have we seen? Let me break this down a little schematically:

(1) we see J. Hillis Miller, watching something, someone, we cannot see. The who and the what do not exclude one another, there is not a choice here. We hear a voice, a recording within a recording, first French, then translating itself to English, the idiom resistant to direct transport. To this Miller responds with laughter.

(2) From this, there is a cross fade, from Miller to Derrida, Derrida "after" Miller, the image "after" the voice, apparently. Derrida "arrives" without arriving, appearing, much as Plato appears after Socrates in *that* Post Card. We have seen Miller already of course, but as yet he has not spoken. Laughter at least does distinguish, for Rousseau at least, the human from the animal. We know we are watching a recording, we can see the laptop on which the recording is being shown. We can no longer see Miller watching. One can either watch the watcher or the watched, not both. There is a point of invisibility, a limit to visibility, much as there is a line one crosses and re-crosses, in drawing or painting a self-portrait. Invisibility, blindness, the difference of the trace, the difference that is the trait, trait of différance itself, not itself. There is thus a displacement, a disjunction, different times introduced, announced, a spacing which is also temporal; and with this, implicitly, the very idea of a difference before presence, of *différance* as that which makes all representation possible,

but which gives the lie to any representation as being anything other than indirect, belonging to a relay and transfer of traces, the one always standing in for, supplementing and substituting the other, all the others.

There is, in this, no absolute sequence. Speaking of a "before" or an "after" is to assume a logic that is both temporal and spatial, when what takes place is a constant interchange. Derrida is talking about wondering what it must be like to be, to feel like, to taste oneself as, to have the taste of, for J. Hillis Miller, of Miller's taste of, for himself. In this too there is an edit whereby the laptop, the technological substrate disappears, giving us in the illusion, through the medium by which film is filmed, that we are no longer watching a film on a laptop, projection within a film, the subject of which is no longer visible but watching from elsewhere, like the ghost of himself that the film would make of him, regardless of whether he is alive (as is Miller) or dead (as is Derrida). One subject, always already absent, assumes a supplementarity for the other subject. These are all provisional positions and can always change.

(3) From Derrida, to a letter. From Derrida on the screen, to a letter, on the screen, by virtue of another screen, one screen on the screen inside a screen, reproduced for the screen, yet another. The "original" letter, transferred to a transparency and thus reiterated, placed on a projector, becomes yet one more in a tissue of traces, the thinnest of leaves overlaying one another, so thin, so seemingly transparent as to have no weight, no depth. Derrida has disappeared; he appears to have disappeared; he appears only to disappear (I say "appears to have disappeared" because in all truth, he has never been there). He has been caused through the agency of tele-technologies, to retreat, becoming in the process his own *retrait*, that which implicitly he is already, if we suspend the narrow logic of representation, and with that its aesthetic-ontological economy in the service of the illusion of presence, and with that any metaphysics reliant on the idea of presence, undifferentiated, metaphysics as exorcism, to keep us, we the living, the survivors safe in the face of the other, in the coming of the spectral. Derrida is become, his proper name the *trait* we affix to the image, eliding the difference, the *trait* made manifest in this form, in this case the voice of a recording, the recording already not Derrida, even as this will not therefore have been J. Hillis Miller. Trace of a trace therefore, trace (film) of a trace (film) of a trace (voice) of a

trace (person), inscribed within a trace (the film); but no, wait, I have got the order, the sequence wrong, even though I do not propose to reorder, to attempt to give order in the realm of the spectral, which disorders both temporally and spatially in the ghostly play of the *trait*, which conventional discourses of representation, mimesis, and so forth would *betray*, in their *translation*. You see the dilemma if one has to come down to enumerating ghosts. The very idea, this is impossible. What we are thus "seeing" so to speak is the impossible, representation of presence, when in fact what we are dealing with, what we must always account for, come to terms with, is that representation only ever represents the act of representation.

To hold off from this though, coming back, allowing to return, the letter: this letter, a letter, read by Derrida, concerning a letter, the letter J. A different order, within the visible, introduces itself: Re-presentation supplementing representation, indirect figuring in the place of apparently faithful image, moving from mimesis and simulacrum to analogy, apophasis. This "represents" without showing us, it re-presents, J. Hillis Miller. Miller is absent. There is no Miller as such. Derrida, reading the letter, and talking about the letter, and also the letter to which he turns his attention, the letter J having arrived before the letter, the simulacrum of which is being screened, signed by the letter "J," about which though it does not matter, the author of that letter tells Derrida who tells us in telling his audience—and the writing is there, on the screen, the screen within and on another screen, and another, etc., *et ainsi, und so weiter,* and so on and so forth...—; once again we are enmeshed in the skein of traces, until

(4) Derrida returns to reassure his audience, not us, though we may take some comfort from this, that the letter will be in the archive.

If my reading thus far has tended towards the febrile in its tenor, this is doubtless because I know that being told the letter (which letter?) is in the archive (to what archive are we referring? Does an archive refer? Can one refer to an archive?) is far from reassuring. The archive, its very idea, the phantom *eidolon* following in the wake but also presaging the material possibility of the archive, is always already haunted by the play of the trace on which the archive relies for its somewhat uncanny existence. But, suspending this torment, the final schema, last skein in the weave

(5), the last path through this labyrinth, in which I have been doing my best to lose you. We return to Miller, who looking now in a different direction, is preparing, apparently, to respond to a question, off camera, issuing from another voice, yet another trace, which question is then doubled, trace of the trace once more, in a subtitle: "what comes to your mind when you see this picture?" The idiom, he phrasing of the question, however unintended, unconscious, is telling, not least for its suggestion that the picture is implied as having the power to call up for the viewing subject, audience of the picture, something that "comes to mind," which arrives as the invisible motion, spacing and temporalisation, of something other momentarily appearing to the subject, for the subject's perception, but invisible, within the subject, unavailable to us except as a relayed trace possibly, re-presented, though not represented, in being treated to translation. Without any slander, Miller is invited to traduce, to lead us over or across, from the invisible to the visible, from the assumed coming of the spectre—what comes to mind—to a re-presentation of that, without the ghost having any appearance, any direct representation.

A diminished chord, possibly a tri-tone, is heard as the question concludes, a musical punctuation, another momentary arrival, aural *trait* as if to emphasise the non-representability of ghosts. It is perhaps worth mentioning at this juncture that at certain moments in *Fanny och Alexander*, a not dissimilar dissonance is heard. There is even an instant when the ghost of Alexander's father is seen sitting disconsolately at the piano, playing notes my memory wants to tell me are very close to those used in the documentary by Miller. Amongst the first of Miller's comments is that the image of Derrida is "very moving" because of Derrida's then apparent ill health. The ghost moves one; Miller confesses to having been moved; the revenant moves in us, revenance there is unseen, but everywhere felt, if felt at all. For Miller, there is not the taste, but the feeling of the ghost. There is, at the mention of death, another cross fade, Miller fades as he returns, shade of himself, almost in the same place, the one, again, supplementing displacing, doubling, as it replaces, its own other. Is this a deliberate or accidental effect of the edit, was this planned, given to be read, or is this merely the revelation of my taste for the ghost, my feeling, the feeling I have, no more than this, the merest frisson, concerning the work of spectrality? That must remain undecidable.

Another piano chord, and Miller begins to consider the tele-technological archive comparing this to the return of a ghost, his figure here being simile. As we know, Derrida has argued, in *Specters of Marx* and also, less directly elsewhere, *Mal d'Archiv* for example, that ghosts have proliferated in the age of tele-technologies. What Derrida fails to suggest is that we have created this world of representation, our tele-techno-mass-mediauratic empire, in order, I would argue, to control, programme, the ghost, not only in its representations but also in its coming. Far from simply living with the spectral, we fear the spectral, we fear the unconscious, memory, the unbidden past, the unexpected and unprogrammable future to such an extent, that we want to protect our selves from the uninvited guest, the unexpected call, we want to screen all our ghosts, keep them at bay. Today we live with an archive of ghosts which is also, auto-co-immunization, the incorporation of the spectral into our realities, as if this would exorcise them, banish them, keep them at the peripheries, to be called up, sent away, played back, played with, through the modes of representation we seek to control. This hypothesis must remain suspended for now, however, hovering perhaps unwelcome, like Banquo's ghost at the feast.

Miller continues, after reference to the recordings of Glenn Gould playing Bach; he considers how the filmmaker can fast forward, rewind, slow down, pause, play over and over again. The spectro-tele-technological archive gives one the illusion of power over the living and the dead, although I have to say it does not appear to occur to Miller that even were he hearing Gould play live, Gould, or whichever pianist you prefer for your Bach, Schubert, or whoever, is, even in live performance, nevertheless acting as a medium, a conduit for the trace of the other. Again we are enchained; moving on, we remain in the snares of the trace, snares which, as I am suggesting, both problematize representation from within itself, whilst retuning to us the Husserlian notion of a re-presentation that can always return to haunt from the future, and additionally serve to exceed and so erase or deconstruct the premise of a separation on which binaries such as "recorded/live" "dead/live," *fort / da*, here / there, presence / absence, and so forth are all predicated. As soon as we acknowledge the trace, there is the ghost in the machine; and the only real distinction to be made between a recording of a piece of music for example and a so-called live, but we must remember, programmed performance, is that the recording remains the same on the condition that the disc, the laptop, the file works, the technology is available, and none of the elements, or components, damaged. The live performance can and may change, from performance to performance, within the same performance. What is not accounted for, what remains as it were on the side of the professional judgement, objective account, academic exercise, is the possible singularity of effect and what takes place when someone, you or I become haunted.

To risk a personal example [**Sound Clip**]: does that move you? Are you moved, touched, haunted, as I have had occasion to be? Can this ghost touch you in the same way? No, you can only understand at most indirectly, by analogical apperception as Husserl puts it. Thinking this voice, these voices: speaking here, but not here, as well as singing. I loved this voice, these voices, I love the voice. Loved, Love, which is it? When it comes back to me, as now it can only in memory or as a recording, is it in the past or present tense that I feel compelled to speak, to respond, to tell you how I loved the voice, how I love these voices. And I have to ask: what is it I love when I say I love the voice? What does it carry in it, in them, the more than one voice in any voice? What do I hear in that voice, no longer a voice, merely its trace, but more than one voice, which at other times I heard. What comes back? What can always come back, but which does not always return? Though I can rewind, fast forward, pause, and so on, I cannot control that return, that which can always arrive from within and overflowing the technological, the revenance in the trace of the voice. I have this feeling that it remains in me touching me, to touch me when I am least aware. We love voices, as we love eyes, Susan Stewart asserts, because there is in these a ghostly "individuation...not synonymous with the individuation of the body as the site of experience." Stewart, in the same passage, suggests that voices, like eyes, are "vessels of that presence we call the soul: to love the voice and the eyes is far different from loving the color of someone's hair or even someone's way of walking" (107). While I would concede the eye as a vessel perhaps, though not the look in the eye when the eye of the beloved looks at you, or when you look into the eye of the beloved, believing yourself to be the beloved of that other, the voice is more ephemeral, evanescent.

Regardless of this minor difference though, what Stewart does capture is that sense of a differentiation between the Who and the What. Where I would take this argument would be to suggest that the look, the voice, perhaps especially the voice, can always return in memory, in unexpected ways, unanticipated moments, to touch one more intimately than one might have been touched when in the presence of the person to whom the eyes, the look, the voice belong.

Listening to Schubert's "Der Leiermann" is not always unbearable for me, let me reassure you. Sometimes it is, and this has less to do with the music or any particular performance than other aspects of spectrality, of one's being haunted, and of haunting being intimately the experience and perception of loss. Not simply loss, wherein one experiences nostalgia, regret, that feeling of *Sehnsucht*; but much more immediately, touching one unconsciously, invisibly all the time, loss as inescapably the ghost at the heart of Being itself. Equally though, it has to be admitted, if we are to accept this tentative definition of Being, what can return unpredictably, beyond any programme, outside of my control to haunt me is not, not necessarily or at all, what haunts you, or you, or you. And of course, everyone can say the same thing; everyone's experience will necessarily differ, the ways in which we represent to others the experience or perception of our being haunted will differ. Haunting cannot be represented directly because every example of haunting, in its singularity, singularity of event, singularity of experience and perception, not only from person to person but from time to time; every example will differ, which is why haunting, spectrality, ghosting cannot by example be exemplified, it cannot by definition be defined: you have to take it on trust, and see, if at all, only in the most indirect of ways, that what I am saying haunts me does, indeed, cause this experience, cause in me, for me and for no one else, the re-presentation of the spectral.

This is why questions of the uncanny, anxiety, déjà vu are so problematic, unresolved. There is in each a matter of an irreducible singularity, a trait the uniqueness of which is irreducible to reproduction, even though the effect it produces is iterable, and this has to be taken into any account of spectrality in its representations; but for which, conversely, there is no accounting, no economic logic or control, no general principle by which one's being haunted can be considered the same for everyone. So, returning to the video of Miller and Derrida, to conclude with the video clip, even if it proves not to have done with us: The limit of Miller's reading is the limit of representation itself and the distinction that remains to be thought through between representation, a mode of human intervention or control (whether more or less technological), and that which is beyond all representation, within but inexpressibly other than representation: the trace, as I have been arguing today. Like justice, like love, the trace is unavailable to any deconstruction or any general theorization or schematization because on the one hand it can only ever be apprehended in the singular experience of its manifestation for someone at a certain time though not necessarily at others, while on the other hand, it cannot be rendered, made over into a generalised ontology, form, concept or, indeed, representation. Certainly, and to emphasise the point through reiteration, the kinds of complex technology we have just seen involved in what Miller calls the uncanny doubling of the ghostly would, from my side, seem to be precisely a technology of control, techno-management or techno-control of the spectral, in its ability to edit, sequence, giving the illusion of order, before and after, a stable manipulated temporality with a visual representation of narrative passage. In this representation conventionally understood cannot "show" the spectral, its economy being one of imitation, direct figuring, transparency of medium in the service of the illusion of presence, manipulability on the part of the human. The trace though does not belong to, nor can it be made over into, such an order, such an aesthetic, even though everywhere and yet nowhere, the trace is that which makes any conventional aesthetic of representation possible.

In order to move then, to continue toward a poetics of the spectral, or rather, perhaps a spectral *poïesis*, thereby indicating not a poetics by which the spectre, the ghost, the phantom are figured or represented, but rather to propose the work that revenants and apparitions cause to appear: we might think this in terms of a "bringing-forth," as Heidegger would have it in his understanding of *poïesis*, or that which is, for Jean-Luc Marion, the givenness of Being; so in moving towards a *spectropoïesis* as that which ghosts make, thereby clearing the way to shift the ground from representation to the Husserlian inflection of re-presentation, it is necessary to recall from amongst his earliest published writings, a few comments of Derrida's on the trace, all from *De la grammatologie* (translations modified). I pursue these here because it is important that we apprehend the relation of non-relation between the ghost, on the one hand, and the trace on the other, as both within, and yet exceeding, other than and invisible within any form of representation conventionally understood. There is, says Derrida, an

> ...irreducible absence within the presence of the trace... announced as such—without any simplicity, any identity, any resemblance... within what is not it.

Neither something nor nothing, neither sensible nor intelligible, one cannot propose a representation or definition of the trace informed or inaugurated by a fundamental or first ontological interrogation beginning with the statement "the trace is...x." To do so is to miss the point precisely of the availability of the trace, if such a thing exists, to representation. At best, we might provisionally propose the following formula, *trace, there is*, signifying spacing, that the trace is not available as or to presence, any more than it is to resemblance, identity, having no being properly its own. This, in effect, opens for us the notion of the ghost, invisible, irreducible to simple or full definition, and yet in its work, in this *spectropoetic* play, causing to bring to mind that which makes meaning possible.

Derrida again, a few pages on:

> ...it is in the specific zone of...this trace, in the temporalization of a *lived experience*...that differences appear....The unheard difference between the appearing and the appearance [*l'apparaisant et l'apparaître*]...is the condition of all other differences, of all other traces, and *it is already a trace*. [emphases added]

If one remains resistant to the idea of the trace as non-synonymous double of the ghost, what Derrida has to say here about the effect of the trace felt, indirectly apprehended, apperceived rather than perceived "in the temporalization of a *lived experience*" within which differences are caused to appear, might move us toward the spectrality of the trace. The trace, Derrida observes, "opens appearance," without being visible itself. Moreover, "[t]he concepts of *present, past*, and *future*, everything in the concept of time and history which implies evidence of them...cannot adequately describe the structure of the trace." Never simply temporal, or containable by reference to, representation through or definition by metaphysical concepts of time, any more than being a question of a mere structural spacing, the trace—ghostwork, ghostplay, spectropoetics itself—reintroduces that which haunts by its very unavailability to representation, reintroducing in the process, as Derrida says of the trace, "the problem of the deferred effect (*Nachträglichkeit*) of which Freud speaks."

To confess therefore: I love nothing better than memory. Memory, as trace, as ghost, as that which returns, experience, the event, become perception, the trace, then re-presented, trace of the trace, not represented. Here is Julian Barnes in a telling non-definition, which indirectly illuminates itself within by its spectropoetic work.

> But no: she didn't mean that....Your first memory wasn't something like your first bra, or your first friend, or your first kiss, or your first fuck, or your first marriage, or your first child, or the death of your first parent, or your first sudden sense of the lancing hopelessness of the human condition—it wasn't like any of that. It wasn't a solid, seizable thing, which time, in its plodding, humorous way, might decorate down the years with fanciful detail—a gauzy swirl of mist, a thundercloud, a coronet—but could never expunge. A memory was, by definition not a thing, it was...a memory. A memory now of a memory a bit earlier of a memory before that of a memory way back when. (3)

The idea of a first, through endless iteration, is made meaningless, the lie given to originary as nothing more than a chimera belonging to our fear of ghosts and our anxiety to fix, to control representation with teleological points of light, Barnes' play of consonance, assonance and alliteration the careful unravelling of priority, the diminution of order and sequence. Memory is always, regardless of its subject, or whatever it may seem to represent directly or indirectly—and I would say in passing that memory is only ever indirect re-presentation—, memory of loss, particularly memory of a loss, of those losses that inform, inscribe, who we are. More than this, let me say, as unequivocally and as affirmatively as possible: memory *as* loss. Singular trace itself, always the revenance of singular traces and the trait of singularity, Memory *is* loss, the trace where by a past that can never return as such is figured in its having passed. Memory confesses to us; it gives to us, as the gift of the other, the revelation in re-presentation that which, in its constitution of our Being and the temporality of Being in its motion of always becoming, the trace that just is loss. Memory remains therefore, the trace of the other, whether as the trace of my own alterity to myself or that of an other at once having been exterior but also incorporated in memory into me, though, poignantly as the sign that the other is never possessed, never possessable, never present, absolutely or directly to me, even though it, trace of the other, can possess, can haunt me. Trace of the other coming to pass, *apparitioning*, memory, always the memory of the singular, never merely memory in general, remains intimately close, impossibly far, touching me, touching on me, but otherwise uncontrollable, ungraspable.

And in this, in the re-presentation of experience encrypted in the initial time of perception, in what remains through the phantom effects of re-presentation, wherein memory is apprehended as trace of the other, memory constitutive of the loss at the heart of Being, as that which remains, to which the ghost of anamnesis bears witness. Coming from what I call with too much ease a "past," my own past, an historical past, memory is what remains, it is the remains, so to speak, but wildly anachronistic, it also remains this unpredictable future revenant, remaining to come. Memory can always arrive from what I have been describing the unprogrammable, from an unprogrammable future for example. It can arrive, remaining in its revenance beyond possession, as that which is unrepresentable as such, but yet as that which is given in re-presentation. If memory is always singular, always a memory for me, for no other, then loss too is singular; it is that which is apperceived, through a kind of memory work that is also at bottom a phenomenological reduction, only truly in what is given to my perception. I am, therefore I am haunted; to say "I am" is to confess to the experience, perception and recollection, re-presentation of the singularity of every instant of an authentic spectrality, authentic because, violently anachronistic, resistant to all historical or temporal containment, the gift of haunting remains other than, and resistant to any mode of conventional, certainly visual, or let me qualify this, directly visual, visibly direct representation or mode of mimesis.

This ghost, the experience of ghosting for which there is no representation; this arrival, the coming of the spectral, is never in doubt. It can always happen, take place, come to pass. However, such a moment of coming requires that we be open to the possibility of the impossible, this arrival of the trace of the other, not seeking to limit it, control it, corral it in the frames of representation. Any spectrality, if there is any, is only known, revealed, in a moment of unexpected, unanticpated *Nachträglichkeit*, that is re-presentation. *Spectropoïesis* is irreducible to any formalisation, to any "theoretical armature" or method, to borrow from Walter Benjamin. Through its flows, energies, upsurges and returns, memory as singular trace of an equally singular experience and perception of the other, coming now, and re-presented in its always already being a loss, irretrievably other, other trace of the trace of the other, comes to be arrested in my memory through "a configuration pregnant with tensions, [giving] that configuration a shock, by which it crystalizes into a monad" (Benjamin 262-63). At the same time though, in exceeding mimetic and related modes of representation, such re-presentation also succeeds in making available to experience translated into archival memory work; with this, there can occur the return of the auratic experience for the subject, for my other self whose perception of experience arrives for me as my own other, and which has therefore been recorded in the anticipation of its iterability. In this manner, only if we understand the most intimate and most familiar aspects of memory's touch in this way, without seeking to fix it in place, or fix it through representation or ontology, or to control its forces through the work of psychoanalysis, then we might imagine the idea of a haunting to come, whereby we can, to cite Giorgio Agamben in somewhat messianic vein, "reopen that breach in which history—in which life—suddenly fulfils its promise" (42). Refusing to lay the ghosts to rest, we admit them; we admit their significance to our Being as all that touches us but which is no longer us.

In conclusion: so, perhaps, and I do not say this lightly, *perhaps* Miller is, if not wrong exactly in his response to the tele-technological ghost, then not quite right either. For as the recording, that which can be played back is only ever a trace, it is different only in degree, rather than as one might at first believe, in kind. A prosthetized archive, memory denatured, made available through an othering, a nonhuman externalisation, the recording *can* always come back, but only on the condition that we understand it not as a representation, though it is this of course. Instead, we must see past the merely visible, the mimicry, the mimetic tendency of tele-technology to be, in its apprehension of the trace, simply representation. Within, other than the visible, the visual, beyond mere representation, the trace of the other is there, the trace in my relation to that trace remains singular. It can always arrive to touch me, because for me, if for no one else, it has about it that singularity phenomenally, by which the trace bears in it the ghost of a chance. This is most eloquently illustrated, I think, in the final scene of another film that treats of ghosts, personal and those of history, Theo Angelopoulos' *Ulysses Gaze*. [**Clip**] A Greek-American filmmaker, having returned to Greece, journeys through the Balkans in search of three missing reels of film, thought to be the first film, the first "gaze." Finally, in Sarajevo, he finds the film. We witness the filmmaker watching the film, but we never see what he sees, by which he is moved to tears, to which he responds with words promising return, the narrative of an other, to which he gives voice. We can never witness the ghost directly. Though I cannot represent to you what is there in the loss I experience in encountering a trace that brings to me my own sense of Being's loss, as well as the loss the other, there, signals in being only captured in the trace, nevertheless, I find myself involved in, profoundly touched by the other, the singular other, an alterity singularly for me, and for me alone, which comes, arrives, returns, and can always return in memory or through the prosthesis of tele-techno-mediatized auratic revenance, to speak of, to, my Being, my Being alone, my Being as a sign, a haunted souvenir, of loss.

## *Works Cited*

Agamben, Giorgio. *Nudities*. Stanford: Stanford University Press, 2010.

Barnes, Julian. *England, England*. New York: Alfred A Knopf, Inc., 1998.

Husserl, Edmund. *Phantasy, Image Consciousness, and Memory (1898-1925)*. Trans. John B. Brough. Dordrecht: Springer, 2005.

Nancy, Jean-Luc. *The Sense of the World*. Minneapolis: University of Minnesota Press, 2008.

Stewart, Susan. *Poetry and the Fate of the Senses*. Chicago: University of Chicago Press, 2002.

# Part 3

*Chapter 7*

# "Like a Beginning of an Interminable Waterway": J. Hillis Miller and the Theory to Come[1]

Dragan Kujundžić

> *"Being a dialectician means having the wind of history in one's sails. The sails are the concepts. It is not enough, however, to have sails at one's disposal. What is decisive is knowing the art of setting them"*
> —Walter Benjamin, *The Arcades Project*, "On the Theory of Knowledge, the Theory of Progress" (1999, 473).

> *"Riddled with light. Ah!"*
> —"Cold Heaven," W. B. Yeats,

> *"We live in a flicker."*[2]
> —Joseph Conrad, *Heart of Darkness*, 2006.

Forty years ago I spent almost two months in the Harrow, Rayners Lane area of Northwest London as a guest of the Styvesant family. Preparing

---

[1] This essay started as a plenary talk given at the University of Lancaster on May 31, 2012, at an event honoring J. Hillis Miller, and which included a conference related to the screening of the film *The First Sail: J. Hillis Miller*. Some of the essays from that conference are in this volume. My own essay thus bears the marks of this occasion. However, it has been since substantially expanded to include references to the subsequently published essays or the relevant literature that has since come to my attention. The essay has been written thus between May 2012 and May 2013.

[2] "Flicker: Noun, 3. movie." In: http://www.merriam-webster.com/dictionary/flicker, accessed May 12, 2013.

for that visit, I, an eleven-year-old boy in Novi Sad, then still Yugoslavia, was glued (*riveted*, about which more later) to the maps of London, particularly learning the names of the bridges on the Thames from the postcards and guide books, in the order as they go from the source towards the Estuary and the offing. I know them to this day by heart, at least the ones in Central London: Battersea, Albert, Chelsea, Grosvenor, Vauxhall, Lambeth, Westminster, Waterloo, Blackfriars, London, they are like photographic snapshots in my memory... They were at the beginning of my own waterway and offing, my own opening to the English language, that led me later on to study in the United States and that bring me here to you today. They reverberate in me like a rhythm of an interminable hospitality, which for me is England, and by extension, the English language.

This, by way of an introduction, also speaks to the interminable hospitality of J. Hillis Miller who was at the beginning of so many of my intellectual and professional adventures, at the University of California, where I had the honor to organize, together with my colleague and our mutual friend, Barbara Cohen, a conference dedicated to him, with Jacques Derrida as the plenary speaker, at the University of Florida where he is a frequent and welcome guest, in Maine, where, in order to film *The First Sail. J. Hillis Miller*, I intruded with the camera operator for two weeks 6-7 hours each day in Miller's house with the camera equipment, moving furniture and lights, to be met with unstinting patience and humor, and now in Lancaster. I am talking, as you can hear, about hospitality, and it is not just a beginning or an introduction of my talk. I am already in it. What I am describing, in many ways for me marks, in the most essential and singular way, the way the work of J. Hillis Miller "works," the way, to paraphrase Derrida on Hopkins and J. Hillis Miller, it *justices*. This "performance" of Miller's texts was powerfully announced in his "The Critic as Host," in the volume *Deconstruction and Criticism*, this "interminable," the word is repeated twice (232,249) movement of interrogation of Shelley's "Triumph of Life," whereby the very act of literary criticism is seen as entangled in the joyful movement of hosting, of opening to the other, of letting the other come, up to and including the uncanniest of guests. You probably all know this justly famous text which describes the age-old scenarios of hospitality and hostility haunting Western metaphysics in its quest to purge the dangerous other.³ Thus, the question of hospitality, of *hostipitality*, to paraphrase Derrida, is from the very beginning implicated in the work of deconstruction as its most immediate task. The task to invent a ground different from the binarism of mythos-logos, nihilist-metaphysical, literary-philosophical, towards what Derrida would call the effect of the *khora*, that which gives space by withdrawing itself, and what Miller called in this essay, the work of criticism as joyous hospitality, the attempt to "move beyond metaphysics to an affirmative, life-enhancing, performative act of language, interpretation as joyful wisdom, the greatest joy in the midst of the greatest suffering, an inhabitation of that gaiety of language which is our seigneur" ("Critic" 229, 230, 231).

In recent years, J. Hillis Miller turned (he himself spoke of his turn in *Conflagration of Communities* and elsewhere), more radically to the question of technology and eco-technology, community and conflagrations of community, the autoimmunitary destruction of the communal, not only as perceived in literary texts, but also as those themes and narrative practices found in literature reverberate with or find themselves cross-referenced in our political reality. It is not surprising that Miller does it in his inimitable way, by closely reading literature. He opens his "Ecotechnological Odradek" with a summary of J.L. Nancy's thoughts on ecotechnology:

> The total environment more and more reveals itself to be "technological," that is, in one way or another machinelike. The "body" is, according to Nancy "linked" to its technological ecosystem in manifold ways, as a prosthesis of a prosthesis. That body, however, is more and more being shown also to function like a machine. It is a technical product of the ecotechnical. "The body" is a complex set of interlocking mechanisms that are self-generating, self-regulating, and self-reading sign systems. "There is no 'the' body," in the sense of a unitary organism, says Jean-Luc Nancy. These corporeal sign systems are the products of chance permutations extending over millions of years, such as those that have produced the

---

3   This essay has been with me since my first trip to the US in 1983, and I have published it in translation into Serbian in Novi Sad, my home town, in a volume dedicated to "Deconstruction, A Merry Science" (1985).

> human genome. These sign systems do not depend on human consciousnesses or on actions based on the choice of a voluntary code-reader in order to function. They just go on working and unworking. (Miller, "Ecotechnics")

These reflections are an introduction to a thirty-page analysis of Kafka's very short story, "The Worry of the Father of the Family." This essay is yet another example of Miller's capacity to weave out of minimal textual and literary material immense theoretical and in this case eco-political consequences, particularly those effects of autoimmunitary destruction of society around us. These realms where our reading of Kafka could be instructive in demystifying and de-ideologizing the forces that are conflagrating the world we live in, are fivefold:

> the environment, the global financial system, the nation-community, the body, and language. These mechanical sign-systems work. They make something happen, often in the end disaster from the human perspective. Each system can be seen as a figure for the others, but no one is the literal of which the others are displacements, figures, supplements, substitutions, or symbols. All are interconnected. Together they make an all-inclusive ecotechnological non-integrated whole into which each one of "us" is plugged, as a flash memory stick is inserted into a USB connection in a computer. (Miller, "Ecotechnics")

From there Miller proceeds to the most troubling consequences of the autoimmunitary destruction of our environment, both political and ecological, the toxic pollution of our water and waterways, and our air and airways. I sense a rising anger in J. Hillis Miller at the sight of such wanton destruction inflicted on us by global warming deniers, by the disgrace of Abu Ghraib and the war on terror inflicted on the United States and the world, by the dismantling of the great American educational system including the once greatest system of higher education anywhere, the University of California where we both worked, which is now being decimated by budget cuts, administrative mismanagement, program closings, and wounded by the aggressive and sometimes downright violent political and police intervention on its campuses. The University of California, alas, is not alone in this predicament, in the US and elsewhere.

Miller is particularly attentive to what in technology, in technics, facilitates certain destruction, just as he is to what in technics and technology, for example personal computers, may still help prevent the more and more inevitable lurch into the global oven. Thus, from a simple reading of Wallace Stevens' "The Man on the Dump," written in 1942.

> What then of the move in the last stanza of Stevens's poem to a claim that the poet is the supreme artificer who will create the supreme fictions by which we can live better lives? The good poet constantly makes up new image clusters that will just as constantly find their way to the dump. I do not think that heroic concept of the poet's role has much purchase these days. A free or transformative reading of Stevens's poem, such I have sketched out, would rather claim that a reading for today is either an instigation to urgent action to do what we can to "stop trashing the climate," or a way of facing up to what is happening to us, as the water rises to inundate our coasts and as species after species goes extinct. You can take your pick. You can be either a watcher or a doer. I claim this essay is a form of doing things with words and other images, even if what it does is only to cry, "Get ready. The end of the world is coming." It is, perhaps, distinctively human to bear witness, to use language to testify that catastrophic climate change is happening and is going to happen. (Miller, "Anachronistic" 89)

The to-come of J. Hillis Miller's ethico-critical gesture consists in pointing out the urgency of reading literature, precisely because there one can find a still perhaps unpolluted cultural space and the instructions how to use it. In the patient reading we discover the urgency of political action, there is no time to be lost. "Where was it one first heard of the truth? The the." The repetition of the definite article in the conclusion of the poem reiterates, and adumbrates the finitude of the world we live in, in an attempt, in Miller's interpretation, to ward off and resist the forces that bring about its conflagration.[4]

---

4   This essay allows us to see, for example, that Conrad's *Heart of Darkness*, among many other things to be discussed shortly, is also a narrative about the piling up of garbage as a byproduct of global colonial expansion: "I discovered that a lot of imported drainage-pipes for the settlement had been tumbled

There is a political turn in Miller, which was, I think, always already there, but has now appeared in its sharper and more acute forms. Miller is more and more interested in global warming deniers, in the Holocaust deniers, in the issues of testimony for which all his career prepared him, and which has now found an outlet in what Eamonn Dunne called "a singular virtuosity of Miller's interpretive ingenuity," *The Conflagrations of Community. Fiction Before and After Auschwitz* (2011). While giving the most patient and astute reading, to texts by Kafka, Kertesz and Toni Morrison, among others (as well as a reading of Jean-Luc Nancy on community, Adorno on literature after the Holocaust, and Celan and Derrida on testimony), Miller turns the consequences of his analysis to the here and now of the tele-technical and political catastrophe, the literal and figural rising tide of all sorts of patriotisms and xenophobia by means of the televisual and mediatic.

Readers will find the author's discussions of these topics most concentrated in the final analysis of *Beloved* in Chapter 7, where there are constant reminders of the urgency of effective and responsible critical responses to contemporary and very real issues of global terrorism, corrupt hegemonic governance and tele-technological and mediatic propaganda: "Now (December 2010) the Republicans have taken over the House of Representatives in the recent election... The most urgent intellectual and ethical challenge today is to understand, and then act responsibly on, a recognition that our present world condition is determined by the complex inter- actions, antagonisms, overlappings, and interdependences among three great forces. These are tele-techno-scientifico-military-medico-mediatic- globalized transnational capitalism; Evangelical, apocalyptic, fundamentalism, rapturous Christianity; and radical 'terrorist' transnational Islamic fundamentalism" (Dunne 365).

One senses a descent of Miller into a heart of darkness increasingly surrounding us, a darkness which is blinding, the blinding of the televisual screen and the multiplication of the rhetorical and political, as well as literal garbage. One hears more and more a question, "Why read literature?" when Rome is burning, why read literature after the Holocaust,

---

in there. There wasn't one that was not broken. It was a wanton smash-up." Marlow is literally the man on the dump. No wonder that the entire nature in this story is in mourning, "filled with mournful stillness."

why read literature in the age of global warming, why read literature at the time of the state and other terrorism, what's the point? Miller is fully aware that we may be living the end of literature as we know it, he has written about it in his *Medium is the Maker* where he traces, alongside Derrida, the possibility that "the entire epoch of so-called literature, if not all of it, cannot survive a certain technological regime of telecommunication" (*Medium* 18). *It may not survive, but that moment has not come yet*, and Miller reinstates, more forcefully than anyone else I know or have read, the urgency of patient reading of literature in the face of this looming Apocalypse. But, in some ways, that is what deconstruction has always already been doing, it was always a transformative practice putting words to do the work of dismantling the dominant ideologies, including the ideologies of tele-techno-communication, of which the ignoble symbol well known here and now in the UK, but a metonymy of the entire FOXification of the televisual, is the Murdoch Corporation.

I will now turn to Joseph Conrad's *Heart of Darkness*, and Miller's reading of this story in his "*Heart of Darkness* Revisited" (a landmark essay, reprinted in 2012) and, of his more recent essay "Should We Read *The Heart of Darkness*?" in his book, *Others*, (2001). It will be followed by a brief account of an even more recent intervention, namely, Miller's discussion of *The Heart of Darkness* in light of a posthumously published essay by Philippe Lacoue-Labarthe (2007; 2012). I am doing it for two reasons. One is already outlined above: in these first two essays, Miller is engaged with the issue of Apocalypse *in* literature but in many ways also the Apocalypse *of* literature. He is attentive as well to what a good reading can do to shed some light on the heart of the darkness marking "the end of Western Civilization, with its ideals of progress, enlightenment, and reason, its goal of carrying the torch of civilization into the wilderness and wringing the heart of the darkness" (Miller, "Prologue" 52). But it also gives a clue as to how he sees his task of critic, directly related to the imminence of what is to come, to the *a-venir* of all our intellectual work, certainly the to-come of Miller's singular signature placed as an apotropaic resistance to "the imminence of that end which has never quite come as long as there is someone to speak or write about it" (Miller, "Prologue" 52).

There is another reason for turning to these particular essays by Miller, pertaining to what his recent reading of the tele-technological in relation to literature allows us to see as the work of the mediatic always already, or in this case singularly in Conrad's short novel, working or unworking the literary text. Miller's readings have been for a long time now, probably from the very beginning, treatises on the rhetorical technicity and mediality of the literary text with its tropological deflections of any finite meaning which they nevertheless *expose* (like one exposes a film), the "images of light and shadow, or of light differentiated from itself," veiling and unveiling of and in the text like "a performative apocalypse" (Miller, "Critic" 237). A performative apocalypse of the technical apparatus put to use, the technical "regenerating itself, interminably in ever new figures of light" (Miller, "Critic" 235), or darkness. I would like also to insist on a certain mediality of Miller's own texts thus announced, an almost cinematic, filmic quality, their capacity to project augmented, blown-up microtextual elements, to give a glow or an aura to the dark or obscure *minutae* of literary texts, to give them a spectacular enlightened afterlife which glows in the dark; just like the darkness in cinema (we all live in a flicker now!) or the one in Conrad's novel, illuminated by the ghostly, reflected moonlight.

The mediatic, tele-technological mode of the production of the *Heart of Darkness* is posited by Miller when he says that "The meaning of the parable appears in the 'spectral' likeness of the story that reveals it, or, rather, it appears in the likeness of an exterior light surrounding the story" (Miller, "Prologue" 42). The narrator appears as a disappearing voice hovering over the river, the figure of a double duty, which "illuminates its own workings and at the same time obscures or undermines it" (Miller, "Prologue" 12). The working of the story is spoken about in terms of a spectral illumination, of the photo-phantomatic, contained in the well known description of the meaning of the story, "not inside like a kernel, but outside, enveloping the tale which brought it out only as a glow brings out the haze, in the likeness of one of these spectral illuminations of moonshine."

The meaning appears in the projection of a reflection of the solar light, thus already as an artifice (we shall see, nature works as a prosthetic device in this story), an apparatic apparition pointing towards the mediatic, towards the medium as the maker of the story which, I would like to claim, is spectral, cinematic, and televisual, a reflection and a reproduction glowing in the dark. The story begins to function like a dark chamber, photographic apparatus, as a camera. The description of its own setting already contains a tightly sealed container in which it unfolds, *exposes* or receives and fixes its own "representation," "the sea and the sky welded together without a joint." Thus, no light but artificial or technically processed light will penetrate this narrative event, though the flickers of the sun may be recorded or reflected in the narrative but only through tightly controlled, shuttered measure.

In this story, everything is already a "specter of a 'televized.' In the nocturnal space in which this image is described, ... it is already night. We are already transfixed by a disappearance which promises and conceals in advance another magic 'apparition,' a ghostly 're-apparition.'" These are Jacques Derrida's thoughts from "Spectrographies," his reflections on the photographic which in an eerily adequate way describe the narrative condition of *Heart of Darkness*. The spectral image described by the narrator and analyzed by Miller, is a "specter, both visible and invisible, both phenomenal and non-phenomenal: A trace that marks the present with its absence in advance" (Derrida, "Spectographies" 117). The spectral, prosthetic tele-technovisuality is already discernible in Miller's analysis, when he writes that "In Conrad's parable of the moonshine, the moon shines already with (twice) reflected and secondary light. Its light is reflected from the primary light of the sun which is almost never mentioned in the *Heart of Darkness*. The sun is only present in the glitter of a reflection, from this or that object, for example, the surface of the river" (Miller, "Prologue" 45). The story is thus a reflection of a reflection, a spectral multiplication of prosthetic reflections, a prosthesis here already encoded in *physis*, in nature, but sealed into the very texture of the narrative as a spectral multiplication of the likeness of the light to itself, a photomimetic phantom of its own production, a "spectral illumination," or to use Benjamin's term, a mediatic aura, an auracity which moved into production, and reproduction of the story, the reproducibility and iterability of the mediatic "itself." "The darkness is in principle invisible and remains invisible. All that can be said is that the halo gives the spectator [notice here the shift in Miller's analysis, a shift not explicated here but essential, from "reader" to "spectator," the shift in the medium from the literary to the cinematic and tele-visual] indirect knowledge that the darkness is there" (Miller, "Prologue" 46).

The story has already sealed, welded its narrative seams at the onset and sunset without a joint, so that no light can penetrate. The only illumination will be artificial, projected from elsewhere, a prosthetic moonlight projected into the haze, the spectral illumination. For a while now we have been shifting Miller's analysis towards something that it itself prepared and made possible, without which our own analysis would not be possible, which Miller's analysis itself already received but has not made explicit. It is time to reveal it explicitly: *Heart of Darkness* is a narrative about its own cinematic, photo-prosthetic production, in the age of the "birth" of the filmic, cinematic, televisual and, anticipating another evolution of the technical, video-tele-visual and video streaming. It is also a narrative that announces the end of literature, its own apocalypse.

After the narrative is sealed within a perfectly welded crypt, the artificial light which penetrates it is captured on the filmic substrate within it: "The moon has spread over everything *a thin layer of silver* [my emphasis, D.K.]—over the rank grass, over the mud, upon the wall of matted vegetation standing higher than the wall of a temple, over the great river I could see though a somber gap glittering, glittering, as it flowed broadly by without a murmur." In the tightly welded narrative crypt an opening shimmers, like an eye or iris of the camera, a somber gap, a shutter, veiling and unveiling the thin layer of silver, the filmic silver gelatin thinly spread over the surface of all things which captures, receives the narrative exposure and the original separation or the final apocalyptic welding together of the light and darkness. "The dusk" thus brings out "the horror, the horror" in the apocalyptic time every time a shutter is opened and closed, a verdict passed in the division and fusion of light in a tele-visual apparatus, the apparition of its own making (*Heart of Darkness*, says Miller, "is a figure for its own mode of working," 2012, 42, or un-working in fact). The "luminous space" only brings the "tanned sails of the barges… to stand still" in the photo-phantomatic *fix*, already covering them with their own reproducibility, "gleamed and varnished" and standing still, instantly and forever, once and for all. ("Tanned," as if burnt by light, and then made to stand still, varnished and fixed into immobility: a photograph). The horror, the horror, repeated twice, stands in for the originary repetition and doubling at work of this narrative. It is also strangely hovering in this doubling (characteristic of Conrad in general), between the mood (the horror) and the genre, the generic description (the horror), "engulphing" (Virginia Woolf, Royle) each other.

In at least two ways: the horror marks and remarks the very sensibility of the text, but also the reflection of the text in itself (an invagination *pace* Derrida). The text "appears" as a mark which inscribes in itself its own survival and mournful testimony, the inscription of its own reproduction and afterlife. The silver surface, like a film, receives the text, developed on the substrate of the narrative, the text indiscernible from the gauzy fog, the river, the halo. The story is also reproduced *doubly*, narrating the process of its making, the cinematic, cine-mimetic, the very generic designation in or on which it inscribes itself: the horror film.[5]

Even the movements of the narrative are opened and closed or delayed by technical parts, not by any human agency. The rivets, for example, which should arrive to seal the hull, are delayed for months, and work to *expose* the narrative time and interrupt it, like a shutter. As Samuel Weber reminds us in *Mass Mediauras*, the word "*riveted*" is today most of all used to refer to being "glued" to a TV set, and "the word is hardly fortuitous" (Weber, 1996, 6).

The rivets also work to seal the hull without seam, thus operating yet another hermetic and hermeneutic sealing of the narrative, the very movement of modernism itself, the production of the technical, prosthetic opening or closure of or to the other. They also serve to enact the separation of waters by sealing the hull, another primordial Biblical motif welded into the narrative (even phonetically, a rive*t* and the rive*r* separated by a consonant, joined, separated). The rivets *qui n'arrivent pas*, like Godot, are the awaited *arrivant*, the techno-messianic without a Messiah, opening and closing the gates of the narrative (both the beginning and the end of) time, captured on the filmic substrate of the silvery surface, or channeled through the mediatic video or digital stream, which then

---

5   Indeed, Miller says that "*Heart of Darkness* is the ideal or a paradigmatic horror story" ("Prologue" 29), followed shortly in the argument on the same page by a reference to "the horror movies."

flickers on the screen. We are all riveted to it but also already captured in or by it, as it were, *in advance*.

*Heart of Darkness* makes visible something Jacques Derrida describes in his "Aletheia" as "what might be called the *photographic* reply: a modern apparatus [*dispositif*], let's call it a technique, becomes a witness without a witness, the prosthetic eye, an eye too many but invisible, at once producer and preserver, the origin and the archive of this insinuation of shadow *at the heart of light* [sic!—DK], of everything that in *physis* thrusts clarity [la clarté] into the night, *light in the dark*, penetrating it without touching it, without the least noise, like an imperceptible thief. ... The *tekhne* becomes the truth of *physis*" ("Aletheia" 172).

*Heart of Darkness* is precisely the genealogy of the photographic reply in literature, at the heart of modernism, thus preparing the disappearance of literature, like this story, which announces it, the thief already at work announcing the theft or the end of the literary epoch, thus developing, like a film is developed, its own demise. The story narrates its own exposure to its own perishing; it fixes it on the "gauzy fabric" of its own silvery gelatinous texture, at once a producer and a preserver—in another medium.[6] The story is a negative waiting to be developed and ruined by every successive reading, a viewing in fact, the horror. But it has not happened yet, as long, as Miller said, there is someone to write of it. But our writing is already marked by that same mediatic and technical archivization which ruins the very attempt to preserve the literary, which here is placed in a *moratorium*. So the same ruination also happens every time we in effect read or counter-sign this narrative. We the readers do not escape its photographic effects of delayed mourning, but neither can we escape the super-vision, being watched over, and the waking vigilance of this text. This super-visory vigilance of the text over its own processes of making (and of us reading) opens the text up to responsibility in the face of horror. The photo-cinematic "reception" within the story also opens up the

---

6   As David Wills writes, this "mediation [is] particular to photography, because of and in spite of its supposed instantaneity, [it] necessarily emphasizes for Derrida what he calls here 'the chrono-dissymmetrical process of the moratorium' (17). In the instant of photographic capture, as well as in such possibilities as delayed shutter release, we experience mourning related to an anticipation" (Wills, review of *Athens...*, manuscript).

time for the story's resilient survival and the space and time for different iterations and interpretations.

This witness without a witness is already described in Miller's essay, as the "relay of witness behind witness behind witness, voice behind voice, each speaking in ventriloquism through the one next further out, characteristic of the genre of the apocalypse" (Miller, "Prologue" 48). A ghostly testimonial apparatus is thus produced, a "witness without a witness" at the heart of the testimonial, the prosthetic iterability as an originary compossibility of literature, testimony, and their limits. It introduces the prosthetic substitute for the witness who has not survived to testify (and where no one can witness for the witness), the prosthetic taking place as the testimony without survivors, as an impossible after-image of the apocalyptic and catastrophic, there where the very narrative speaks about the disappearance of the live agency of writing, where only a spectral glow of the mediatic projections remains to make and unmake the reality, to testify to it. The snapshots taken in *Heart of Darkness* announce a "seriality in mourning," as Derrida says in another essay on photography, *Athens, Still Remains* [Athens Demeure], *Heart of Darkness* being not unlike Derrida's own book "a book of epitaphs, which bears or wears mourning in photographic effigy" (Derrida, "Aletheia" 2).[7]

In Miller's essay too these multiple witnesses are already technical, machinic, prosthetic, "like Kurtz, one of those speaking tubes or relay stations through whom the darkness speaks" (Miller, "Prologue" 53). At the heart of darkness and proximity of Kurtz, described as a relay, an antenna, or an amplifier tube, is a Herz or Hertz, the kilohertz of electromagnetic oscillation, the heartbeat of modernity, the Herz and Hertz of darkness and modernity itself (this is my translation of the story's title for

---

7   We have used the word crypt to describe the operation of this story. Let us remember that it itself names the "sepulcher" as the place from which Marlow's expedition gets to be launched, the sepulchral city (presumably Paris) from which, like from a photographic dark chamber, the entire story is being projected on the silver substrate, and then developed and re-viewed as a halo in London. Paris happens to be the city encrypted in the most famous sepulchral structure of modernity, the tomb-pyramidal like Eiffel Tower, itself a huge projector of flickering light into darkness. Cf. Nicholas Royle's essay on Conrad and the *cryptaesthetics* of his writing, which produces the effects of doubling, seeing everything as "double," or I would say, photographically and mediatically reproduced. Ghostly, spectral, mummified.

this occasion: *Hertz of Darkness*), the flickering oscillation of the artificial light: "The glow of light alternates fifty times per second in European lightbulbs, sixty times in American ones: the uncomplicated, and hence imperceptible, rhythm of our evenings and of an antenna called the body" (Kittler 122).[8]

The oscillation measured in Hertz, the discovery of the heartbeat of the alternation of light and darkness, directly leads to the invention of the stroboscopic event and the cinema: "the stroboscopic illumination transforms the continuous flow of movement into interferences... Coupled with the afterimage effect, Faraday's stroboscopic effect became the necessary and sufficient condition for the illusions of cinema. One only had to automatize the cutting mechanism, cover the film reel with a wing disk between moments of exposure and with a Maltese cross in the moments of projection, and the eye saw seamless motion during moments of projection rather than 24 single and still shots" (Kittler 122).

In his *Athens, Still Remains*, Jacques Derrida offers a reflection on the wing disk, the shutter, the mechanism essential for the oscillation of shadow, darkness and light, the oscillation between an instant, imminence that is to come like a verdict, an infinite finitude, like death itself, and eternity, spectral immortality, the prosthetic survival captured and saved in a photographic image. "Speaking of which, what would Plato or Heidegger have thought of this thing called shutter or, in French, using a name that has been part of the vocabulary of photography since 1868, the *obturateur*? Would they have even considered this little mechanism that allows one to calculate the light passing though, the impression of

---

[8] The story refers to Kurtz's words as to "the pulsating stream of light [again, a very good definition of cinema—DK], or the deceitful flow from the heart of an impenetrable darkness," binding "the pulse of light" (the pulse, as in *pulsus venarum* means "beating from the blood in the veins") with "the heart of darkness," thus techne and physis separated by only a heartbeat from each other. This story bleeds technology. Furthermore, the noun in German for the heart, *Herz*, and the name of the inventor of the electric frequency, *Hertz*, are of the same etymology: "Hertz," Jewish (Ashkenazic): ornamental name from German *Herz* 'heart,'" just as "Kurtz" is German and Jewish (Ashkenazic): nickname for someone who was short in stature, from Middle High German *kur(t)z*, German *kurz* 'short' http://genealogy.familyeducation.com/surname-origin/hertz, accessed May 18, 2013.

the sensible subjectile, and the delaying of the 'right moment' [*moment voulu*]" (Derrida, "Aletheia" 3).

The shutter is in full swing, almost in rhythm with the riverboat wheel (we'll come back to this), throughout the novel. It is placed on the highest promontory, the observation deck, the figure of the colonial sovereign (Kurtz will be brought here to die while shouting, "Close the shutter!"), and controls the rhythms of observation, revealing and hiding behind it, like a visor of Hamlet's father's ghost, letting in light or shadow, protecting from or letting in death. But nature itself, from the second mention of the shutter in the novel (as indicated by the word search I conducted as I re-read the story on my Kindle, glowing in the dark), works like a prosthesis, *tekhne* the truth of *physis*, letting in the light or protecting from it: "When the sun rose there was a white fog, very warm and clammy, and more blinding than the night. It did not shift or drive; it was just there, standing all around you like something solid. At night, perhaps, it lifted as a shutter lifts.[9]

The shutter also opens and closes like the rhythm of the steamboat wheel, when "being shot at! I stepped in quickly to close the shutter on

---

9   Cf. "Haze: Nebular Modernism" by Michael Connor (2006): "The associations between photography and spiritualism at the end of the nineteenth century may have been at work somewhere behind that image of the fog lifting and coming down again like a vast eyelid or the shutter of a camera. Photographers of mediums and séances not only sought to capture the spectral masses of spirit-bodies, or the billowing cumulus of ectoplasm, they also seemed to see an analogy between the actual apparatus of the photograph, so given to producing silvered mistiness, and this gelling of light or spirit-energy into indeterminate form. Conrad's interest in undulatory and radiation theories may also have helped him appreciate the effects of X-ray radiation, discovered only four years before the writing of *Heart of Darkness*. On the one hand, X-rays penetrated the flabbily obscuring veils of the flesh, to reveal the bony essence of what lay within. But X-rays also left visible traces of that pervaded flesh, dissolving it to a spectral haze or plasma, which, as Martine Hennard Dutheil de la Rochère suggests (2004), seems close to the hollow, insubstantial bodies found in *Heart of Darkness* (the figure of Kurtz, for example, whose form will appear 'unsteady, long, pale, indistinct, like a vapour exhaled by the earth' (Conrad 1971, 66)." I am grateful to Michael O'Rourke for pointing out this essay to me. For further discussion of the invention of x-rays and *Heart of Darkness*, see "Sounding the Hollow Heart of the West: X-rays and the *technique de la mort*," de la Rochère, in Latwoo (2012).

the landside… I had to lean right out to swing the heavy shutter, as though a veil had been removed from my eyes… The twigs shook, swayed, and rustled, the arrows flew out of them, and then the shutter came to." The shutter opens and closes the entrance of death, which will soon befall the steam master. It is also a prosthetic machine of veiling and unveiling, the lifting of the shutter lifts the veil from Marlow's eyes, thus again operates as an interruption and photographic fixing of the narrative. Like a blinking of a camera, a shutter could be thought of as a cinematic, prosthetic eyelid. But death is also lurking behind the shutter, the mechanical death, the weaponized gaze here coinciding with the lifting and closing of the shutter: "a loaded Martini-Henry leaning in one corner, a tiny table, and the steering-wheel. It had a wide door in front and a broad shutter at each side." "The steam master had dropped everything, to throw the shutter open and let off that Martini-Henry," a gun seen on page thirty has to go off at page fifty, to paraphrase Chekhov. In turn, death will come through the shutter: "I threw my head back to a glinting whizz that traversed the pilot-house, in at one shutter-hole and out at the other." "A spear came in, thrown or lunged through the opening," and killed the helmsman.

"'Close the shutter,' said Kurtz suddenly one day; 'I can't bear to look at this.' I did so. There was a silence. 'Oh, but I will wring your heart yet!' he cried at the invisible wilderness." And immediately after in the narrative, "One morning he gave me a packet of papers and a photograph."

Close the shutter, a photograph.[10]

The rhythm of the steamboat wheel, the rhythm of the wheel paddle, throbs or *pulses* like the heartbeat, the *Herz/Hertzschlag*, throughout the text, moving or exposing the narrative on the silvery surface of the river, and then capturing and retaining the story by the movement of the shutter, the snap shots both photographic and weaponized. *Heart of Darkness* exposes or writes down, in this way, the very genealogy of the cinematic, by tying together the wheel paddle, the invention of the semi-automatic revolver weaponry, and the photo-cinematic.

"It was in 1861," Paul Virilio writes in his *War and Cinema, the Logistics of Perception*, and all this follows as a genealogy, without interruption,

---

10   *Shutter* and *shudder*, as in "shudder with horror," are practically indiscernible when pronounced, and separated only by a voiced/unvoiced consonant phonetic opposition. A double consonant, in fact.

one from another, "whilst traveling on a paddle-steamer and watching its wheel, that the future Colonel Gatling hit upon the idea of a cylindrical, crank-driven machine gun [named after him the Gatling gun]. In 1874 the Frenchman Jules Janssen took inspiration from the multichambered Colt (patented in 1832) to invent an astronomical revolving unit that could take a series of photographs [when attached to a telescope]. On the basis of this idea, Etienne-Jules Marey then perfected his chronotopographic rifle, which allowed its user to aim at and photograph an object moving though space" (Virilio in Kittler, 124). Commenting on this quote, Friedrich Kittler concludes: "The history of the movie camera thus coincides with the history of automatic weapons" (Kittler 124), originating in the movement of the steamboat wheel paddle to which in *Heart of Darkness* are attached a shutter and a loaded Martini-Henry, the colonialist's rifle of choice.[11]

That steamboat operating like a weaponized camera has already been encountered during Marlow's travel to Africa. That is, the description of the warship, and the construction of the other as enemy, has already been established by the time Marlow starts sailing on the steamboat up the river.

> It appears the French had one of their wars going on thereabouts. Her ensign dropped limp like a rag; the muzzles of the long six-inch guns stuck out all over the low hull; the greasy, slimy swell swung her up lazily and let her down, swaying her thin masts. In the empty immensity of earth, sky, and water, there she was, incomprehensible, firing into a continent. Pop, would go one of the six-inch guns; a small flame would dart and vanish, a little white smoke would disappear, a tiny projectile would give a feeble screech— and nothing happened. Nothing could happen. There was a touch of insanity in the proceeding, a sense of lugubrious drollery in the sight; and

---

11   The steamboat is thus at the origin of the cinematic, just as Disney's "Steamboat Willy" (1928) is at the origin of cinematic animation. We will soon see the symbolic relevance of the two furnaces blazing in the ship and energizing this narrative, one for operating the steamboat, and the other in the boat metal shop for fixing it, the very *in-animation* of modernity (Cf. Wills, *Inanimation*, forthcoming).

it was not dissipated by somebody on board assuring me earnestly there was a camp of natives—we called them enemies!—hidden out of sight somewhere.

*Nellie* is thus already an extension of the war machine, even before Marlow boards the ship. One should note two things, however: the description of the warship is given at a distance ("empty immensity"), as if filmed by a tele-lens camera, with a very ironic depiction of the "ensign," the flag, as a rag, flown in "one of their wars," all of this had a touch of insanity. Because, precisely nothing is what unfolds in this "war" enterprise, "nothing could happen"! The war machine is the nihilistic machine, it produces, precisely, nothing. Except madness, and curiously, appears as if followed by a canned laughter, as if it were a TV show, a sense of lugubrious drollery. And while this firing into the continent is going on, "the men in that lonely ship were dying of fever at the rate of three a day." The ship, engaged in the production of enemies (notice the invisible quotation marks, a subtle rhetorical distinction, a doubling within the story itself, between the use and mention of the word "enemy,"—"enemies" they called them) and building the protective wall against them, is all the while dying from within, the autoimmunitary effect of protection turning against those who serve on this "lonely ship." Does one not see in this description the sad enterprise, funny if it were not catastrophic, of the production of enemies in the United States as we live it, the enormous investment of money, materiel, and simply human bodies, precisely into nothingness in Iraq and Afghanistan ("one of their wars going on thereabouts") while the returning soldiers die of suicide and post-traumatic madness in the thousands, mission accomplished! And while the country is spiraling into more and more cuts, social and political self-amputations and self mutilations, autoimmunitary suicides imaginary or real, self-inflicted destruction of the very functioning of the state discerned immediately after the so called "9-11" by Miller and Derrida. J. Hillis Miller wrote about it in his essay on "Derrida's Politics of Autoimmunity," which he delivered at the University of Florida and which was featured in *The First Sail*:

> We were promised that invading and occupying Iraq would make us safer at home. Exactly the opposite has happened.

Iraq has now become what it was not before our occupation, a breeding ground for terrorists. Iran is winning control of Iraq as a result of our invasion. Our standing or credit in the world has diminished immeasurably. We are now the object of widespread hatred, distrust, and disdain, in part because we are a rogue state that ignores international law and the Geneva convention, not to speak of our own Constitution. Nobody can be sure what mad act we will next commit. We torture and hold indefinitely without charge detainees in a prison falsely claimed to be extra-territorial. We operate secret prisons around the world where prisoners are held and tortured through what is called, in an extraordinary example of double speak, "Extraordinary Rendition." We have suspended our own precious civil liberties through something with the chilling Orwellian name of The Patriot Act. The Department of Homeland Security has conspicuously failed to secure our ports, our borders, or our chemical plants and nuclear power plants. We are immensely more insecure than we were before, trembling in a terror that we have ourselves created. (Miller 2009, 225)

This wholesale dismantling of civil liberties and the autoimmunitary destruction of the society by means of the mechanisms of purported protection is also related to a certain techno-mediatic transformation of the world we live in and as we know it, an apocalyptic end of it, in fact: "It will be nothing less than the end of the world as we have come to think of in these days of teletechnoeconomicomediatic globalization" (Miller 2009, 226). Thus, we are still in the heart of darkness, "trembling in a terror that we have ourselves created," the terror one step away from horror.

*Heart of Darkness* thus operates something like a self-consuming, auto-devouring of the world, what Russell Samolsky ingeniously calls "the apocalypse as consuming cannibal" (Samolsky 2011, 93). The emblem of this devouring is the mouth which appears in the story on several occasions, most notably as Kurtz's mouth, the voracious appetite of capitalism, swallowing via Kurtz "Earth with all its mankind." The other mention of the mouth, that of the river, makes this into a geo-political, global auto-consumption, the mouth of the Thames and the mouth of the Congo, swallowing each other's tail/tale, forming a Moebius strip whereby each other's tail/tale refers to the destruction of the entire Earth, and all men with it. There is a doubling of these geopolitical mouths and a quasi-symmetrical relation between the "primitivism," "darkness" of Africa, and the gaze of the colonial Roman soldier cast on the primitivism and wilderness of the marshes of London (nothing fit for a civilized man to *eat*), darkness that was here "yesterday" (preceded by "we live in a flicker"). Thus, the story consumes itself in a kind of eternal hunger, prefiguring the hunger of capitalism qua an imperial war-like civilizing mission (the destining of the West, as Heidegger would put it) by swallowing the entire Earth.[12] This voracity lingers in the seemingly quiet environments of "civilization" too, barely suppressing the capitalist hunger: in the sepulchral city, "As we sat over our ver*mouths* (my italics—DK) he glorified the Company's business."[13]

The relationship between a certain techno-mediaticity, and the warmachine, it has been established, constitutes the very fiber of this narrative. *Heart of Darkness* is a story of the mediatic conquest, the shocking voracity of techno-mediaticity, in its appropriation of the racial other. The story after all explicitly thematizes the hyper production and accumulation of ivory *whiteness*, something that Kurtz excels in over all other merchants, the blinding whiteness at/as the heart of darkness. There is one remaining element of the techno-mediatic apparatus which has not been mentioned, which binds the technical and the racial, as it were in an

---

12  Cf. Royle, about "The Secret Sharer": "Conrad's opening comes strangely to bear the tale's ending, the tale sending its tail-end to be swallowed up in its mouth. The episode circles back into retelling and rereading."

13  In Martin Heidegger's 1942 seminar about another river, the Danube, the *Ister*, the civilizational, geo-onto-political loop ("the essence of Western humankind" 1996, 43) closes itself between Greece and Germany. The river Danube flows "rückwertz," backwards, and finds its true destination in Schwarzwald, coming to "one's own" and to "mother earth" (1996, 21, 43), swallowing itself in this journeying, by coming to the mouth of German language: "'Hertha' is the Germanic name for mother earth" (1996, 43). And "what is one's own in this case is whatever belongs to the fatherland of the Germans" (1996, 49). This seminar, written in 1942 (1942!), starts with the quote from Hoelderlin's poem *The Ister*: "May the fire come!" "Jetzt komme Feuer!," it starts by a welcoming invocation of the advent of the Holocaust. The great err greatly. I addressed the seminar on *The Ister* in "Nonbiodegradables" (2007) and in my film *Frozen Time, Liquid Memories* (2013).

electric shock performed by the narrative. It is the blow Marlow receives when, watching through his binoculars, he spots the shrunken heads on the stakes, four turned away, and one gaping at him: "and its first result was to make me throw my head back as if before a blow." What he sees is not "ornamental, but symbolic," thus already marked by an internal narrative distance, re-working and reproduction. Nothing can be seen "as is" in this story, everything is already processed and doubled by the mediatic ("symbolic"), and in this case, explicitly prosthetic gaze. Not only does the ship have a shutter, but it also has a lens attached to it, and is engaged in the tele-technological representation or symbolic appropriation of the racial other. The gaze cast on the shrunken heads, decapitated and serialized, preserved or mummified by light, reminds one of Bazin's dictum that the mummy is the ontology of the photographic and cinematic gaze. This is what Marlow sees: "black, dried, sunken, with closed eyelids—a head that seemed to sleep at the top of that pole, and, with the shrunken dry lips showing a narrow white line of the teeth, was smiling, too, smiling continuously at some endless and jocose dream of that eternal slumber."

Two effects of these "symbols" (repeated twice) on Marlow are worth mentioning. One, that he is "blown back" in shock of this magnified apparition, his head is "thrown back," he suffers a shocking revelation. But that shock may have something to do not only with the gruesome image, which in the narrative is not without parodic elements, but with the very realization of the machinic and technical production and reproduction of the racial other, which is opened up by the prosthetic gaze cast at the heads (the heads in fact resist this appropriative colonizing gaze by smiling back at it). Another sense of shock is that Marlow's whole body suffers a shudder (shutter?) of displacement, having been traversed by the prosthetic gaze which dispossesses him as a gazing sovereign subject, inasmuch as it seemingly empowers him. "I put down the glass, and the head that had appeared near enough to be spoken to seemed at once to have leaped away from me into inaccessible distance." The medium has taken over and the sense of displacement (what is near is actually in "an inaccessible distance": this is a definition of the mediatic or, say, televisual, *par excellence*) is now haunting Marlow himself.

The source of the shock may also stem from the fact that the scene stages the mediatic, technical, representation of the racial other (as

People gathered in the forest, at the passage of Conrad's steamboat "Roi des Belges" ("King of the Belgians") in 1888. From Alexandre Delcommune, *Vingt Années de Vie Africaine* (Brussels: Ferdinand Larciers, 1922)

"symbol" or image) now in captivity of a machine much larger than the immediacy of the warring ship, the serialized techno-mediatic reproducibility of the racial and racialized other. As the effect of that technical reproduction, the racialized bodies have started to pile up as the effect of tele-techno-mediatic massification of death. From the desiccated heads that Marlow sees to the images of the camps in *Night and Fog* is only a step.

The gaze cast at the racialized African other, and that may be the shock experienced by the white master, will soon be turned much closer to home, to Europe itself (the *whole of Europe made Kurtz*, as the narrative has it). In this lies the proleptic, "futurological power" (Royle) of Conrad's writing, the paradigmatic conditions which the following history will fill in, already being written up, photographed and archived, en-crypted *in advance* in Conrad's narratives. They "encrypt 'the worst to come,' and hauntingly inscribe a figure of the traumatic as the return of the unknown. As Derrida remarks in *Philosophy in a Time of Terror*, 'traumatism is produced by the *future*, by the *to come*, by the threat of the worst to come, rather than by an aggression that is 'over and done with' (Auto 97)" (Royle). For Kurtz is a kind of shortcut between technomediatic modernity, colonial capitalism and the racialization of the other, a blow, a mediatic or electric shock, a *short-circuit* of modernity, as well as its terrible goal or finitude, a *Kurtzschluss*, the worst yet to come.[14]

Kurtz, the white master and the master accumulator, aggregator of whiteness who turned native, surrounded by *impaled* bodies, touched by the unspeakable horror of cannibalism, thus a cannibal himself (the voracious mouth swallowing the whole world), reminds one of that other master of darkness, arising with and in the darkness of the tele-techno mediatic and cinematic at the turn of the century in London, Count Dracula, Vlad Draculea, the Impaler. He also lives at the heart of darkness, his pale, white skin can be burnt by the sun, his skin, like the little film skin, *pellicule*, cannot be exposed to the light without burning; he is surrounded by impaled bodies (supposedly erected after Dracula's "going native," after his encounter with the Muslim, Ottoman Turk, the other, Dracula "the avenger of the Battle of Kosovo," practically a modern day Slobodan Milošević). In "real" history Dracula was the protector of Christian Europe who then turned into a demonic Messiah (*Hic est enim corpus meum, hic est enim calix sanguinis mei*). Dracula is the cannibalistic and cannibalizing Other, the dark incorporated underbelly and the unseen mirror/horror image of the empire/vEmpire, sucking at the very heart and veins of it, hunted by the imperial war machine and the tele-techno-medico-mediatic "gang of light" led, of course, in their search for Dracula in the darkness of so many ruins, crypts (one is tempted to say "caves" too), by a gun slinging *Texan*, Quincey P. Morris. (Hundred, and ninety years respectively, in 2012, since the publication of *Dracula* and *Heart of Darkness*). As the "West" projects the cannibalizing onto the other, it itself is *doubled* down with hunger. That *projection* is also part of the cinematic hunger of these two narratives.

But to remain close to the issues of technology and the production of both narratives. The novel, *Dracula*, was the first text to feature the Kodak camera and make use of photography, just "as a testimony of its accuracy," "Joseph Conrad's portrayal of circumstances in the Belgian Congo was headed 'Kodak from the Congo'" (Wicke 583).[15]

---

14  *Kurzschluss*, German, "short-circuit," *Collins German-English Dictionary* (2013).

15  Cf. Kittler's pioneering analysis of *Dracula* and technology in his "Dracula's

As to the worst yet to come. When Conrad made his voyage to Congo, a family friend, a certain Professor Kopernicki, a well-known Polish craniologist and phrenologist, professor at Krakow University, asked him to bring him back a few skulls for his museum collection of cranial racial profiles. In his *Physical Characteristics of the Population of Galicia*, Professor Kopernicki distinguished himself by his research in phrenology, which "sought to confirm in physical anthropology that the Jews were not 'native' to Galicia" (Wolff 243). There is no evidence that Conrad actually brought back to Professor Kopernicki any skulls for his research in physical anthropology, or that he shared with the professor such racial geo-political convictions.[16] However, the skulls in the story ("'I always ask leave, in the interests of science, to measure the crania of those going out there,'" the doctor tells Marlow) are inscribed in the long history of the representation of racial others by means of cranial features, the medical and scientific essentialization and stereo-typing of race preparing the Holocaust. When Marlow looks at the skulls, already a symbol, at the racialized other processed by the technical apparatus and the gaze of the white master, himself the sovereign on top of the observation deck like a watchtower in a camp, he is setting the scene for the serial,

---

Legacy," in which he describes various ways by which technology (typewriters, for example), devours, vampirizes from within the literary text of the novel: "Under the conditions of technology, literature disappears (like metaphysics for Heidegger) into the un-death of its endless ending" (Kittler 1997, 83). For the relationship between the vampire and the vEmpire, as well as for the notion of the vampire as a cinematic substrate, film, burnt by light, and the discovery of the first appearance of the Kodak brand name in literature, or for the war over Kosovo in the former Yugoslavia as if it were an episode from Stoker's *Dracula*, see Kujundžić, "vEmpire, Glocalisation, and the Melancholia of the Sovereign," *Comparatist*, Spring 2005. Russell Samolsky makes a convincing case that "Kurtz is ultimately a figure of the undead" (108, and repeated several times), but does not make a connection with Bram Stoker's novel, the initial title of which was, indeed, *The Undead*. Cf. also Miller: "The illumination by the tale is 'spectral'" ... it turns everything into a phantom, something that has come back from the dead..." (Miller 2001, 125).

16  See the analysis of *The Heart of Darkness* by Russell Samolsky, in his *Apocalyptic Futures* (2011), a book wholeheartedly and deservedly welcomed and endorsed on the back cover by J. Hillis Miller, which briefly mentions Kopernicki but does not extend the analysis or draw the conclusions I propose.

industrial production and processing of the racialized others, by means of tele-technic and scientific apparatuses (a technical stereo-typing), tied to the work and ideology of scientists proving that "the Jews were not native to Galicia." Setting the stage which should blow not only Marlow's but anyone's mind, which is the mind-blowing explosion of European rationality, leading to the nihilistic (Nellieistic?: *Nellie* has not one but—as with everything else in this story—*two* furnaces on board) conclusion of modernity, the end, the *Schluss* and *Kurtzschluss* of all modernity in the camps. Krakow, the cradle of European science, with one of the oldest universities in Europe, the Jagiellonian University, where Professor Kopernicki worked, is also only a short hour away from Oswiecim, Auschwitz, the short-circuit, the blazing, flickering *Kurtzschluss* of European rationality, the burning "proof" that the Jews were not native to Europe. *Ashenglorie. Nothing* to see there, you see?

When Marlowe looks at the skulls with their cranial orbs, while experiencing the effect of tele-technological displacement, he is gazing at the anamorphic history of all those bodies circulating around (*orbiting*) the white master suddenly alone in the universe with an infinite capacity for destruction. Sigmund Freud, writing about various scientific revolutions in the Renaissance and on (we are in the middle of the eco-technical as described by J. Hillis Miller on numerous other occasions), in his *Civilization and Its Discontents*, called modern man, a man "become a prosthetic God" (Freud 44). That experience was started in many ways by the Copernican revolution which first posited the heliocentric theory, in *De revolutionibus orbium coelestium*. It placed the sun in the center of the universe, a displacement of God from the center of the universe, and prompted the tele-techno-scientific revolution which soon followed by the invention of the telescope, which will place man in the position of the prosthetic god.

When Marlow looks at the cranial orbits of the heads, is he not himself that almighty prosthetic god, armed with the tele-technical apparatus, and inscribed in the heart of the history of modernity, both on the side of the scientific racialization of the other, and on the side of the scientific and telescopic revolution and rationalization which started in Krakow, at the Jagielonnian University by Copernicus, which placed man at the center of the world as the prosthetic god? Of this illustrious forefather, Copernicus, according to Larry Wolf, the authoritative historian of East and Central Europe, Professor Kopernicki is, quite literally, a direct descendant.

The prosthetic eye which sees the eye of the other, which beholds and is looked back by the eye of the other, conflates the tele-prosthetic gaze and death, the empty orb of the skull which looks back at me, it is the I/eye who is looked back through the prosthetic machine, the I/eye, inflicting the shocking blow to Marlowe, in that he becomes controlled by the spectacle and the specter. We are at the very heart of the society of the spectral, which, like a ghost, like a specter, may be discerned, in the phantomatic, prosthetic glow. "The society of the spectral, where I am sovereignly controlled by the specters, subjected by phantoms, where I am not anymore except as a subject of my death, represents a grand theater, a total *mise en scene* of the eye of the other.... This eye is my body become prosthesis of power, is at that place the point of confusion [a shortcurcuit, a *Kurtzschlus*] of indecision, of indifference, between an automaton and death, where the flow of the borders of the living manifest themselves, the borders between living and non-living" (Margel 2012, 60). Marlow's gaze is the gaze of the prosthetic biopolitics, the biopower projecting in the spectral halo all the automated production of the non-living racialized other, the racialized other as the mechanically, tele-technologically reproduced non-living, in order to anesthetize the viewer "back home" in the glow of the TV, to its destruction from Auschwitz to Rwanda, from Srebrenica to Iraq.

Thus *Heart of Darkness* has a capacity to receive the subsequent history of which it is a photographic or mediatic lure. In Philippe Lacoue-Labarthe's essay published in 2007, and recently published in English in a volume dedicated to it, with an extensive introduction titled "Prologue: Revisiting '*Heart of Darkness* Revisited' (in the company of Philippe Lacoue-Labarthe)" by J. Hillis Miller, this history is identified as the entire destining of the West: "L'horreur occidentale," the horror of the West. In the overt colonial instrumentalization of the world Lacoue-Labarthe discerns the very "revelation d'une technique de la mort," "revelation of the *technique of death*" of the Western will to power. When Marlow recoils (like a gun recoils after a shot) from seeing the sculls through his lenses, he has repeated the very barbarity of the West: "To recoil from the horror is the Western *barbarity* itself" (Lacoue-Labarthe in Lawtoo, 2012, 118). Such is the lesson from Lacoue-Labarthe's essay on *Heart of Darkness* taken, for example, by François Warin. In his reading of Lacoue-Labarthe in the same volume, this story is the model representative of the "techne that works as a dangerous supplement, and the West that defended itself through a technical and colonial inspection of the totality of the planet" (Warin 2012, 134). Warin discerns in *Heart of Darkness* a coupling of "the most powerful and dangerous media," with the stereotyping of racialization, which "is inextricably tied to the name of Auschwitz" as it is to the "case of Rwanda": the horror "of the West" (2012, 134, 136).

The story reveals something which in a recent book Jean Luc-Nancy analyzed, in light of the catastrophe at the Fukushima nuclear power plant, as a "nihilism," "le revers exact de ce que nous avions confié à l' Espérance de la technique comme maîtrise d'un destin," the "exact reverse of what we have confided to the hope of the technique as the mastery of our destiny" (Nancy, 56). Nancy does not mention Conrad on this occasion, unlike Nick Royle in a similar context. In his essay "Reading Joseph Conrad: Episodes From the Coast" (2013), Royle brings into direct correlation the proleptic, futurological power of "The Secret Sharer" and "Typhoon," with the catastrophe of Fukushima, "the black gully," "the pit" "the awful depth," left in the wake of this catastrophe and as if described or snap-shot in advance and deposited in the dark chamber (the "black and secret chamber of the sea" in which "darkness palpitates" in "Typhoon," for example). This "secret chamber, " this "pit" is deposited there for future *development* by and of Conrad's narratives, thus forcing on the readers the recognition of the urgency of "ecological thought" or action (Royle references Timothy Morton's book by the same name). Because, as Nancy says, "there are no more natural catastrophes: there is only one civilizational catastrophe which propagates itself on all occasions" (Nancy, 57).

*Heart of Darkness* receives this horror, but does not reproduce it "directly." By means of technical mediations, it deflects the ultimate apocalypse, it is "parabolic, an allegory, and following Derrida's essay on apocalypses, this is a quasi apocalypse or a parodic apocalypse, an apocalypse that unveils the impossibility of an ultimate unveiling" (Miller,

"Prologue" 26). This insistence on the technicality of the story itself, its rhetoric, or what I discern as mediatic photo-cinematic reproducibility, marks a difference from Lacoue-Labarthe's insistence on this story being "literal," "not allegorical," with a meaning of words "not different from the meaning they enunciate" ("Prologue" 120); in that regard, Miller's interpretation differs from Lacoue-Labarthe's. Nevertheless, regardless of this difference (one tropological or techno-mediatic, the other literal), Miller and Lacoue-Labarthe ultimately come to the same conclusion of the epochal significance of Conrad's writing. The prominence given to the essays by Miller and Lacoue-Labarthe in this volume also recognizes the epochal, groundbreaking power of their writing about Conrad.

Why insist on the technicity and mediaticity of this story? The technique of death which is the West, and which gives form to the story or history of destruction, horror and terror, the very myth of the West, is juxtaposed in the story to another type of technics, that of the receptacle of the dark chamber, a cinematic, photographic prosthetic *khora* which gives place in reverse to the represented world, an active and passive (*actipassive*—Derrida) receiving of the narrative thus opening a possibility of inversion, of uprooting and revolution of the visible beyond realistic aesthetization (Nick Royle calls *crytpoaesthetics* this kind of aesthetics found in Conrad). The narrator's very body experiences this shock when it recoils as it receives the images of skulls through the binoculars. "Now I had suddenly a nearer view, and its first result was to make me throw my head back as if before a blow. Then I went carefully from post to post with my glass, and I saw my mistake." The story does not set up some pristine nature, *physis*, or bios, bare life, etc., as a counter model to the predictable repetition of technical destruction, but *another* type of technics in life or as life, of survival, operating as a passive photo-cinematic receiver of the narrative, exposing it and at the same time attempting a reverse and a revolt (maybe even a realization of a "mistake"), in the dark, thus opening it also to the unseen and perhaps a different, non-programmed future. *A pulsating light in the heart of darkness.*[17]

---

17 These reflections owe a lot to David Wills' *Dorsality*. Cf. his reading in *Dorsality* of Sade's novels figured as a cinematic projection. His more recent work is a book called *Inanimation*. I am particularly grateful to him for sharing with me this work in progress. See for example this ingenious formula, eminently applicable to *Heart of Darkness*, in Wills' work tracing "the animation

The cinematic reception (the volatile silver substrate, both reflective and receptive) inscribed in the story functions as a proleptic and prosthetic opening to the Other, as Hillis would say in the "Critic as Host," the risky opening, maybe even to the "uncanniest of guests." Without such risk no event takes place and no one or nothing arrives. This risky opening also allows the story to perpetually, like *in a flicker*, prepare and receive future readings/viewings, in the time yet to come, for better or for worse. *Heart of Darkness*, to use Wills' interpretation of Paul Celan on the issue of survival, is "traversed by a radical otherness, an otherness whose structure, as we have consistently insisted, cannot not include the non-natural, the prosthetic, the artificial, the inanimate," ... "the substitution for life of an inanimate, inorganic, artificial form of continuance or survivance."(Wills, *Inanimation*, forthcoming).

The technical reception of the narrative opens it up to a disorientation and uncalculated arrival, "heterogeneous to myth ... and its philosophical *telos*" (Derrida, *On The Name* 113). By means of the techno-receptivity, it operates like a *khora*, "a story that is reported and in which another story will take place in its turn" (Derrida, *On The Name* 117). Such doubling within the story, a receptive non-dis-closure, gives hope that the epochal trajectory of the West, the *telos* of its arrival to the violent self, can be postponed, deflected, or reoriented to different, *heterogeneous* shores. At the very least this difference of the story with itself opens a space/delayed time for reflection, distances the reader from the immediacy of the "horror," postpones it, and forces a reflexive distance and spacing. In that space lies our last chance before the ultimate auto-immunitary self-digestion of the Entire world, and all mankind with it.

∼

All of the above is a response to the provocation to reading, of Hillis Miller's reading of *Heart of Darkness*. It abides in the direction of these great essays, particularly towards the conclusion of his "Should We Read *Heart of Darkness*?" which speaks of:

---

of inanimate marks, from something that *pulsates* otherwise in the conjunctive play of blank and *blackened space*" in the work of Paul Celan and Hélène Cixous (my italics).

> The promise of universal prosperity made for the new economy dominated by science and transformative communications techniques,... It also echoes the promises made by the right wing ideologies, even the most unspeakably brutal, for example the Nazi promise of a thousand-year Reich. We are inundated, swamped, and engulfed every day by the present form of these promises—in newspapers and magazines, on television, in advertising, on the Internet, in political and policy pronouncements. All these promise that everything will get bigger, faster, better, more 'user friendly,' and lead to worldwide prosperity. These promises are all made by language or other signs, "the gift of expression, the bewildering, the illuminating, the most exalted and the most contemptible, the pulsating stream of light, or the deceitful flow from the heart of impenetrable darkness...." [*Heart of Darkness*] should be read as a powerful exemplary revelation of the ideology of capitalist imperialism, including its racism and sexism. (Miller 2001, 135)

At the intersection of the tele-techno-mediatic, racist and capitalistic, *Heart of Darkness* navigates an interminable waterway, operates like the task of deconstruction "of the idea of Western culture" (Wolfreys 1998, 181) an interminable analysis. That is the conclusion suggested by Julian Wolfreys, in his response to Hillis Miller's reading of the story. In the words of Jacques Derrida, which Wolfreys quotes, "deconstruction is always incomplete, of an incompletion which is not negativity of a lack, it is interminable..." (Derrida in Wolfreys 1998, 181).

### A Koda(k): The First Sail: J. Hillis Miller and the Theory to Come

In his *Athens, Still Remains*, a reflection on photography, Jacques Derrida describes something that can be termed the birth of theory out of the tele-techno-mediatic. Out of that which in theory (but not "in theory," but in truly everyday practice as well), binds a certain sense of finitude with ethics and philosophy. The scene of Socrates' verdict is well known, Plato writes about it in *Phaedo,* and Derrida retraces it in his book.

The Roi des Belges, the Belgian riverboat Conrad commanded on the upper Congo, 1889. From Alexandre Delcommune, *Vingt Années de Vie Africaine* (Brussels: Ferdinand Larciers, 1922).

"'It happened that the stern of the ship which Athenians sent to Delos was crowned on the day before the trial.' What ship? The one, following an ancient Athenian tradition ... that once carried *seven boys and seven girls* whom Theseus led to Crete and whom he then saved in saving his own skin. It is in short this saving, and the pledge that followed, that is responsible for granting Socrates a reprieve of a few days, a provisional salvation, in this case, the time for an unforgettable discourse on true salvation, salvation by philosophy. Because in order to give thanks for the safe conduct of the young boys and girls led by Theseus, the Athenians had made a pledge—a pledge to Apollo. They pledged to organize a yearly pilgrimage or a 'procession,' (*theoria*) to Delos. The law (*nomos*) of Athens thus prescribes that the entire time of the *theoria* 'the city must be pure and no one may be publicly executed until the ship has gone to Delos and back' (Phaedo 58b). This time is not calculable, and neither is the delay, therefore, because the voyage took a long time and the winds were unpredictable.... Such an uncontrollable delay mechanism (what is called *physis*), such incalculability, granted Socrates an indeterminable reprieve. One knows where the *theoria* begins, but one does not see the end. One can determine the *arkhe tes theorias*, the moment when the priest crowns the stern of the ship, but one never knows when the *theoria* will end, and when a sail will announce the return from Cape Sunion. ... One never knows when the *theoria* will end." (Derrida 33)

The arrival of the first sail [a sail, as J. Hillis Miller says in his essay on *Heart of Darkness*, a synecdoche for ship: "I see a sail" means "I see a ship"] visible from the Cape Sunion will be the last sail. Like a shutter on the camera coming after a delay, the *techne* and *physis* sharing the heartbeat interrupted by *inanimation*, it will bring the verdict, the pronouncement of truth, to theory and to Socrates.

Thus, philosophy, theory, if they are worthy of their Attic salt, are always turned towards and live between that first sail as the last sail, towards the to-come of the inevitable, the only time we have, life itself, waiting for the first sail to be the last, and in that waiting *expose* that which is or what gives in fact the time for the theory to come. That delay opens theory to life and the waiting for the other at the moment of death, and thus to responsibility, but it also opens theory, in our finitude, in the infinite finitude which is our life, to all the questions of ethics, murder, capital punishment, state terror, eco-catastrophe, theory unfolds as a work of delay in life itself, as life itself, deconstruction or postponement of the worst. Because the worst has already happened, on its way; the theory is always as a task ahead of us, of the yet to come.

J. Hillis Miller's is a theory that has always already been ahead of us, *a-venir*. Which is what deconstruction, what every theory worthy of its name is: a vigil, out of the profound sense of the finitude of our lives and the finitude of the world, or of our shared resources, over the urgent task of reading as a resistance and warding off of so many catastrophes, a counter signing or a counter sailing or counter smiling as an affirmation and joy. Theory as the knowledge of how to set the sails and harness the *pneuma*, the wind and breath-turn, the very soul in the sails. One should and ought to read J. Hillis Miller, precisely as an emblem of such theory of "joyous affirmation," theory to come and theory that comes, *jouissant* and *a-venir*. The theory to come which makes possible, like the movement of the water beneath a boat, like a *Khora* which gives place in the movement of withdrawal, all our theoretico-critical sailings and adventures. Like a gentle version of the Ocean in Shelley's *Triumph of Life*, J. Hillis Miller floats our boats; he certainly rocks *my* boat.

In the last scene of *The First Sail*, after he has disappeared, dissolved in the light-house which then began blinking, pulsing in the dark, blinking as a warning to ships and thus preventing a disaster, and flickering in the film, in the very flickering of the flicker, riddled with light, ah, after all the credits have gone by, at the very end of *The First Sail*, J. Hillis Miller appears in his boat, and pronounces the verdict. Let these be the last words, or the last sail as the first, these words arrive and project an *aletheia* of the cinematic image on a screen, veil or sail, they launch everything ahead of us, incalculably, interminably.

Picture this: J. Hillis Miller to the camera, smiling, sailing: "Everything was put together wrong!"[18]

---

18 The following is an exchange I had with J. Hillis Miller after the screening

of *The First Sail* at Brown University on September 24, 2013. It has occurred to me, during the screening, and in the discussion during which Hillis again commented on Yeats' "Cold Heaven," that Hillis himself was "riddled with light" in the video, in all ambiguities of the term: he was shot through with light, but also turned into a riddle, a secret, a shibboleth. This is the reading of "The Cold Heaven" I proposed to him, as well as to use the line from it as an epigraph. Here is our correspondence:On Sep 27, 2013, at 12:55 PM, "Kujundzic,Dragan" <dragan@ufl.edu> wrote:

> Dear Hillis,

> Greetings from New Haven, I am at the train station waiting for the train to NYC. I gave a talk on the Danube yesterday at Yale, a colleague in Slavic invited me to talk to her class. Afterwards I had a lunch with Henry, it went great. We discussed the project, his introduction to the film book, and spoke of you a lot and fondly. It has been agreed that he will do the intro by December. So we are all set. In the meantime I will be editing the volume. I will include all your suggestions, of course.

> The screening at Brown also went well. They hosted a dinner afterwards, all was very friendly and generous.

> Your talk was great, could I have a copy? I may still include some elements of it in my essay. We had a bit of problems with the connection, that's why you may not have had as many questions afterwards.

> May I run something by you? I am also tinkering with an idea that Cold Heaven may be related to the production of the cinematic. It is all (well, not only, but to me it seems suddenly predominant) about being "riddled with light," "rook deLIGHTing heaven," etc., which are captured by the ice which burns (the silicate lens and the burning of the light on the film), producing more and more ice capturing naked life (bio-scope), becoming a quick ghost. In a word (or entire "books"), a camera. Every frame a freeze frame. Does this sound plausible?

> "Riddled with light," I am thinking of making this the epigraph of the whole volume.

> It fits my analysis of the Heart of Darkness as a cinematic apparatus, so I am thinking including a paragraph in my essay.

> Thank you again for your participation in the screening event, it was as always an honor to appear with you on the same stage.

>> I'll be in touch.

> All my best,

> Dragan

From: J. Hillis Miller [jhmiller@uci.edu]

Sent: Saturday, September 28, 2013 1:09 PM

To: Kujundzic,Dragan

Subject: Re: greetings from New Haven

Dear Dragan: Nice to catch a glimpse of you before Skype died entirely. It had worked with Brown's technician when we tried it out a week earlier and worked flawlessly earlier in the summer for a long interview with someone at Pittsburgh. My guess is that my feeble DSL was overloaded at that time of the day by multiple users, as it is at this moment on a Saturday, with, I'd guess, my neighbors watching streaming video and taking up the meager bandwidth. So emails are not getting through either way. This will go through later today, I hope. Extremely annoying. Boondocks.

Glad you saw Henry, an old and dear friend, and I'm greatly flattered he will write intro.

I attach two files in pdf, one the Brown talk more or less as I gave it, the other the somewhat differently oriented Daedalus essay that is coming out Jan. 2014.

It certainly would never have occurred to me to connect "The Cold Heaven" to the cinematic, and I don't remember any place where Yeats mentions cinema, though of course he lived and wrote well into cinematic times. Nevertheless, it is a plausible reading, though a greatly surprising one, to me at least . I hold that it is a free country, that is, that the reader always cooperates in the production of meaning. If that is the way you see the poem, then that reading (or seeing) should be recorded by you. "Riddled with light" would make a terrific epigraph. Illumination (the ah ha moment) is always overwhelming and puzzling, leads to unanswerable riddling questions, as in this poem.

warm best, Hillis

## *Works Cited*

Benjamin, Walter. *The Arcades Project*, "On the Theory of Knowledge, the Theory of Progress." Translated by Howard Eiland and Kevin McLaughlin. Cambridge: Harvard University Press, 1999.

Conrad, Joseph. *Heart of Darkness*. Public Domain Books. Kindle Edition. (2006-01-09).

—. *Typhoon*. Public Domain Books. Kindle Edition. (2012-05-16).

Derrida, Jacques. *Khora*. In *On the Name*. Edited by Thomas Dutoit. Translated by Ian McLeod. Stanford: Stanford University Press, 1995.

—. (With Bernard Stigler). "Spectrographies." In *Echographies of Television*. Translated by Jennifer Bajorek. Cambridge: Polity Press, 2005.

—. "Aletheia." Translated by Pleshette DeArmitt and Kas Sagafi, *The Oxford Literary Review*, 32.2 (2010): 169-188.

—. *Athens, Still Remains. The Photographs of Jean Francois Bonhomme*. Translated by Pascal-Anne Brault and Michael Naas. New York: Fordham University Press, 2010.

Dunne, Eamonn. "J. Hillis Miller, *The Conflagrations of Community. Fiction Before and After Auschwitz*. Chicago: The University of Chicago Press, 2011." *Textual Practice* 26.2 (2012): 364-368.

Freud, Sigmund. *Civilization and Its Discontents*. Standard Edition. New York: Norton, 1961.

Heidegger, Martin. *Hoelderlin's Hymn "The Ister."* Translated by William McNeill and Julia Davis. Bloomington: Indiana University Press, 1996.

Kittler, Friedrich, A. *Gramophone, Film, Typewriter*. Translated by Geoffrey Winthtrop-Young and Michael Wutz. Stanford: Stanford University Press, 1999.

Kujundžić, Dragan, "Non-biodegradables." *Art Margins*, 2007, www.artmargins.com, Accessed May 19, 2013.

Lacoue-Labarthe, Philippe. "L'horreur occidentale." *Lignes* (Mai 2007). Lawtoo Nidesh. Editor. *Conrad's* Heart of Darkness *and Contemporary Thought. Revisiting the Horror with Lacoue-Labarthe*. New York: Bloomsbury, 2012.

Margel, Serge. *La Societé du spectral*. Paris: Nouvelles Édition Lignes, 2012.

Miller, J. Hillis. "The Critic as Host." *Deconstruction and Criticism*. New York: Continuum, 1979.

—. "*The Heart of Darkness* Revisited." *Heart of Darkness (Case Studies in Contemporary Criticism)*. Ed. Ross C. Murphin. Boston: Bedford, 1996. 206-220.

—. "Joseph Conrad: Should We Read *Heart of Darkness*?" *Others*. Princeton: Princeton University Press, 2001.

—. *For Derrida*. New York: Fordham University Press, 2009.

—. *The Medium is the Maker. Browning, Freud, Derrida and the New Telepathic Technologies*. Brighton: Sussex Academic Press, 2009.

—. "Anachronistic Reading." *Derrida Today* 3 (May 2010): 75-91.

—. *The Conflagrations of Community. Fiction Before and After Auschwitz*. Chicago: The University of Chicago Press, 2011.

—. "Prologue: Revisiting 'Heart of Darkness Revisited' (in the company of Philippe Lacoue-Labarthe)." *Conrad's* Heart of Darkness *and Contemporary Thought. Revisiting the Horror with Lacoue Labarthe.* Ed. Nidesh Lawtoo. New York: Bloomsbury, 2012.

—. "Ecotechnics: Ecotechnological Odradek." In *Telemorphosis: Theory in the Era of Climate Change, Vol. 1.* Edited by Tom Cohen. Ann Arbor: Open Humanities Press, 2012. 65-103. http://quod.lib.umich.edu/o/ohp/10539563.0001.001/1:5/--telemorphosis- theory-in-the-era-of-climate-change-vol-1?rgn=div1;view=fulltext, accessed May 12, 2013.

Nancy, Jean-Luc. *L'Équvalence des Catastrophes (Après Fukushima).* Paris: Galilée, 2012.

Royle, Nicholas, "Reading Joseph Conrad: Episodes From the Coast" (manuscript, February, 2013).

Samolsky, Russel. *Apocalyptic Futures.* New York: Fordham University Press, 2011.

Weber, Samuel. *Mass Mediauras. Form. Technics. Media.* Stanford: Stanford University Press, 1996.

Wicke, Jennifer. "Combining Perspectives on Dracula." In Bram Stoker, *Dracula.* Edited by John Paul Riquelme. New York: St. Martin's, 2002.

Wills, David. "Revolutions in the Darkroom. Balász, Benjamin, Sade." *Dorsality: Thinking Back through Technology and Politics.* Minneapolis: University of Minnesota Press, 2008.

—. Review of Jacques Derrida. *Copy, Archive, Signature: A Conversation on Photography.* Trans. Jeff Fort (Stanford: Stanford University Press, 2010). Also, Jacques Derrida, *Athens, Still Remains: The Photographs of Jean-François Bonhomme.* Trans. Pascale-Anne Brault and Michael Naas (New York: Fordham University Press, 2010), manuscript.

—. *Inanimation.* Forthcoming.

Wolff, Larry. *The Idea of Galicia: History and Fantasy in Habsburg Political Culture.* Stanford: Stanford University Press, 2012.

Wolfreys, Julian. "Heart? Of Darkness? Reading in the Dark with J. Hillis Miller and Joseph Conrad." *Deconstruction. Derrida.* New York: St. Martin's Press, 1998.

*Postscript*

## Thanks a Lot and What I Would Say Now

J. Hillis Miller

This book is an immense honor for me. I am honored not only by the splendid film, *The First Sail*, represented here in transcript, but also by the generous and brilliant essays by so many distinguished scholars that take up the major part of the book. I thank first Dragan Kujundžić, who has turned out to be a film director of genius, not least in putting together a wonderful film that succeeds in making me look human and in getting across much about me in little, that is, in succinct filmic form. I thank also the gifted camera-man Georg Koszulinsky, and the equally gifted film editor Dave Rodriguez, who gave Dragan's conceptions wonderful cinematic life. The admirable original music by Natalia Pschenichnikova is another great honor for me.

Though I much like the film, even in transcription of just the words, the accompanying essays are the life of this book. They are really wonderful tributes, not only in their generosity toward me, but also in their brilliance as essays. Hearing them in Dublin and reading them again now has been deeply moving for me. I thank all the authors from the bottom of my heart. I thank especially Éamonn Dunne and Michael O'Rourke for organizing the conference in Dublin so efficiently, so generously, and for contributing such witty and profound papers themselves, as indeed all the papers are. The conference was a great event for me.

Rereading the transcript to write this Postscript brings home to me how much has changed, and by no means all for the better, just since the film was made in 2010. If the film were being made today I'd still mention climate change, financial meltdown, our foreign wars, the digital revolution, and the present state of literary studies, but what changes in all of them! All the things I mentioned have progressed, but mostly in the wrong direction.

The effects of climate change have been more rapid than was then foreseen, with already more destructive hurricanes, floods (think Colorado at this moment), widespread fires caused by drought (think the Rim Fire near Yellowstone), melting glaciers and disappearing Arctic and Antarctic ice, along slowly rising sea-levels.

The political situation in the United States is truly catastrophic, with congressional gridlock and the looming of yet another threatened default on the debt. Disastrous decisions by our Supreme court, injurious to our democracy, have 1) declared corporations, absurdly, people, so that they can give unlimited money secretly to political campaigns, effectively trying to buy the government; 2) erased a key provision of the Voting Rights Act. This has allowed installation of new voter identification rules that will deprive many poor and minority citizens of the right to vote or of access to the polls. Widespread climate change denial is only one of many idiocies. The Republican Party in Texas had as one of its planks in the last election a proposal to forbid the teaching of "critical thinking." The Texas School Board as I write this is proposing that all science textbooks used in Texas must teach creationism along with Darwinism.

The persistent attempt to repeal or defund "Obamacare" is another proof that Derrida was right about self-destructive auto-co-immunity being the doom of any nation. Healthcare costs are creeping up toward a predicted 25% of GDP, immensely higher than any other "developed" nation. This will certainly happen if the Affordable Health Care Act is repealed or defunded. Any intelligent person can see that universal single-payer health care, as exists in most developed countries, is the way to go.

We have left Iraq, and are in the process of leaving Afghanistan, but both are pretty much in chaos, with constant suicide bombings, as the various factions kill one another. Our invasion of both countries has led to hundreds of thousands of deaths and to even more exiles and displacements. We have for the moment suspended in the nick of time Obama's plan to bomb Syria in retaliation for their use of chemical weapons, but who knows how that will play out? Finding those 10,000 tons of sarin gas Assad has stored at so many different sites will be extremely difficult.

Financial institutions have still not been seriously regulated, so that another financial meltdown is widely predicted. The banks are back to making out like bandits, while our middle class is gradually disappearing. Income disparity grows apace, with the top one percent now having twenty percent of the wealth, as was just last week announced.

Few people in 2010, certainly not I, had any idea of the extent of NSA (National Security Agency) secret spying on our emails, our Skype communications, our phone calls, our mail. Two enormous facilities store all this data, one in the east, one in the west. The cover of every letter sent in the United States is now photographed and stored. This document I am now writing will be available to the NSA, especially when I email it to Dragan as an email attachment. The digitalizing of everything proceeds apace. One effect of this is the NSA secret domestic spying.

Over 70% of College and University teaching in the United States is now done by adjuncts. They are underpaid, have no job security, and few if any benefits. Many of these adjuncts in the humanities are nevertheless faithfully teaching writing and literature, often in difficult situations (unprepared and indifferent students, an ideology that says you should go to college primarily to prepare for a well-paying job, etc.). These faithful teachers are my heroes in these bad days, as are those many young scholars and teachers who are publishing brilliantly learned and original essays and books about literature and about teaching literature. Since 2010 more and more statistics have been released about the radical decline in humanities majors, especially in those studying English and foreign literatures. More and more humanities courses are about race, gender, class, performance studies, film, "digital humanities," the use in the humanities of cognitive science and brain science. These are entirely worthy topics. They are where the action is these days, but they are not the same thing as courses involving a careful reading of *Hamlet* or *Middlemarch* or *The Crying of Lot 49*. The cultural entities that really shape the ethos of our citizens in the United States these days are video games, films, popular music, television, Facebook, Twitter.

Were I answering Dragan's questions today I'd also have something to say about the way MOOCs, or Massive Open Online Courses, are rapidly changing higher education, among other things by threatening the need for all those adjuncts.

I'd also have comments concerning the recent noble statement about the importance of the humanities and social sciences by a commission of fifty experts assembled by the American Academy of Arts and Sciences ("The Heart of the Matter: The Humanities and Social Sciences for a vibrant, competitive, and secure nation"). I have said without irony that it is a "noble" document (everyone should read it), but I note that only one of the fifty members is president of a community college, while the other eleven university or college presidents on the commission run Yale, Harvard, NYU, Cornell, Amherst, Stanford, Penn, etc. Not one of that horde of adjuncts was represented on the Commission to tell it like it is down in the trenches teaching the humanities and social sciences these days.

I'd also have something to say today about the "Common Core Curriculum," now widely adopted by a majority of the States in the United States. Who could be against setting some standards about what all young people should learn about science, math, writing, argumentation, reading, and literature? On the other hand, the one size fits all aspect of the Common Core plan worries me, in spite of its emphasis on flexibility. We have an immense diversity of students in the United States. Teachers have to take what they get in a given classroom and start from there with clear-eyed recognition of where their students are at. An unmanageable disparity may exist between what the Common Core prescribes and where a given classroom full of students are in Common Core knowledge and skills, though most of them would be whizzes with iPhones these days, with Facebook, with video games, and with texting. These are difficult skills to learn. They involve a lot of linguistic expertise, as well as a high level of hand-eye coordination.

To end on a more joyful note: Were I being interrogated by Dragan Kujundžić today I'd stress four indispensable uses reading and teaching literature can have even in these days of rapid social and technological change:

1) Readers can learn from literature a lot about social, personal, technological, and ideological conditions in the "real world" at this or that time in history. I see no reason to deny the "representational" aspect of literature, as long as you recognize that you are reading a fictional transposition of the real world. *Alice in Wonderland*, fantasy though it is, tells you

a lot, particularly if the great Tenniel illustrations are taken into account, about the life and milieu of a well-to-do little girl in Victorian times.

2) Literature is an exemplary place to learn how "ideological mistakes" are most often made by taking a figure of speech literally, for example by assuming that because a family should balance its budget, running up big Federal deficits in the United States is a bad thing. The two entities are not commensurate. For one thing, families can't print money, whereas the Federal government can, and the inflation predicted by doom-sayers has not materialized. As George Eliot's narrator in *Middlemarch* says, "We all of us, grave or light, get our thoughts entangled in metaphors, and act fatally on the strength of them." Novels are full of examples of that.

3) Even more important, as an indispensable function of reading literary works, is the sheer pleasure of entering an alternative imaginary world. We do this by way of the words on the page. Every work opens a different and unique world. This pleasure of entering a new world is a good in itself, as I have claimed for my pleasure in reading Yeats' "The Cold Heaven." It needs no further justification. The need for the imaginary seems to be a basic feature of human nature.

4) Literature is the best place to enjoy wordplay, puns, linguistic jokes, and so on. This is a particular form of what Roland Barthes called *jouissance*. Films, video games, and television sit-coms are no doubt also alternative worlds, but they cannot easily match the pleasurable linguistic complexity of literary works, as the relative thinness of language in films made from classic novels attests, however closely they try to follow the text. Films cannot present, except with great awkwardness, the interiority of personages. Those faces and their talk on the screen have their own great power, but it is a different sort of power from the words on the page as they report, among other things, internal thoughts and feelings. Film is only partly linguistic. One often waits in vain to hear in a film version some piece of word play that has caused *jouissance* in reading the print text original.

So "Long live print literature!" For all these reasons.

*September 18, 2013*

## Postscript to Postscript

Now, just a year after the *Postscript* above, my concerns have veered or modulated a good bit. This *Postscript to Postscript* sketches those out. My abiding concern remains the justification of literature and literary study. I think the social and global context in which the study of literature must be defined and defended, if that can be done at all, has changed markedly for the worse since September 2013. I have a much clearer idea than I did a year ago of the interrelation of all these elements. They all hang together. They make a single structure or web, set of concomitants, not a causal chain, though "aesthetic ideology" and the human gift for language may be the aboriginal "cause." I agree with Tom Cohen's claim that this is the case. He says that and much more, in a brilliant essay to appear with essays by me and by Claire Colebrook, in a book to be called *The Twilight of the Anthropocene*. This *Postscript to Postscript* owes much to Cohen's admirably original essay. I had the elements, but he shows me how to put them together in these ecocidal (Cohen's word) days. Cohen argues persuasively that 2014 will be seen in retrospect (if there is anyone left to look back) as the crucial turning point or tipping point in all the areas I mention in the *Postscript* above. I have a stronger sense now, thanks in good part to Cohen's essay, of the way all these areas are interrelated.

Climate change is now irreversible and accelerating rapidly, with species die off already occurring. Half the bird species in North America will soon be affected, a recent study predicts. Climate change means the likelihood of the end of "us" hominids too, as the planet comes to be no longer able to sustain us. Handy signs of this are 1) the polar vortexes of last winter, caused by arctic ice-melt, and 2) wildfires in California, prolonged drought, and excessive heat there that are causing the vanishing of California's water, so that California will before long be uninhabitable. Big wildfires and high temperatures in California right now, as I write this.

As Cohen argues, the climate change deniers have accomplished their goal. (Conscious? Unconscious? Hard to tell.) That goal was to put off doing anything about "the end of the anthropocene" until it was too late. Ecocide is being hastened by rapidly accelerating $CO_2$ emissions globally and by unchecked exploitation of oil and gas reserves, for example by "fracking" in the United States. Putting off by the success of climate change deniers allowed time to transfer most of the world's wealth to that famous .01% or .001% of the population, so they could, they (falsely) imagine, survive on their hilltop mansions.

Irreversible climate change is, paradoxically, as Cohen and others (Bernard Stiegler for example) argue, a result of language structures, what we call "aesthetic ideology." That ideology has built-in programs of self-destructive "ecocide." Derrida and I would call these programs the bringing about of an auto-immune effect. The reigning ideology, intended to produce "security," turns disastrously against itself. Here is Derrida's description, in "Faith and Knowledge," of the auto-immunity he claims inhabits every community: "Community as *com-mon auto-immunity* [*com-mune auto-immunité*]: no community <is possible> that would not cultivate its own auto-immunity, a principle of sacrificial self-destruction ruining the principle of self-protection (that of maintaining its self-integrity intact [*du maintien de l'intégrité intacte de soi*]), and this in view of some sort of invisible and spectral survival."[1]

One concomitant of climate change (I do not say "cause") is an almost unbelievably self-destructive political and media situation, in the United States and around the world. This is once more a language-based auto-immune effect. One current example of this (September 2014) is the way the media and politicians both Republican and Democratic have persuaded most Americans that it is in our interest to go to war with ISIS, even though a few courageous and wiser heads, in the Pentagon and elsewhere, have asserted that ISIS is not a threat to our national security. We have once more fallen into the trap, as we did in invading Iraq. The ISIS leaders must be laughing their heads off, since, among other things, our aggression against ISIS will work as a fantastic recruiting tool for them. Imagine how you would feel if a country on the other side of the world were raining bombs and missiles on the United States. You would want

---

1   Jacques Derrida, "Faith and Knowledge: The Two Sources of 'Religion' at the Limits of Reason Alone," trans. Samuel Weber, in *Acts of Religion*, ed. Gil Anidjar (New York: Routledge, 2002), 87; also in *Religion*, ed. Jacques Derrida and Gianni Vattimo (Stanford, California: Stanford University Press, 1998), 51; ibid., "Foi et savoir: Les deux sources de la 'religion' aux limites de la simple raison," in *La Religion: Séminaire de Capri sous la direction de Jacques Derrida et Gianni Vattimo*, ed. Thierry Marchaisse (Paris: Seuil, 1996), 69. I have discussed Derrida's thinking about community auto-immunity in *For Derrida* (New York: Fordham University Press, 2009).

REVENGE, as we have been seeking ever since 9/11. The war with ISIS will also divert attention from the forest fires, water shortages, and weird weather in the United States. We'll be too busy watching on TV news the latest air strikes on Iraq and Syria, as well as hearing pundits tell us that we must put "boots on the ground" in both countries if we are to "stamp out" ISIS.

The digital revolution has even in the last year gone further toward changing every corner of our lives. This includes our relation to "literature," as more and more people play computer games or "text" rather than read literature, even though much literature is now abundantly available as e-texts.

The degradation of our colleges and universities has also proceeded apace in the last year. They are turning more and more into trade schools focusing on training in STEM (science, technology, engineering, and math), as preparation for a job in information technology or the like. The fantasy that on-line courses and MOOCs (Massive Open Online Courses) are just as good as real classrooms with real teachers has taken more and more a firm hold. Large amounts of money can be made from online teaching. These changes mean the not so gradual vanishing of the ideal of a "liberal education" as preparation for life and good citizenship, not to speak of the not so gradual disappearance of training in "critical thinking" or in foreign language competence. In spite of lip service to the teaching of how to read literature, it matters less and less in higher education, less now than a year ago. You do not need to know how to read Shakespeare or George Eliot's *Middlemarch* in order to be a good computer programmer. One tiny example: The Trustees of the University of Maine system will meet soon (deliberately in an out of the way place in Maine, far east in Fort Kent, where there is a remote branch of the University). The trustees will, among other things, act on a proposal to eliminate entirely the program in "Arts and Humanities" at one of the University of Maine's branches.

Any attempt to justify the continued reading, study, and teaching of literature, my life-long vocation, has in 2014 to take place in this complex context. I am no longer so sure as I was a year ago that reading literature can be justified on the grounds that it is good to enter into imaginary worlds. Those imaginary worlds are often the persuasive embodiment of some form or other of "aesthetic ideology," even though they may contain some element of "critical thinking" directed against that ideology. *Middlemarch*, for example, does that deconstructing of ideology brilliantly, as I have tried to show in a recent book, *Reading for Our Time: Adam Bede and* Middlemarch *Revisited* (2012). Nor am I so sure that reading literature can be plausibly defended, in these bad days of 2014, beyond the tipping point, as a good way to find out about the "real historical world." No doubt one learns what it was like to be a Victorian by reading Dickens, Thackeray, Elizabeth Gaskell, George Eliot, or Anthony Trollope. But who cares? Or who can afford to care, as the water rises along our coastlines and we have yet another "warmest summer on record," or as we plunge blindly into yet another war in the Middle East?

That pretty much leaves training in the "rhetorical reading" (in Paul de Man's sense) of literary works as a concentrated way of developing procedures for at least trying to understand what is happening to us. This might teach us to understanding how politicians and the media get away with telling such whoppers, and how people gullibly believe those whoppers. It should always be remembered, however, that if de Man emphasized the power of rhetorical reading, he also stressed the irrepressible power of recuperation of aesthetic ideology or of what he called "hermeneutics." Here is a notable passage by de Man that states this clearly:

> When you do hermeneutics, you are concerned with the meaning of the work; when you do poetics, you are concerned with the stylistics or with the description of the way in which a work means. The question is whether these two are complementary, whether you can cover the full work by doing hermeneutics and poetics at the same time. The experience of trying to do this shows that it is not the case. When one tries to achieve this complementarity, the poetics always drops out, and what one always does is hermeneutics. One is so attracted by problems of meaning that it is impossible to do hermeneutics and poetics at the same time. From the moment you start to get involved with problems of meaning, as I unfortunately tend to do, forget about the poetics. The

two are not complementary, the two may be mutually exclusive in a certain way, and that is part of the problem which Benjamin states, a purely linguistic problem.[2]

My current work is attempting to see what can be said for literary study in the light of our new situation in 2014, when more and more people, including erstwhile climate change deniers, are openly or tacitly recognizing that climate change is humanly caused and that it is already irreversible. This new situation means, among other things, that it no longer makes sense to argue that we can learn from literature how to be good readers of all the signs and then try to persuade people to do something about climate change before it is too late. It is already too late. That is just what the self-destructive auto-immunity programmed into aesthetic ideology made bound to happen, in a machinal effect.

*September 15, 2014*
*Deer Isle, Maine*

Here is a bibliography of my books, essays, and interviews published or recorded since *The First Sail* was filmed in 2010. The veering or modulation I began this *Postscript to Postscript* by asserting can be followed from year to year in these texts.

### *Books*

*The Conflagration of Community: Fiction Before and After Auschwitz.* Chicago: University of Chicago Press, 2011.

*Theory and the Disappearing Future: On de Man, on Benjamin,* co-authored with Claire Colebrook and Tom Cohen. London and New York: Routledge, 2012.

*Reading for Our Time:* Adam Bede *and* Middlemarch *Revisited.* Edinburgh: Edinburgh University Press, 2012.

*Communities in Fiction.* New York: Fordham University Press, 2014.

*An Innocent Abroad: Lectures in China.* Evanston: Northwestern University Press, in press, forthcoming 2015.

---

2   Paul de Man, "Conclusions: Walter Benjamin's 'The Task of the Translator,'" in *The Resistance to Theory* (Minneapolis: University of Minnesota Press, 1986), 87.

Arabic translation of my *On Literature: Thinking in Action*. El Gabalaya St. Opera House, El Gezira, Cairo: National Center for Translation, 2015.

## Essays

"Foreword" (in Japanese translation) to a volume in Japanese, *Society and Culture in the Times of Elizabeth Gaskell: A Bicentennial Commemorative Volume*, ed. Mitsuharu Matsuoka. Hiroshima: Keisuisha, 2010. vii-xiii.

"A Salute to Harold Bloom," in *Harold Bloom 80*. New Haven: Yale University, 2010. 43-4.

"Hands in Hardy," in *The Ashgate Research Companion to Thomas Hardy*, ed. Rosemarie Morgan. Farnham, Surrey: Ashgate Publishing Limited, 2010. 505-516.

Review of Avrom Fleishman, *George Eliot's Intellectual Life* (Cambridge: Cambridge University Press, 2010), in *George Eliot-George Henry Lewes Studies*, Nos, 58-59 (September 2010): 118-22.

"Performativity$_1$/Performativity$_s$," in Lars Saetre, Patrizia Lombardo, and Anders M. Gullestad, eds., *Exploring Textual Action*. Aarhus: Aarhus University Press, 2010. 31-58.

"Challenges to World Literature," *Comparative Literature in China* (a journal in Chinese and English), No. 4 (Shanghai: Shanghai International Studies University, 2010). 1-9.

"The Sense of an Un-ending: The Resistance to Narrative Closure in Kafka's *Das Schloß*," in Jakob Lothe, Beatrice Sandberg, and Ronald Spiers, eds., *Franz Kafka: Narration, Rhetoric, and Reading*. Columbus: The Ohio State University Press, 2011. 108-22. (This is a version of part of my chapter on Kafka in *The Conflagration of Community*.)

"Anachronistic Reading," in *Derrida Today*, vol. 3 (May 2010): 75-91.

"Robert Browning," in *The Cambridge Companion to English Poets*, ed. Claude Rawson. Cambridge: Cambridge University Press, 2011. 392-407.

"Resignifying Excitable Speech," in *Women's Studies Quarterly*, vol. 39, nos 1 &2 (Spring/Summer 2011): 223-6.

"The Act of Reading Literature as Disconfirmation of Theory," in "Theory Today," *Frame* 24.1 (May 2011): 18-31.

"*Exergue*"; "*Brisure*"; "*Jeu*," "Trace," in *Reading Derrida's Of Grammatology*," ed. Sean Gaston and Ian Maclachlan. London; New York: Continuum, 2011. 38-51.

"Should We Read or Teach Literature Now?" *Literature and/as Ethics*, ed. Martin Middeke et. al, a special issue of *Anglia*, vol. 129, #s 1-2 (2011): 1-11.

"Globalization and World Literature," *Neohelicon*, Special number on "Comparative Literature: Toward a (Re)construction of World Literature," Guest-edited by Ning Wang, vol. 38, No. 2 (2011): 251-265.

"The Presence to Oneself in Decision-Making," in *Le Concept de presence/The Concept of Presence*, ed. Mircea Martin, a special issue of *Euresis*, no. 1-4 (2011): 18-31.

"Imre Kertész's *Fatelessness*: Fiction as Testmony," in Jokob Lothe, Susan Rubin Suleiman, and James Phelans, eds., *After Testimony: The Ethics and Aesthetics of Holocaust Narrative for the Future*. Columbus: The Ohio State University Press, 2012. 23-51. (This is a version of a chapter in my *The Conflagration of Community*.)

"How to (Un)Globe the Earth," in a special issue on "Globing the Earth: The New Eco-logics of Nature," ed. Ranjan Ghosh, of *SubStance*, 127, Vol. 41. 1 (2012): 15-29.

"Paul de Man at Work: What Good is an Archive?" in *The Political Archive of Paul de Man: Property, Sovereignty, and the Theotropic*, ed. Martin McQuillan. Edinburgh: Edinburgh University Press, 2012. 149-156.

"Some Versions of Romance Trauma as Generated by Realist Detail in Ian McEwan's *Atonement*," in Jean-Michel Ganteau and Susana Onega, eds. *Trauma and Romance in Contemporary British Literature*. New York: Routledge, 2012. 90-106.

"Prologue: Revisiting '*Heart of Darkness* Revisited' (in the company of Philippe Lacoue-Labarthe," a reprint of "*Heart of Darkness* Revisited," in Nidesh Lawtoo, ed. Conrad's *Heart of Darkness and Contemporary Thought: Revisiting the Horror with Lacoue-Labarthe*. Bloomsbury: Bloomsbury Academic, 2012. 17-35, 39-54.

"Po co czytac literature?" [Polish trans. of "Why Read Literature?," 4th ch. of *On Literature*] *Przestrzenie Teorii*, 17 (Poznan, 2012): 219-243.

"The Truly Critical Critic," Preface to *Critic*, ed. John Schad and Oliver Tearle. Brighton: Sussex Academic Press, 2011. xi.

"Absolute Mourning: It Is Jacques You Mourn For," in *Re-reading Derrida: Perspectives on Mourning and Its Hospitalities*, ed. Tony Thwaites amd Judith Seaboyer. Lanham, Maryland, Boulder, New York, Toronto, Plymouth, UK: Lexington Books, 2013. 9-21. (Also in my *For Derrida*).

*Stray Savages All Around: Performative James or Fiction as Forgery* J. Hillis Miller Literary Imagination 2013; doi: 10.1093/litimag/imt003. Also in print version: "Stray Savages All Around: Performative James or Fiction as Forgery," in *Literary Imagination*, 15.1 (2013): 52-64.

"Cold Heaven, Cold Comfort: Should We Read or Teach Literature Now?" in *The Edge of the Precipice: Why Read Literature in the DigitalAge?*, ed. Paul Socken. Montreal & Kingston: McGill-Queen's University Press, 2013. 140-55.

"Literature Matters Today," in a special issue *SubStance* entitled *Literature Matters*, ed. Ranjan Ghosh, 131, Vol. 42. 2 (2013): 12-32.

"Preface," to Éamonn Dunne, *Reading Theory Now: An ABC of Good Reading with J. Hillis Miller*. New York, London: Bloomsbury, 2013. ix-xiv.

"Response" to *Forum on J.Hillis Miller*, with essays by Éamonn Dunne, Peggy Kamuf, and Justin Halverson, in *Comparative Literature Studies*, 50. 2 (2013): 358-63.

Translation into Korean as part of a translation into Korean of Virginia Woolf's *Mrs. Dalloway*, with critical essays, of all or part (can't tell) of "*Mrs. Dalloway*: Repetition as the Raising of the Dead," from my *Fiction and Repetition*. Cambridge: Harvard University Press, 1982.

Translation into Chinese by xialin ding of Nanjing University of the first half of "Literature Matters Today" in Beijing University's *Guo Wai Wen Xue* (*Foreign Literatures)*, issue no. 2 (2013): 3-8.

"Should We Read or Teach Literature Now?" in *Narrative Ethics*, ed. Jakob Lothe and Jeremy Hawthorn. Amsterdam; New York: Rodopi, 2013. 13-24.

"'Waves' Theory: an anachronistic reading," and "La theorie des Vagues: lecture anachronistic," in *Virginia Woolf Among the Philosophers*, ed. Chantal Delourme, special issue of *Le tour critique*, 2 (2013): 113-120; 121-129; http://letourcritique.u-paris10.fr/index.php/letourcritique/issue/view/3 (accessed 1/26/14). (A revised and much lengthened version of this essay appears in my *Communities in Fiction*.)

"Text; Action; Space; Emotion." In *Exploring Text and Emotions*, ed. Lars Saetre, Patrizia Lombardo, and Julien Zanetta. Aarhus: Aarhus University Press, 2014. 91-117.

"Grenzgänge mit Iser und Coetzee: Literature lessen—aber Wie und Wozu?" trans. Monika Reif-Hülser (Konstanz: UVK Universitätsverlag, 2013). Pamphlet. Translation of the first annual Wolfgang Iser Memorial Lecture, 2011.

"Derrida and de Man: Two Rhetorics of Deconstruction, *A Companion to Derrida*, ed. Zeynep Direk and Leonard Lawler. Chichester, West Sussex: Wiley Blackwell, 2014. 345-61.

## *Interviews*

Interview by Vincent Kaufmann, in Vincent Kaufmann, *La faute à Mallarmé: L'aventure de la théorie littéraire*. Paris: Seuil, 2011. 270-75.

"Literature, Community, and Contestation, An Interview with J. Hillis Miller," conducted by Margaret Barrow, Robert Savino Oventile, and Manya Steinkoler, in *Teaching Literature in Community College Classrooms: Traversing Practices*, ed. Margaret Barrow and Manya Steinkoler. Boston, etc.: McGraw-Hill, 2013. 8-16. Available as an online post for Literature Lab:

Interview by David Sherman, "Why Read? Thoughts from a Cold Heaven" ( http://www.brandeis.edu/departments/english/literaturelab/miller.html https://itunes.apple.com/us/podcast/literature-lab/id523653479?mt=2).

Interview with J. Hillis Miller: "For J.," Lyn Chapman's undergraduate Introduction to Critical Theory class at JKS, Naropa University, February 28, 2013

Interview by Éamonn Dunne et. al. in on-line journal, *Australian Humanities Review*: "You see you ask an innocent question and you've got a long answer" (http://www.australianhumanitiesreview.org/archive/Issue-May-2014/miller.html; http://www.australianhumanitiesreview.org/archive/Issue-May-2014/AHR56_1_Miller.pdf)

Interview by Bradley Fest: "Isn't it a Beautiful Day," An Interview with J. Hillis Miller," *boundary 2*, 41.3 (Fall 2014), 123-158."

www.ingramcontent.com/pod-product-compliance
Lightning Source LLC
Chambersburg PA
CBHW030854170426
43193CB00009BA/610